WEDGWOOD GLASS

WEDGWOOD GLASS

Susan Tobin

2001

First published 2001

Printed by Fergies, Hamilton, Queensland, Australia
Design and typesetting by Wintercourt Pty Ltd, Caboolture, Queensland, Australia
Cover design by Philippe Vipathkun
Black and white Illustrations (except those on page 6 and lower photo on page 16); also fig. 1–4, 8, 10, 44–45, 53, 55, 57 and 66–67 © The Wedgwood Museum Trust Limited, Barlaston, Staffordshire, England. Fig. 76 ©Dartington Crystal 2001.
All other colour plate photography by Peter Wanny.

ISBN 0-9580234-0-9

Acknowledgements

Glass has been used for centuries. Once a luxury for the very rich and a source of taxation revenue, in contemporary society glass is taken for granted. It is almost everywhere in the lives of most people. Sheet glass in window panes protects us from the weather but allows in light, while science allows makers to construct panes of strengthened glass large enough to be used as walls. Glass is part of daily life through mass-produced bottles, jars, and tableware. These items may be as prosaic as clear milk or brown beer bottles. They may be plain jam or condiment jars. They may be the ordinary tumblers in the kitchen cupboard. Away from the prosaic and mundane, glass items may be as beautiful as elaborate finely etched, cut or enameled crystal goblets, decanters, vases and bowls.

Glass may be used for decorative wares. As such, the item may be as small as a bead or as large as a statue or a glass wall. The only limits are the creativity of the designer and the skills of the glassmaker. Yet creativity is not limited. This small publication attempts to record some of the work done by Josiah Wedgwood & Sons Limited between 1969 and 1987. It focuses on the glass factories at King's Lynn, Norfolk, and Torrington, Devon, in England, and Galway in the Republic of Ireland, and examples of the products unique to each.

This work would probably never have been started if I had never seen a Lilliput whale and duckling at a local auction in 1995. They were curios rather than significant items. No one seemed to know anything about them or when they were made. In the two years following, I saw a two ring amethyst candleholder (which I subsequently found was from the pattern called 'Sheringham'). Then came the Christmas paperweights (which were purchased and passed on to collectors) and a smoky blue glass goblet bearing the portrait cameo medallion of Princess Anne. My curiosity was aroused when I first saw a topaz squirrel. I had seen animal figures in clear and coloured glass, candleholders, paperweights and goblets. What else was there? In what colours were they made? How many and for what events were made? Where was the factory and was it still functioning? No one could answer all my questions, but from that point I was no longer alone. My search took me down many informational cul-de-sacs, but gradually I found lanes leading out to vistas of new facts.

Here it is my delight to record appreciation to the many people who have helped me on my search. Firstly, I must thank the former Chairman of Josiah Wedgwood & Sons Limited and current Chairman of the Wedgwood Museum Trust Limited, Sir Arthur Bryan whom I met in Melbourne during a lecture tour in 1997. Then thanks must go to the people at The Wedgwood Museum Trust Limited, at Barlaston, Staffordshire, England, Gaye Blake Roberts—Curator, Lynn Miller – Information Officer and those who work with them, Martin Chaplin—Archives Supervisor, Jo Riley—former Secretary to the Curator, Joanne Nutt—Secretary to the Curator, Sue Howdle—former Secretary to the Curator.

It took a little detective work, but I found the glass designer and founder of King's Lynn Glass, later to become Wedgwood Glass, Mr Ronald Stennett-Willson, who kindly invited me to speak with him at his home and who also provided information about the factory and photocopies of many details of his work. For all of which I am sincerely grateful and thank him.

Also in the county of Norfolk, thanks must go to the three glass blowers from 'Creative Glass of King's Lynn' and later of Caithness Crystal Limited, Philip Tuddenham, Steven 'Ginger' Bone and Paul 'Beaver' Payne, all of whom worked at Wedgwood Glass; to engraver Richard Stephenson from Caithness Visitor's Centre at King's Lynn; to Otmar Schoss, Paul Miller now of Langham Glass, and John Dowe all of whom worked at King's Lynn. Otmar was an employee for the full time Wedgwood owned the glass factory and one of the last four men, another of whom was John Dowe, to leave when it finally closed. The hospitality of Otmar and his wife Ottie in talking over 'old times', clearing up points of uncertainty relating to glass production, and visiting local places of interest around King's Lynn were most gratefully appreciated. Thanks to Eric Dancer CBE Managing Director of Dartington Glass Limited; to Peter Lewis Curator of the British Golf Museum, St Andrew's, Scotland, and who established and was first curator of the Dartington Glass Museum, Torrington; to John Barker, the last Managing Director at Wedgwood Crystal, King's Lynn. There are several other people who requested not to be named, but whose information proved invaluable.

Away from people directly associated with Wedgwood Glass there are others who provided assistance in a variety of ways. Margaret and Roy Swift gave their hospitality to a fly-in antipodean and 'e-mail pal'. Margaret's finds always surprise and delight me. Margaret's mother, Ivy Blackburn, had old Home Sales Invoices which held historic information. My contacts at British fairs are paperweight experts, Anne and Peter Metcalfe, and Lynn and Bob Heyes. A most avid collector, Ann Goodridge, through a pleasant visit to her home enabled me to see so many of the Wedgwood Glass items that I knew only from advertising fliers and many others of which I still had no idea.

Thanks to John Regan, James Robertson, and especially Bruce Strachan for their time in reading drafts of the manuscript.

The most special thanks go to my cousin, Penny Francis MBE, who gave me a home away from home while I was in London. Her kindness enabled me to travel in the United Kingdom from a safe and welcoming base.

This has been an exciting tour of discovery. It has opened doors of knowledge. It has enabled me to meet very helpful people. It has taken me from two small glass figurines into a world of glass, a world of which I was largely oblivious and in which there is so much more to learn. What I have gathered I believe is a large part of the Wedgwood Glass story. I know that there may be patterns, particularly for the North American market, of which I still have no knowledge at present. There are also commissions which I have never seen or of which I have never heard. Any further information would be gratefully received at smtobin@telstra.com or through P O Box 596, Mt Gravatt, 4122, Australia. In my work, I have found that one sentence or one referral has often led to a new line of research. This is certainly not a closed topic.

Contents

This work is dedicated to the men and women who worked at Wedgwood Glass.

PROLOGUE

What is 'Lynn Glassware'? This title is usually applied to wine glasses, tumblers and decanters characterised by between two and eight shallow, horizontal bands encircling the glassware. Collections of eighteenth and nineteenth century glass tumblers, wine glasses, a decanter, tankards and finger bowls held in The Museum of Social History, King's Lynn, in Norwich Castle, and in the Elizabethan House Museum, Great Yarmouth provide evidence of old glass in this form. It appears, however, that none of the glass held in the above-mentioned museums can definitively be traced to production at King's Lynn. (The town is variously referred to as King's Lin, King's Lyn, Lin Regis and Lynn Regis).

There are also pieces held in private collections. Local stories in King's Lynn mention a piece held privately, and referred to in family tradition as 'King's Lynn Glass'. The piece held privately is a somewhat lopsided stem glass which could have been made in the late 18th or early 19th century. Though it contains some impurities it still rings true, whereas a similar piece, also lopsided, and held by the King's Lynn Museum does not have a true ring. As with the pieces held by the museums, there is no evidence that any pieces in private collections were produced at King's Lynn.

Francis Buckley in his work, *Old English Glass*, published in 1925, referred to Albert Hartshorne as the originator of the term 'Lynn Glassware' in 1897, without any stated evidence for the title to this type of glassware. So what evidence is there of the production of glassware in King's Lynn prior to the 20th century?

The port of King's Lynn could for centuries have been a natural centre for the production of glass. Raw materials not naturally occurring locally could be easily transported from The Wash down the Great Ouse River and its tributary the Gaywood River. The Tollage Roll of 1300 indicates glass for the town hall windows being made by a Jordan le Verrer. While there is no physical evidence of glasshouses, seventeenth and eighteenth century cartographical evidence refers specifically to two separate sites of 'The Glasshouse'. During the early years of the seventeenth century, King James I sold the monopoly for glassmaking in England to Robert Mansell, a one time member of parliament for King's Lynn. Of all his factories throughout the country, it seems at least one may have operated at King's Lynn, though at exactly what time is also unknown.

General mention is made of glasswrights and glasiers (glaziers), but there was only one specific reference to a glassmaker, Israell Harrison, who was a freeman of the borough about 1650. There is no reference to the site of the glassworks.

John Houghton, a Fellow of the Royal Society, in 1696 published a list of the locations and numbers of glasshouses in England and Wales. On this list were two in the town of King's Lynn, but no specific addresses were given. These two glasshouses were said to produce bottles, and flint, green and ordinary glass. For Houghton 'flint' glass referred to what George Ravenscroft had discovered through experimentation, possibly with the assistance of an Italian, da Costa, at Henley-on-Thames and probably at his glasshouse in the Savoy by the Strand in London, glass-of-lead. This brilliant crystalline glass was made on the Continent, but not previously in England. By the end of the seventeenth century flint glass was made widely throughout the country. The nett effect was public acceptance of the hard brilliant glass and the consequent reduction in importation of foreign glass.

If Houghton's list did not refer to particular sites of glasshouses, several years earlier there is reference to a glasshouse in Pilot Street by the Gaywood River, appropriately sited for the importation of sand and coal. It appears on Henry Bell's *Groundplat of King's Lyn* c1680. It is possible that it was owned by Jonas Phillips. It is also possible that it was owned by one Francis Jackson, a glassmaker who also operated a glassworks with John Straw at Southwark in London. Whether the factory in King's Lynn was successful, or the one in London was not, is not recorded, but by 1695, their stock of drinking glasses, ornamental glasses and bottles, as well as their London factory, had been sold by auction. It would appear the partners Jackson and Straw ran only the King's Lynn operation after that date, but for how long is not known.

What local industry there was in the town unfortunately fell victim by the 1690s to the excise tax on glass to finance the wars against France. This tax consisted of one shilling a dozen on common glass bottles and a duty of approximately twenty percent on flint glass and glass plate. Although there is no evidence that only bottles, and not drinkware, were made at King's Lynn, glass production and its usage were greatly reduced. As a consequence, there was a negative impact on the quality of life of proprietors and workmen. A petition was sent in the mid-1690s to the House of Commons explaining the plight of glassworkers of King's Lynn and pleading for the discontinuance of the tax. It was partly successful with the tax being halved in 1698. In 1699 a second petition was sent. This one resulted in the repeal in the same year of the remaining duty on glass bottles so that the glasshouse was able to re-open for a time, as 'Port Books' show glass was fairly regularly exported from King's Lynn at the beginning of the eighteenth century.

No physical evidence of any of these glasshouses exists, but about 1710 the 'Prospect of Lin Regis from the West' identified a glasshouse with a domed roof in Spinner Lane. This building appears also on the 1725 Rastrick map, but by then it had been converted to a Presbyterian chapel. (By the late twentieth century a bus station covered the site near old St John's School on the corner of Market and Albion Streets, and only blocks from The Exchange, later the Customs House, which was renovated and used as a Tourist Information Centre). There is no reference to the Pilot Street factory on the Rastrick map.

Was glass produced next door to the Presbyterian chapel by Gilbert Dixon, glassmaker, during his lease of the property between 1726 and 1729? Was the 1747 glass auctioned by the Glass House Company produced or merely sold by the firm as a result of the 1745 Excise Act? Were there other glasshouses in King's Lynn between the Rastrick map of 1725 and 1830 when the next large-scale map of the town was drawn? There is no reason why there would not be, but also there is no current evidence of their existence. None of these factories, if indeed they existed, is believed to be the source of Lynn Glassware. If the glasshouses of which there is cartographic, but no physical evidence, were short-lived, it is quite possible other small factories were established, operated on a small-scale and closed within that one hundred and five year period. Still the question remains unanswered—were any of these the source of Lynn Glassware?

Whatever the origins of the so-named 'Lynn Glassware', by the end of the nineteenth century there were no glass factories in King's Lynn.

I

KING'S LYNN—A NEW PROJECT

Although the term 'Lynn Glassware' is given to certain types and shapes of glass, with current evidence the first truly identifiable Lynn Glassware was not made until the twentieth century. In June 1966, a new company, King's Lynn Glass Limited, was privately formed by a group of individuals who were supported financially by the Industrial & Commercial Finance Corporation. During the next ten months the glass factory was built on Oldmedow Road in the Hardwick Industrial Estate. New industry was being attracted to the town under an industrial expansion scheme. At the time, King's Lynn was not classified as a development area, consequently the factory was built entirely with private capital. There was no connection between the new and former factories, but it was the desire of the new factory's founder, chief designer and managing director, Ronald Stennett-Willson, F.S.I.A., a well-known glass designer, to develop quality modern glass in Britain. It was his intention that products would be functional and decorative. He also recognised the need to employ other designers to prevent the company's products from becoming stereotyped. It was also his hope that there would be considerable expansion in the first ten years of its operation. King's Lynn Glass Limited originally provided employment for about fifty people. At the time it was said to be the most modern factory in Britain making handmade glass.

To succeed, the factory had to be viable from inception in June, 1967 by producing a minimum output of two tons per day. Initially there were four furnaces. They produced colourless soda lime glass and light lead crystal glassware mainly for export, but the plan was to include a broader range of items as soon as possible. Many of the first glassmakers employed at King's Lynn Glass Limited were craftsmen from Sweden and other parts of Europe, with the master glassmaker being an Austrian, Gerd Elstner, who had been working in Sweden. Initially there were two teams, the first and more experienced was led by Gerd Elstner with Leif Svenson, Sune Svenson and Otmar Schoss. Percy Goodchild was the first of the English masters. Others to join as early team members brought a range of complementary experiences. These men included John Munnelli, Billy Robson, Colin Dupois, Andy Moncrief, David McCallum, Bob Watts and Eddy Manelli (who mixed the basic ingredients for the glass). Two of the first local young men to commence their glassmaking careers at King's Lynn were Paul Miller and Philip Tuddenham. Sydney Wilkinson was the cutting and finishing shop foreman while Jack Snell was chief engineer in charge of the furnaces.

Although he had had many years of association with Scandinavian glass factories, the aim of the founder, Stennett-Willson, was not to establish a Scandinavian factory in Britain. Rather, it was to utilise the skills of the European master craftsmen on a temporary basis to train the British, who in turn, would become masters of the craft of glass making. This was a wise move, as within a short period, local employees soon became very skilled in the factory. Together with men who had come from the Continent and stayed to make their home in King's Lynn, they formed a talented workforce.

As part of its diversification into the production of glass, it was this factory, most appropriately, that Josiah Wedgwood & Sons Limited purchased in 1969. The Chairman, Arthur Bryan was pleased to announce the acquisition. As reported in the *Stone Guardian* of May 2, 1969, he 'welcomed the opportunity for Wedgwood to enter the crystal and glass tableware field by means of this acquisition.' He was enthusiastic about the prospects of Lynn Glass for both the home and export markets.

An encouraging article in the *Wedgwood Review*, Vol 4, No 11, June 1969, on p. 15 reported that 'Although the company is relatively small and requires much to be done to extend its production facilities, it is capable of considerable and early development, and we are confident with the Wedgwood marketing division behind it, Lynn Glass will grow quickly and strongly. We very much appreciate the manner in which a quick and satisfactory agreement was reached in negotiation with the Industrial and Commercial Finance Corporation and the part played in developing this important glass factory'. Though there was no immediate plan for expansion, the factory was designed to be extended to treble, and when necessary, quadruple its original size onto adjacent vacant land.

Following a tradition and company policy to employ talented artists with training or teaching experience at the Royal College of Art, the former head of its industrial glass department, Ronald Stennett-Willson, was appointed as managing director of Wedgwood Glass at King's Lynn. He held this position, and that of chief designer, till his retirement at age 65 in December, 1980.

Ronald Stennett-Willson is recorded as saying 'it gives us the benefit of a very vigorous worldwide marketing organisation. This will speed up our expansion and I welcome it' (ibid). The headline in the *Eastern Evening News* Lynn Edition on 30th April, 1969, heralded 'Big expansion plan—BID FOR LYNN FIRM IS ACCEPTED'. The article reported on the announcement of the agreement of the terms of take-over whereby King's Lynn Glass would become a wholly-owned subsidiary of the Wedgwood Group. For Stennett-Willson the good news was threefold. The take-over firstly gave him access to the worldwide market of 'the largest pottery group in the world'; secondly his planned expansion would be much quicker - 'within the next two or three years I can get to where I envisaged getting within ten years'; while finally employment within the firm would increase significantly as young people were trained in the skills of glass making.

He also looked forward to the introduction of a new technique—engraving. The *Lynn News & Advertiser* of 13 May, 1969 reported Stennett-Willson as saying 'England lags behind in this field'. Engraving at King's Lynn was not to be of the traditional kind, but modern, to suit his designs. To achieve this, Alan Knights undertook a training course in Birmingham. This training and his natural skill enabled him to engrave items not only for sale to the public, but also for specially commissioned prizes or awards, for gifts for dignitaries and for royalty, including Her Majesty, Queen Elizabeth, the Queen Mother and Her Royal Highness, Princess Margaret, both of whom were frequent visitors to the King's Lynn factory.

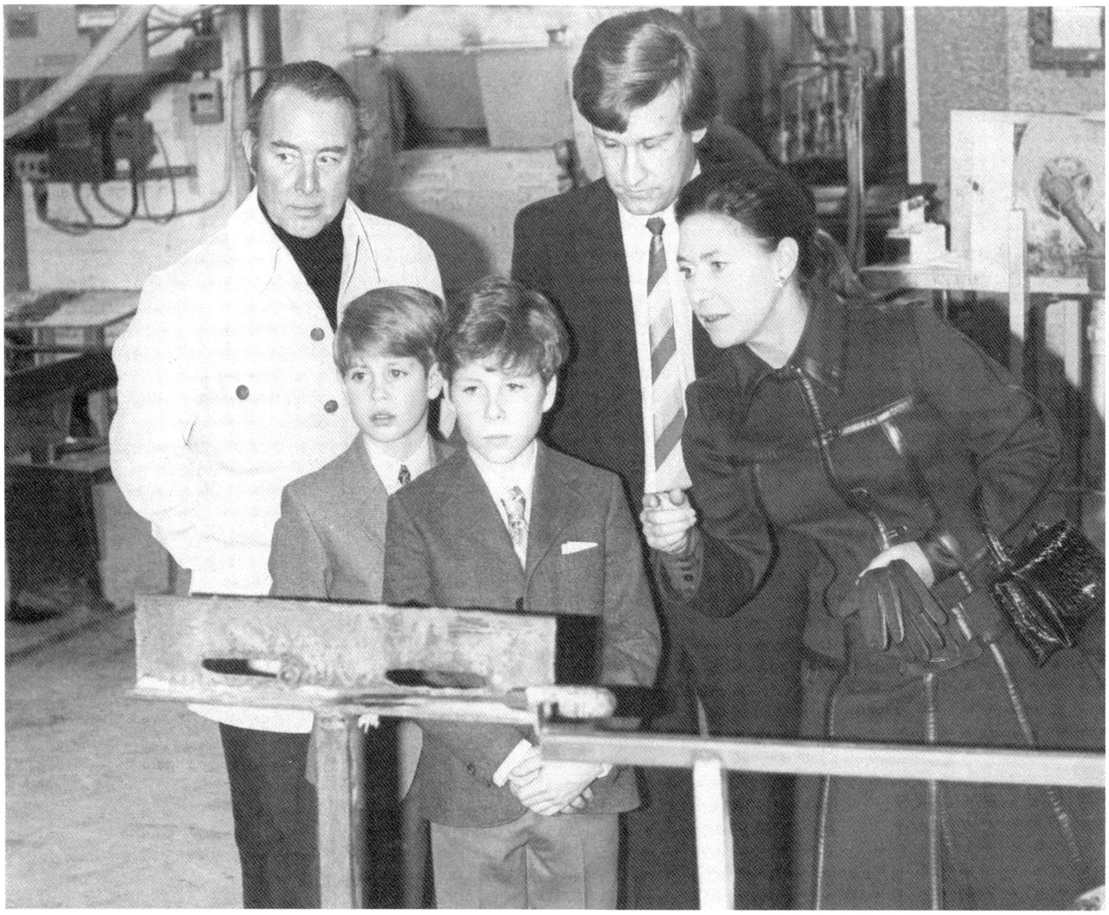

Factory tour—Ronald Stennett-Willson and Ray Duly with HRH Prince Edward, Viscount Linley and HRH Princess Margaret.

On certificates in many Wedgwood boxed items a few lines informed purchasers that the new factory restored a 'long-lost art and industry to the town'. Glass making is an ancient craft, but it was not small or dying. Quite the contrary, there was an increasing place for well-designed, well-made, high quality glass. The factory at King's Lynn was able to meet that need.

Before Wedgwood purchased King's Lynn Glass Limited there were fears among employees that the company would be moved from the area, but this proved groundless. At the height of production at King's Lynn, the Wedgwood Glass factory employed over one hundred and thirty people. Among the employees, the local highly skilled artisans included glass blowers and cutters. At its busiest it had up to twenty chairs or teams, depending on what was being made, and each chair could have from three to twenty men. Some of the implements used were similar to those of earlier periods such as blowing irons and simple hand tools for shaping glass, but mid- to late-twentieth century improved manufacturing methods, equipment and technology, as well as more refined materials, gave wider scope to the glassmakers.

By September 1969, Colin Wright, Director and General Manager of Wedgwood Rooms announced the introduction of Wedgwood glass, both tableware and decorative items, to the existing Rooms in Britain. He included specific areas for display of glass in the next Rooms to be constructed, because of initial success of the items available.

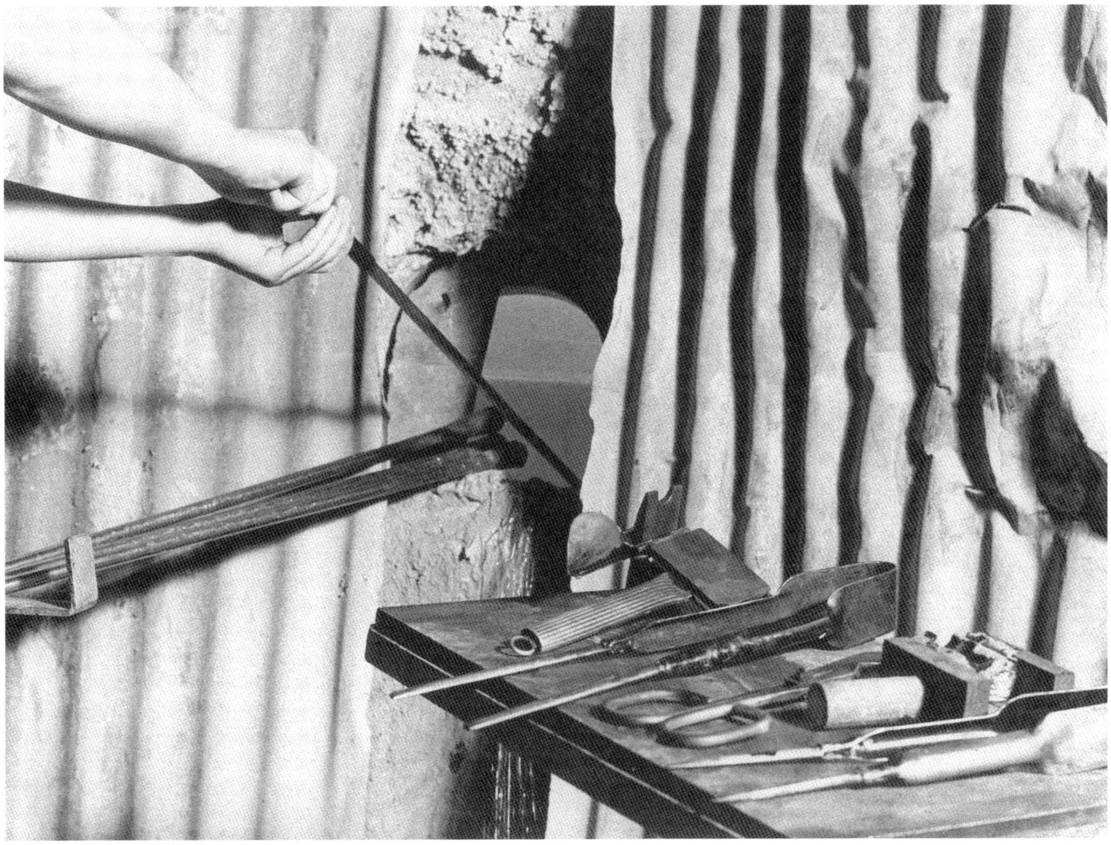

Glass-making tools laid out at the mouth of a furnace.

As a result of this success and expansion of the glass division, on 27 June 1974, Princess Margaret, sister of Her Majesty, Queen Elizabeth II, opened an extension to the glasshouse. It was single-storeyed, covering 20,000 square feet and equipped with nine furnaces, the last of which was lit by the Princess. The occasion was one of community as well as company celebration. It was attended by the Chairman of the West Norfolk Council, Mr Clifford Burman, King's Lynn Town Mayor and Mayoress, Mr and Mrs Eddie Edgley, Chief Executive of the West Norfolk Council, Mr J. Bolton, and the Council's Central Area Manager and his wife, Mr and Mrs K. Faulkner. Also present were the architect of the extension, Mr Peter Skinner, and his wife, and the chairman of the building company, Mr R. Carter and his wife. The Chairman, Mr Arthur Bryan, Chief Designer, Mr Ronald Stennett-Willson, and Production Director, Mr Ray Duly, represented Wedgwood Glass. It was a day of celebration. As the Princess unveiled a commemorative plaque, both employees of Wedgwood Glass and those of neighbouring factories watched. Inside the factory, she was treated to a guided tour, a demonstration of the glassmaker's skills, and showed a display of the range of Wedgwood glass. The Princess was presented with a pair of decanters. Alan Knights, a young craftsman who was achieving the success originally desired for British glassmakers and decorators by Mr Stennett-Willson, engraved grouse and the opening date of the factory extension on them. The event was widely reported and photographs appeared in local and national press.

Reported on the front page of the *Lynn News & Advertiser*, of Friday 28 June, 1974, Arthur Bryan said of the glassworks that 'this factory, although small, has secured for itself an important place in modern design and in the high-quality tableware field'. He hoped it would 'continue to play an increasing part in the crystal and glass trade in the country'. The extension became the new glasshouse while the original section was converted into a cutting, decorating and finishing shop. A special feature of the extension was the louvred windows which could be entirely removed in the heat of summer. Regular guided tours were organised, and from the visitors' gallery there was a panoramic view of craftsmen at work. Advertising had attracted more than 20,000 visitors from all over the world by 1976. Facilities were over-stretched. By reorganising the warehouse and offices new space was available. In 1977, Mr Tom Legge, Chairman of West Norfolk District Council, officially opened a new reception hall. The Mayor of King's Lynn, Mrs Joan Panks was also present. Both were welcomed by Managing Director, Mr Alan Lodey.

It was at this factory that Wedgwood Glass produced modern hand-made items. They were well designed, elegant, sophisticated and simple—both decorative and functional glass. A Company advertising booklet informed all interested in the product that there was a choice of 'table glass, bowls, vases, candlesticks, and other *objets d'art* in clear and coloured glass. The colours are modern, the hand making superb and the design is sensible. The best of modern glass can be British.'

This was evident in the range of items produced for the Silver Jubilee in 1977 of the accession of Queen Elizabeth II to the throne. Ronald Stennett-Willson and Alan Lodey concurred that the items were not only a commercial success but also aesthetically pleasing. They were something to be used and enjoyed, not just collectors' items to be hidden away in a cupboard. This was the purpose of the design and manufacture of glass—beauty and usefulness.

2

GLASS MAKING

Two distinct processes in the age-old manufacture of glass are melting and moulding. Before melting attention must be given to the raw materials which have to be as pure as possible through the removal of impurities. It is the fusion of silica—sand, quartz or flint, and an alkali—soda or potash, which acts as the flux to enable the silica to melt—that are the basic ingredients of glass. Other chemicals are added to give specific properties. Magnesium gives glass its clarity by neutralising the effects of impurities in the silica. Lime provides lightness and stability. Lead oxide adds weight and brilliance and is a major ingredient of crystal glass. Each factory has its own jealously guarded 'recipe'. Small variations in materials used give the end-products their specific, readily recognisable characteristics.

In ancient times, the chemicals added to provide colour covered the undesirable natural brown, green or purple tints that were the result of impurities in the silica used. Colour was also used so that glass could imitate semi-precious stones. Contemporary glassmakers can produce a far greater range of clear and opaque colours than was possible previously, although cost and scarcity of some chemical additives, for example, gold used for making ruby glass, has required experimentation with replacement minerals. The use of colour and colour combinations can be ends in themselves. Colour can give the product its intrinsic value.

Among the commonly used chemicals are oxides, sulphides and selenides which, when dissolved in the flux, give the glass its specific colour. From the Egyptian era, antimony was known to produce yellow as well as opacity in other colours. During the Roman period antimony was also used as an agent to neutralise impurities and to produce opacity. Chromium came into use much later and produces a yellow green, while cobalt produces blue in many of its shades. It, too, can be used to neutralise impurities. Copper is more versatile. Depending on the furnace conditions, it will give red, turquoise or green. One of the most commonly occurring chemical ingredients in glass making is iron as it occurs in minute quantities in silica (sand). Left untreated it can pollute the flux. The result will be the brown or green common bottle glass. If used alone and in sufficient proportion, it will produce a deep emerald green. If controlled, and combined with antimony or manganese, it will produce a range of yellows, ambers, browns, and even the appearance of black.

Depending on quantities used, manganese can produce amethyst and deep purple or softer shades of rose pink. In combination with cobalt it produces an extremely dark colour which resembles black. (In the early 1880s, in Zechlin (Germany) and Bohemia, 'black' glass articles were produced that imitated the shape and design of Wedgwood's basalt). Manganese can also be used as a decolourising agent, 'glassmaker's soap', to neutralise the effect of iron. Nickel is another versatile element in that when used in making soda glass, the result is yellow. When used in making potash glass it gives violet. It has also been used to neutralise impurities. Silver sulphide results in yellow, while tin or stannic oxide gives opaque white. Selenium reacts differently in making soda and lead glass. In the former, the result is pink, while in the latter it is amber. A different colour again results if selenium is combined with cadmium sulphide—sealing wax red, yet selenium can also be used as a decolourising agent. Less commonly used now is uranium which gives the fluorescent green-yellow of vaseline glass. In combination with antimony, amber or topaz is the result.

Using its own recipe, each factory combines basic materials of silica, soda, potash, and other chemicals specific to the task at hand. Some of the chemicals are only added in minute quantities. Each batch requires the same amounts to attain the same finish in the products. Contemporary measuring equipment used is so precise as to achieve this consistency.

Batches of raw material are mixed before being shoveled into the mouth of the pot. Contemporary single pot furnaces are much easier to control accurately than those of earlier periods, and the finished products more precise. During the night, furnaces are watched and controlled so that they are ready for the first batches of each day's production. The furnace temperature has to be raised as quickly as possible to 1400 degrees Celsius or higher to melt the batch to turn it to glass. Furnace temperatures must be precisely maintained during every melt. At the beginning of the working day the furnace temperature is reduced to approximately 1150 degree Celsius. Electronic instruments controlling fuel and air maintain a flame of particular temperature and enable the consistency of molten glass to be kept constant. This results in clear glass, free of minute undissolved bubbles of air or gas (known as 'seeds') or striations of varying consistency ('cords'). A cord is an almost invisible difference in density in the glass which occurs by reason of the fact that it reflects light. When a glass with a cord in it is filled with water, no light is reflected and the cord becomes invisible.

In decorated glass seeds and cords are not always noticeable, but they detract from the perfection of high quality drinking glasses, bowls or vases and are serious in flint glass for lenses. It is interesting to note that although Wedgwood's production of glass occurred during a very short period in the twentieth century, reference to glass making and problems that can confront manufacturers occurs in Josiah Wedgwood's manuscripts.

Although he never produced glass, in the 1780s Josiah Wedgwood had problems with glazing his ceramics. He used a frit of ground flint glass which resulted in an unsatisfactory product. (The preliminary heating of raw materials in a moderate furnace gives a partly-vitrified mass which is called 'frit'. For use, this is broken up and ground to powder). Being a man of science Wedgwood consulted glassmaker, James Keir of Stourbridge, about the problem. Keir suggested a better result would be achieved with the use of the raw materials of flint glass rather than the ground glass frit.

In return, Wedgwood tried to help Keir with problems of the appearance of streaks and veins in glass. The causes of these seeds and cords, and therefore their prevention, were not known at the end of the eighteenth century. Keir believed them to be caused by use of materials with different densities. Following his own experiments reproducing imperfections in glass, Wedgwood wrote a paper about 1783, and possibly presented it to the Royal Society. It was entitled—'An attempt to discover the causes of cords and waviness in Flint Glass, and the most probable means of removing them'. The focus of his paper was on imperfections in glass used for achromatic telescopes. It ended by recommending that glass be stirred constantly to preserve homogeneity or that batches of glass be taken from different levels in the pot and that these batches be kept separated to be used for different purposes. (This system for the prevention of imperfections was also put forward by Louis Guinand about 1798. It was never used for glass manufacture in England). Current knowledge indicates that as little disturbance as possible to the surface of the molten glass in the furnace reduces the likelihood of seeds and cords.

The clear glass is the good beginning. From that point in the production process the glass blower and his team, the 'shop' or 'chair' takes over. (Chair is the title both of the work group and the long armed seat on which the glass blower sits). It is his and their efforts that transform a gather of glass into the required finished article. The master glass blower who does the most skilled work is also known as the gaffer. Gathering glass requires skill and judgment to take the right amount of molten glass accurately but not too quickly to cause bubbles to form, yet fast enough to avoid the intense heat of the furnace opening, and the fellow worker next in line to gather his glass. With a deft twist of the gathering iron, blow pipe or pontil (or puntee) rod any of which may be over five feet long, the bit gatherer takes a blob of molten glass with a minimum of disturbance from the

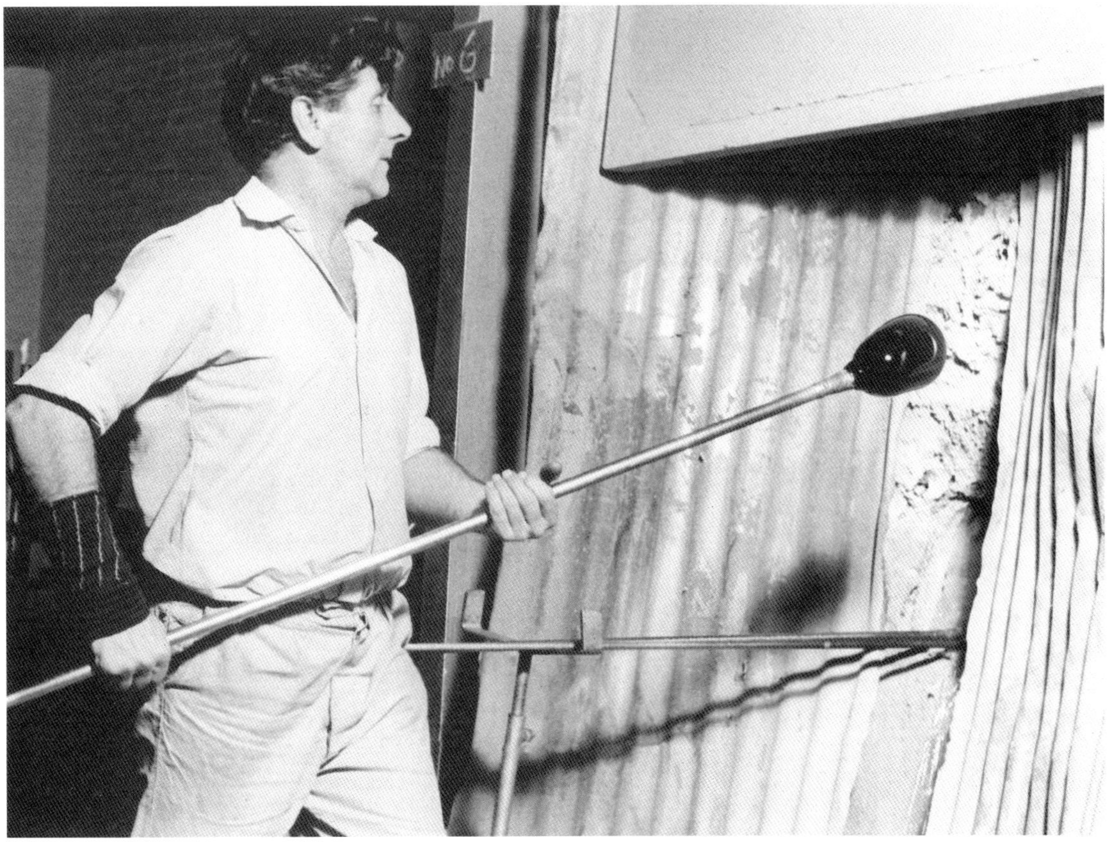

Roy Talbot gathering molten glass.

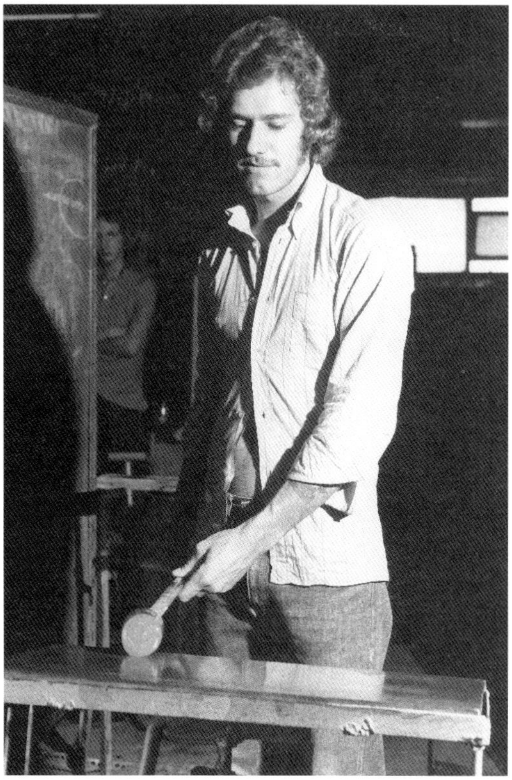

Malcolm Flegg at a stainless steel marver shaping a gather.

surface in the centre of the pot. This ball is taken to the 'marver' (once a slab of marble, now more likely a sheet of polished steel) to be rolled accurately into a symmetrical shape.

From this point, the blower puts the iron down, puts his thumb over the mouth piece and waits as the heat of the iron and glass cause the air to expand as a bubble into the lump of molten glass. He can now manipulate the glass bubble. Depending on what the finished item will be, he can use a wooden, steel or carbon mould to give the finished product its partial or complete shape.

In the manufacture of some drinking glasses, candleholders, small bowls, and vases, the bubble is lowered into the mould while the blower gently blows into the bubble. Once the glass reaches the top of and overflows the mould, it is allowed to cool sufficiently to hold its shape. At this time it is withdrawn, ready for the attachment of the stem and foot by the gaffer. Care must be taken with the soft bowl. Until the bit of additional glass is attached, the bowl must be rotated so that gravity does not cause it to deform under its own weight. To obtain the required size for the piece, the gaffer regularly checks the diameter with a pair of callipers and adjusts the piece until it is the correct size.

On a solid steel pontil rod, the bit gatherer collects a small amount of glass firstly for the stem and then for the foot. The gaffer guides the bit iron with his shears to attach the new glass. The bowl must be cool enough to hold its shape, while at the same time the stem piece must be at the right temperature to control. Time and temperature range are the essence of success. The attached glass stretches as the bit iron is pulled away from the bowl. The gaffer uses the same shears to cut the stem to the exact length required. At this point he is in control, laying the blowing iron across the arms of the chair, he rolls it back and forth. He also stretches and shapes the stem with the 'tool', an implement similar to a large pair of sugar tongs. To form the foot, a similar procedure is followed where the gather is brought then shaped with the aid of flat wooden boards. The size of the foot, too, is measured accurately with callipers. Any surface decoration, such as the attachment of flat discs or seals

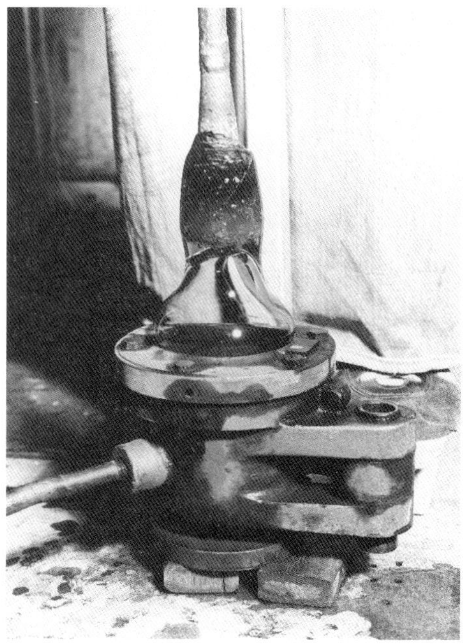

Glass within the mould is still attached to the blowing iron.

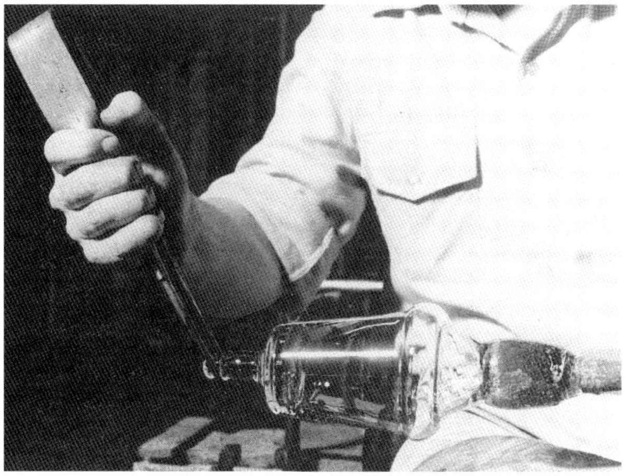

The gaffer draws the newly attached stem away from the goblet bowl.

stamped with simple patterns is done at this time while the glass is sufficiently plastic to work.

Before the finished glass is detached from the iron, a pontil rod is attached to the foot by a small lump of glass. The point of detachment is either scored with a diamond or tungsten point, revolving on a small turntable. A fine flame is directed at the incised line or cold water is dribbled onto the position where the mouth of the glass is wanted. The iron is given a sharp tap, and the glass comes off in a process that takes only a few seconds. The rough edge of the glass is accurately cut away with shears. The pontil rod is detached (leaving the well-known mark), but the glass is not allowed to cool naturally. If this occurred, the stresses that built up when the glass cooled and was reheated several times during shaping and when a stem and foot were added to a wine glass or a handle to a jug or tankard would cause the glass to shatter. With thicker glass this is particularly the case. To prevent loss of work, the 'taker-in' or apprentice carries the still-hot glass in a forked piece of wood or metal to a long kiln, the annealing lehr, through which a moving belt carries the glass. The cooling temperature in the lehr is low enough to prevent the glass melting and losing its shape but high enough to even out stresses. Final cooling is gradual, being up to fourteen hours, with the end product being stable to sudden temperature changes.

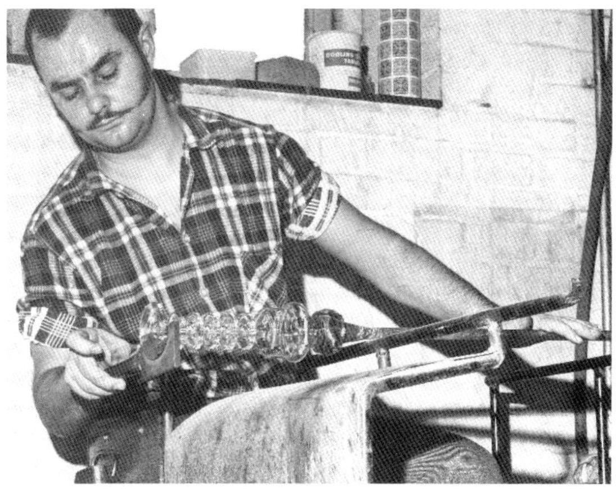

Helmut Morgenfurt measures the foot of a 'Sheringham' *candleholder.*

The final process in finishing the glass, candleholder, bowl or vase occurs when it is passed over a moving band of fine emery or carborundum under a spray of water to smooth the sharp edge. (Thick glass is firstly cut with a diamond saw). Both inner and outer edges may be bevelled. The inner is done on a cork wheel, the outer on an emery belt. The matt edge is finished by passing the glass which is placed on a rotating disc on a rotating platform through gas flames to melt the edge to give it a polished surface. The three processes can be done automatically, but for fine work where the glasses are of different heights and thickness, they are finished individually. Bases are ground on a carborundum wheel, polished and cleaned before being inspected. Perfect pieces can then be stamped with the company's mark.

Both moulding and blowing may be required in the making of drinking glasses, candleholders, small bowls and vases. In moulding alone, age-old techniques and tools in the hands of masters turn glowing molten glass into objects of beauty and utility. Each piece is individually made.

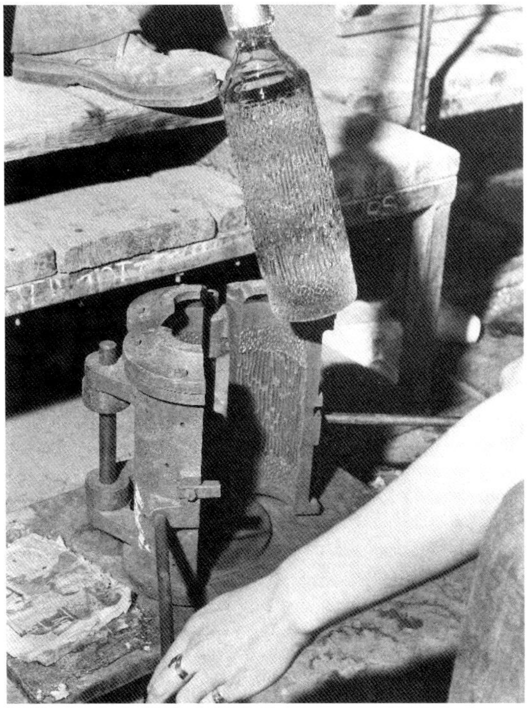

Textured vase — Shape 626 — is removed from the mould.

No two are identical, and minute bubbles may appear — evidence that the item is handmade. Molten glass is pressed into metal two- or three-piece moulds fitted with hinges. On the surface of the moulds the desired pattern is formed as an intaglio. Plaques, bowls and vases can be made in this way and the finished product requires no cutting.

The manufacture of vases and bowls may use moulds fully or partially to shape the item or they may be made entirely freehand. Procedures for making larger items are different from those in making drinkware as much more glass is needed. It is necessary to add extra gathers when the first has been blown to a certain size. The glass blower's skill in manipulating molten glass, heat of the furnace, working with and against gravity combine to form the desired shape. He may use a piece of wood, the tool or even his own hands protected by wads of wet newspaper. Large pieces cool during manufacture. To enable them to remain workable, they are taken to the 'glory hole', formerly a hole near the pot furnace mouth, now a separate oven with a flame hot enough to melt the glass so that it is soft enough to continue the formation process.

There are situations where an artist does not want an item to be made entirely of solid coloured glass but to have the final item appear as solid colour. To achieve this, the bit gatherer collects a batch of clear glass from the furnace, allows it to cool slightly, then takes the batch to a furnace in which is the selected coloured glass. He covers the clear batch with the coloured glass, then removes the second batch. This, too, is allowed to cool before being taken back for a final layer of clear glass to be added.

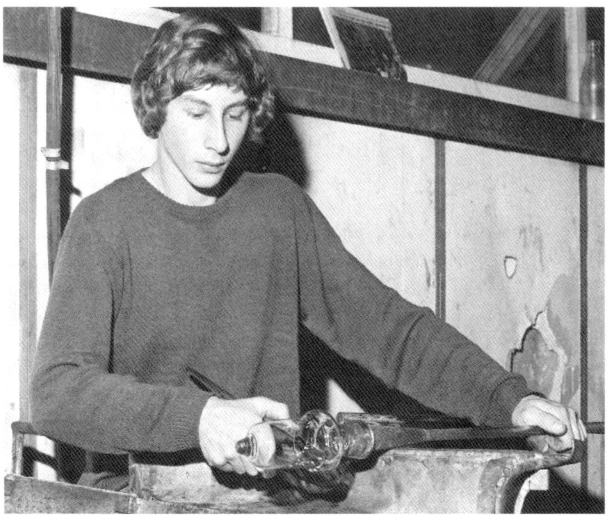

Philip Tuddenham scores the top of a goblet.

To make speckled glass, a batch of clear glass is rolled, where the colour on the finished item is required, into selected grades of powder or granules of coloured glass. These adhere to the hot batch. It is important that work proceeds sufficiently quickly that the coloured pieces soften sufficiently to be worked into the desired shape, but not melt into solid colour. Once the colour is attached, the batch is taken back to the furnace to be covered in a layer of clear glass. Once these processes have been completed, either with solid colour, pow-

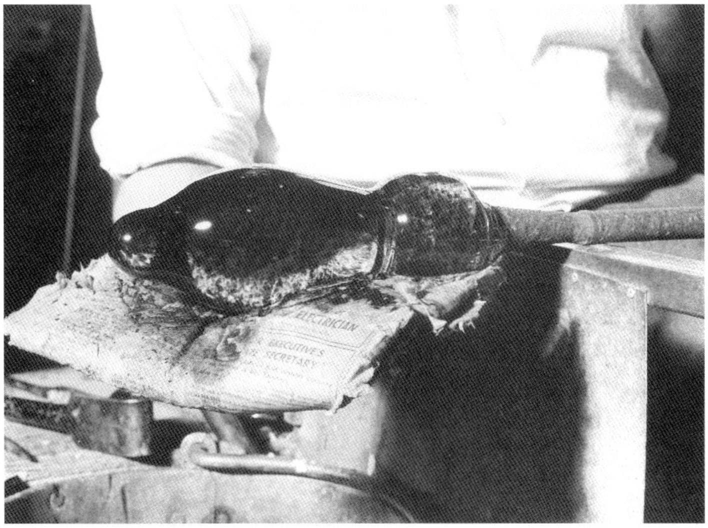

Using a thick wad of newspaper to shape a partridge

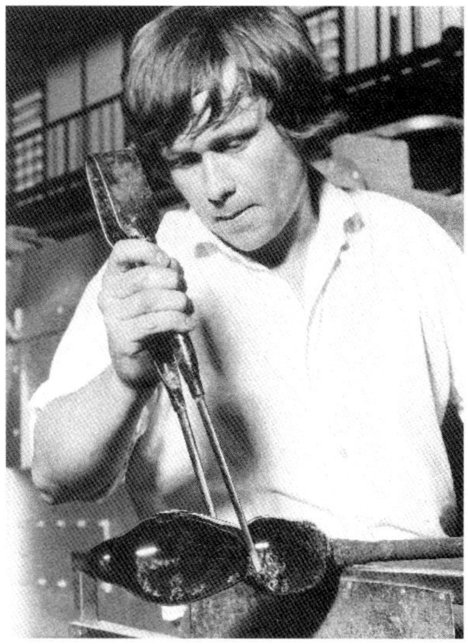

Paul Miller marking the base where the partridge will be detached from the pontil rod.

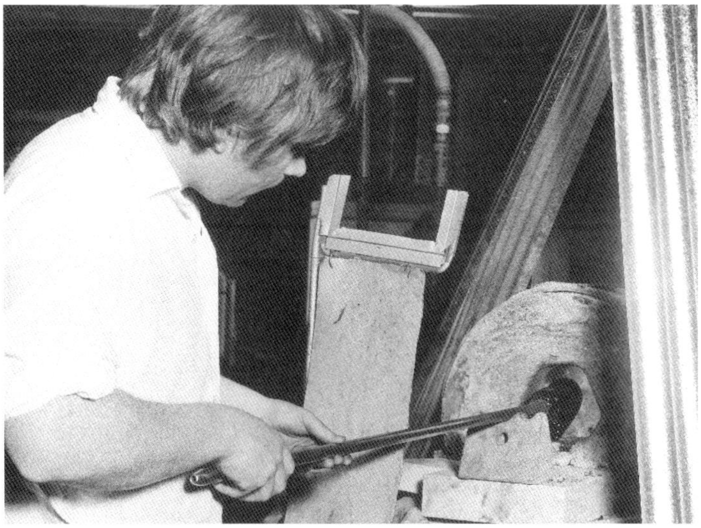

Reheating at the glory hole to keep the partridge soft enough to continue its formation.

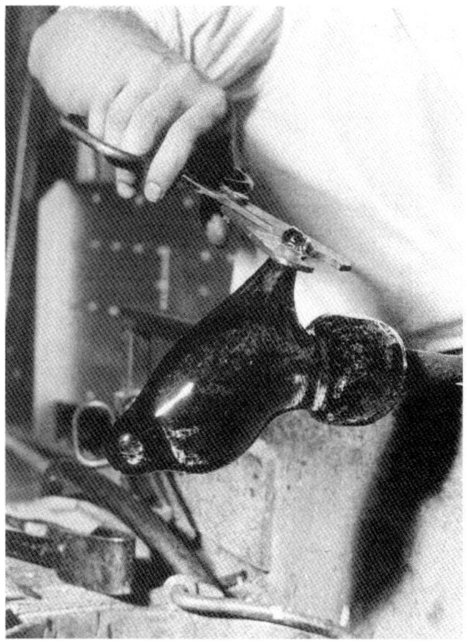

Excess glass is cut off the partridge's tail.

dered or speckled glass, the craftsman can shape the soft glass to the artist's intent.

The making of glass items combines the ideas of the artist/designer and the skill of the master glass blower. The former has the creative ideas, but rarely the skills to be able to blow the glass him/herself. The latter has the responsibility to manipulate, add, cut away and mould the glass to produce a finished object which exemplifies the designer's idea. The two must work in close collaboration to transform an idea into a reality.

Before reaching the stage of master glass blower, traditionally an apprentice learns his trade as part of a chair. During this period he will be required to make various objects as part of his training and to show his increasing skill in the trade. In his own time, such as lunch breaks and after-

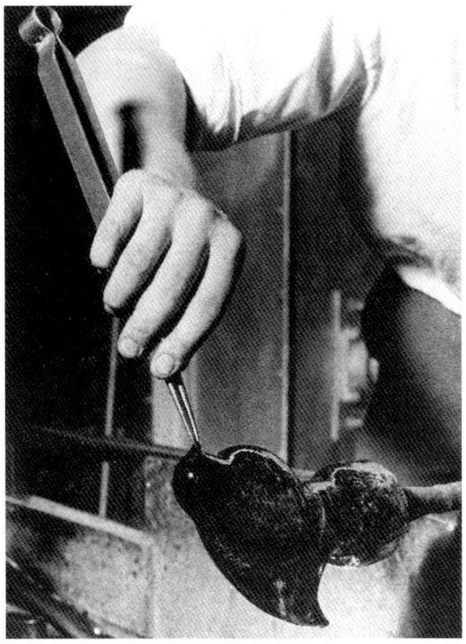

The final shape takes place as the partridge's beak is formed.

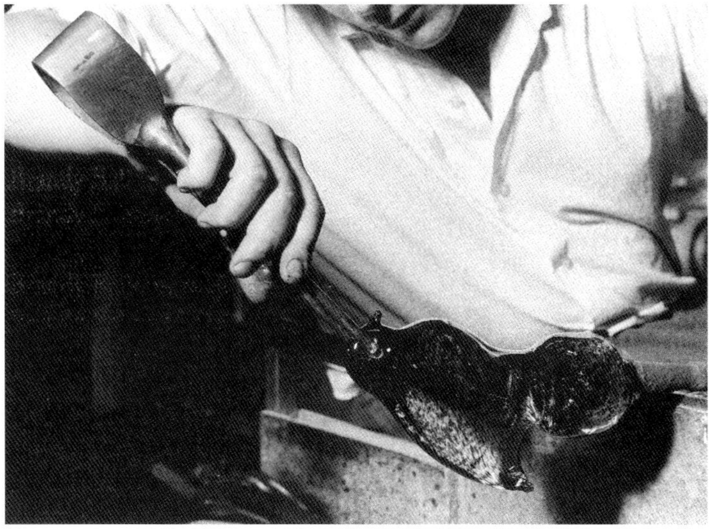

Paul Miller adding eyes to the partridge.

hours, the apprentice will be able to do this. The result may be used to assess his progress. At other times the apprentice may be making small objects without assessment in mind but nevertheless to increase his skills. Objects made in this way are called 'friggers' (or 'friggars') or end-of-day glass. The production of friggers is an essential part of training. Some are of high quality, depending on the stage of an apprentice's training. They are clearly not copies or fakes. Friggers are also produced by glass blowers in their own time, usually from molten glass remaining at the end of a day's work or on Saturdays when the glasshouse is not operating.

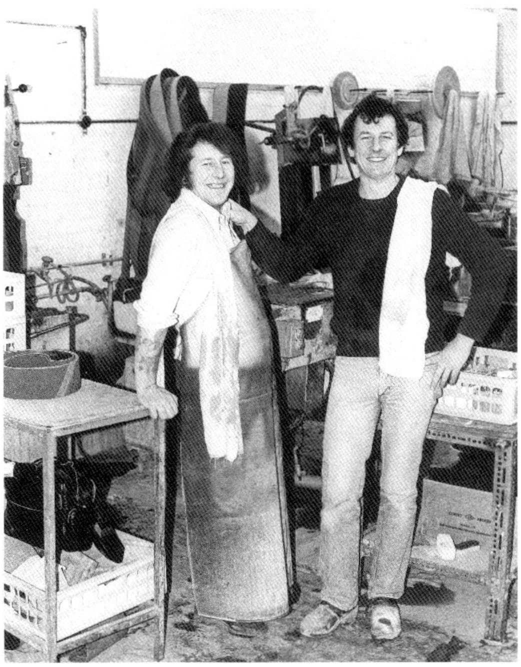

Ken Tiler and Otmar Schoss in the finishing room.

For centuries it has been the right of the glass blower to produce such items. Some friggers were taken home and used as family decoration. Others were sold at local fairs to bring the maker a little more income than could be achieved through his regular and sometimes very small wage. In past times the glass blowers paraded their friggers through the town in which the glasshouse was located. Stops were made at the public houses for the items to be assessed and voted on. The most popular received a prize and the item could be put into factory production. Friggers were never intended to be passed off as company products. Over time many friggers from different companies have passed into general circulation. They will not bear a company's signature mark. Their finish may be inferior to the company's product. Because of the different colours remaining in the glass pots at the end of a day, some specimens use colour combinations not normally used by the company.

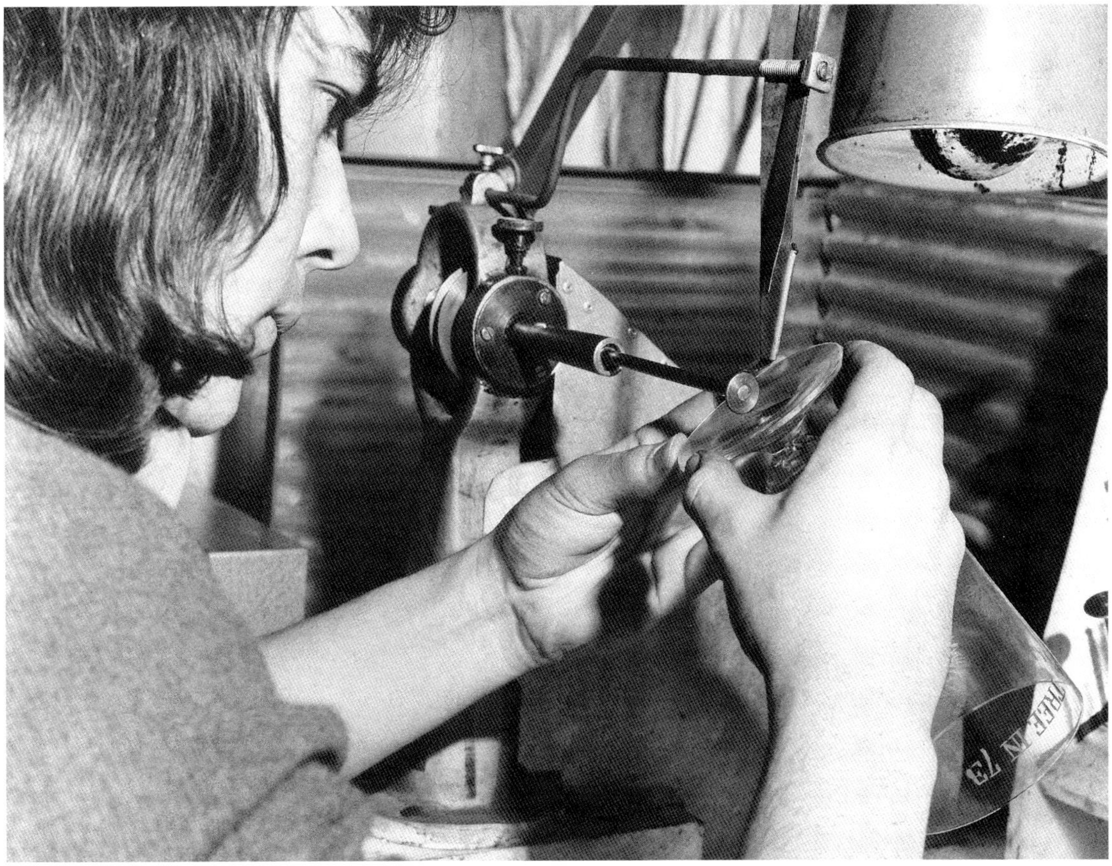

Alan Knights engraves the item number under the foot of a Plant a tree in 73 *clear glass goblet.*

DECORATING GLASS: Engraving

Most contemporary engraving is done with a copper wheel on a drive similar to that of a dentist's drill. Although some engravers use a diamond point, the more versatile engraving implement is the copper wheel using an abrasive such as emery powder in oil. The craftsman/woman usually has a selection of wheels, varying in size from about one-eighth of an inch (.2 cm) to three or four inches (7.5 cm or 10.25 cm) from which to choose. These are interchangeable on a rotating spindle allowing the engraver to work quickly and efficiently.

The engraved area may be left grey or matt to provide contrast. Alternatively the cut area may be polished. Either way the varying texture adds its own special character to the finished product. On one hand, a simple engraving of inscriptions for special events for which the glass item has been commissioned is an end in itself. On the other hand, the engraving may be extremely complex. It may highlight the transparency or thickness of the glass. It may complement the beauty of the shape of the piece being decorated. Glass most suitable for engraving will have a high lead content and be of sufficient thickness to produce brilliance when cut.

Cutting

To exploit the ability to reflect and refract light, decorative cutting grinds away selected parts of the surface to increase the number of facets on the glass. The cutter's tools are much larger than those of the engraver. The size of wheels can range from eight to ten inches (20.5 cm—25.5 cm) to two or three feet (61 cm–91.5 cm) in diameter with the largest being used to cut flat flutes or panels. There are four stages in the cutting process. In the first, the pattern outline is marked onto the surface often with a mixture of red lead and turpentine. The second is the roughing, in which the glass cutter uses wheels of carborundum of varying degrees of hardness or less frequently, sandstone, and water instead of oil. The cutting edge of the wheel may be V-shaped, which will give a mitre cut, or convex, which will give shallow olives, flutes or circles. Smoothing, the third process, refines the cut pattern with a copper or sandstone wheel fed with fine sand, pumice or emery.

In the final process, the matt surface of the cut sections requires polishing. This is done by hand, using a wood or cork wheel with fine abrasive such as jeweller's rouge, or by a bath of a mixture of hydrofluoric and sulphuric acid which is quicker. This last method of polishing is not specific to the area that has been cut. Consequently the whole surface of the glass will be affected lessening the contrast between the cut area and the remainder of the surface. This may be a desired effect, but the reason for cutting is to add reflective surfaces that will in turn add light and sparkle.

Etching

Sand blasting removes part of the surface of glass by directing a stream of abrasive sand at high velocity in a stream of compressed air to the surface area to be decorated. Parts of the surface not requiring decoration are masked by a stencil which will resist the blasting by sand. The area removed may be only a fine layer of the surface, but sand blasting may produce deeper, bolder more sculptural effects. This treatment gives a matt finish to the decorated area. This process was first used in the 1870s and is currently is wide use. Wedgwood Glass decorated and base marked its items using this method only.

In less environmentally conscious times surface decoration was achieved through the use mainly of hydrofluoric acid. Acid etching is used less frequently because of the need to dispose carefully of the chemicals. In this process, the surface is covered with an acid-resistant protective coating of wax, varnish or drying linseed oil. The design is scratched on. The essential composition of hydrofluoric acid, sulphuric acid, potassium fluoride, hydroflourosilicic acid and water is applied to the exposed area. The hydroflourosilicic acid is formed as part of the chemical reaction between the glass and the other acids. Consequently when a new acid bath is required, some of the old acid must be added to it or cullet must be dissolved in the bath to achieve the polishing conditions. (Cullet consists of broken pieces of imperfect or damaged glass objects discarded during production or remnants left on the blow pipe or pontil rod. When cullet is melted with fresh ingredients a new batch is formed). During the polishing process, the level of hydroflouric acid reduces and more of the acid must be added to the solution to maintain the efficiency of the bath. Each manufacturer that uses acid etching has its own particular chemical 'recipe' for the combination of the bath. This mixture cuts through the glass to the depth required for the particular design. The depth of etching is dependent on the time to which the glass is exposed to the acid. When the etching is complete the remaining protective coating is removed.

The end product of acid etching on glass is a soft surface that reflects light gently and has a silky texture. The reverse of acid etching is satin glass in which the design area is covered and the remainder of the background exposed to the acid.

3

THE PEOPLE, THE PRODUCT

The Major Designers

The major designers for Wedgwood Glass were Ronald Stennett-Willson and Frank Thrower. Items produced by Wedgwood Glass included candlesticks, vases and bowls, drinkware, decanters, ornamental and fruit paperweights, hand-blown paperweights some of which had fine surface cutting, and wide choices of jewel toned interior colouring or interior air designs, and commemorative wares. They were made in lead crystal and/or glass both clear and coloured.

Ronald Stennett-Willson was born in 1915 at Padgate, near Warrington, Cheshire. His love of designing and making glass was greatly stimulated from the age of 20 when he began work for the Swedish glass import company, Rydbek and Nordstrom, who acted as agents for Orrefors. During World War II he served as a Captain in the Tank Regiment, but at the end of the War he returned to Rydbek and Nordstrom where he remained till 1951.

From 1951 till 1964, Ronald Stennett-Willson worked for the glass importing company, Wuidart, firstly as sales manager and later as joint managing director. Through this position he collaborated with various glassworks including Lemington in Britain and Bjorkshults and Nazeing in Sweden. It was through his work designing vases for Lemington that he won the Duke of Edinburgh's Award for Elegant Design. During this period he wrote his first book, *The Beauty of Modern Glass*, which was published in 1958.

Between 1961 and 1966, he was founder and Reader in the Department of Industrial Glass at the Royal College of Art. Being multitalented and a man of many interests who was not satisfied with

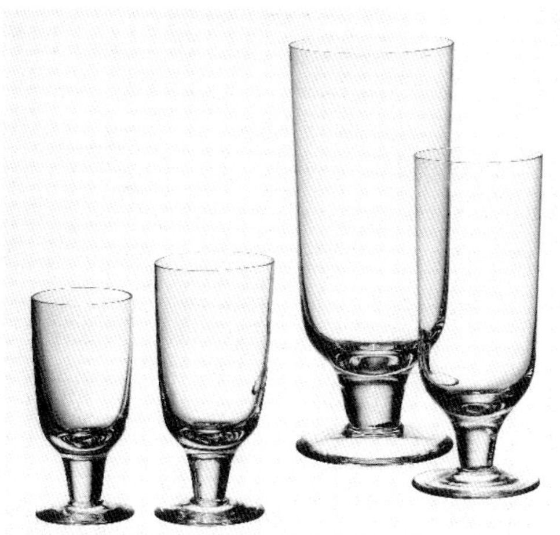

Liqueur, sherry, champagne and beer glasses from the 'Tower' *suite (RSW1).*

working at only one job at a time, during these years, too, he ran the 'first *avante garde* glass furnishing and interior decorating shop in London—Choses—in Hampstead' *(Eastern Daily Press,* 27th November, 1988*)*.

Some of his designs were used on the luxury liner *Canberra* and for Pullman railway coaches. His tableware design, 'Tower', was created for the Rib Room of the Carlton Towers Hotel in London. The 'Tower' suite (RSW1) was the first tableware to be offered to the public bearing the Wedgwood trademark. 'Tower' was produced in clear, blue and topaz.

It was Ronald Stennett-Willson who started one of the first modern glass factories in Britain. The initial work of establishing the factory commenced in 1966, with the first items being produced there in 1967. Some of the earliest designs were still being made after his retirement in 1980. Between these two years, not only was he chief designer for Wedgwood Glass, but also in 1975 his second book, *Modern Glass* was produced.

In 1980, it was the company policy at Wedgwood for employees to retire at age 65. In this year the working relationship between Wedgwood and Ronald Stennett-Willson was severed. He reached the mandatory retirement age. It was not the end of his love of glass or his working life. Creativity knows no chronological age barrier. He joined Paul Miller, master glassmaker and designer who had been one of the original apprentices at King's Lynn Glass, who had formed Langham Glass at Holt in northeast Norfolk. This also became a centre of creative glass making, but on a smaller scale than at King's Lynn. At Langham they were able to make individual pieces which could not be made in an industrial process.

Among his other activities, Ronald Stennett-Willson has served on the Norfolk County Council, was a founder of the Wells Arts Centre and been a member of the executive council of the East Anglian Tourist Board. Through the decades of the 1980s and 1990s, Ronald Stennett-Willson continued his publishing in a series of books on Norfolk churches. He also established the *Norfolk Journal.* Though officially living in retirement, he continued to involve himself in several projects. In 1999, he published *Towards Inner Freedom.*

Frank James Thrower was born on 11th April 1932. His early years were less than uneventful. It has been said he flunked not only at Stationers' Company School but also at his first jobs, particularly office jobs. *Who Was Who* tells of how he 'bought a hat and tried to sell carbon paper, failed, 1951; sold hat and tried to sell pottery and glass, 1953-1960, succeeded' (p.1). This was the irrevocable turning point in his career. It was during this period that both he and Ronald Stennett-Willson worked at Wuidart. Where Stennett-Willson was sales manager, Thrower was one of the salesmen.

In 1960, Frank Thrower joined Portmeirion Potteries as sales director. Within a month he had sold a year's production. He realised there was scope for new ideas and improved design and was given opportunity to have some of them put into production. This was the beginning of twenty-five years of design. The first few years were with Portmeirion, but for twenty-five years from 1962 with Dartington Glass.

It was in that year, a series for interrelated events occurred. Peter Sutcliffe, Director of the Dartington Trust, held discussions with Euan Cooper-Willis from Portmeirion and adviser to Dartington on several matters. Cooper-Willis convinced Sutcliffe a rural glass rather than a ceramics industry would be viable in Devon, and the most suitable person to design for the group was Frank Thrower. Glass produced could be marketed through Portmeirion. The idea was good but the establishment of Dartington Glass took another five years to eventuate.

In 1969, Frank Thrower received the Observer Award for Design. It was followed in 1972 by the Duke of Edinburgh's Award for Design and the Design Council Award. In all he created over five hundred pieces for Dartington Glass, over ninety percent of the company's range. Some reflected designs from the Regency Period but most were thoroughly contemporary. Following the formation of English County Crystal Limited on the 9th July, 1982, he was designer for both Wedgwood Crystal and Dartington Glass, a position he held until January 1987. Later that year, Frank Thrower was appointed a Member of the British Empire, not long before his death on 29th June.

King's Lynn Giftware and Tableware

The first products from King's Lynn displayed a distinct similarity in design to those of Scandinavia, particularly those of Orrefors and Kosta. This comparison did not last long. The British products hand made at King's Lynn were to be well designed ranges of decorative and functional glass, elegant, sophisticated yet simple, and in contemporary colours. The *Financial Times* on May 17, 1969, displayed photographs of matching decanter and tumbler sets, which could be bought either as sets or separately. The set was sold in clear or blue. The paper also advertised a range of

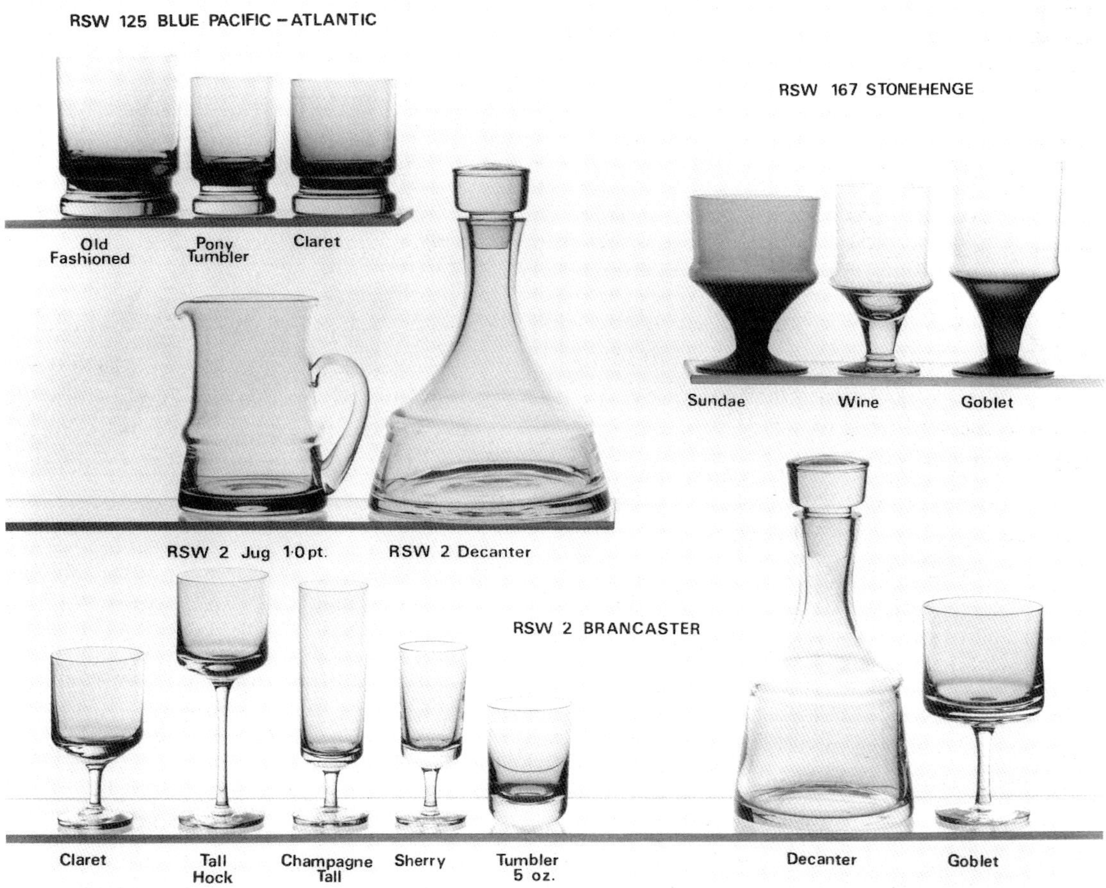

Drinkware, decanters and a jug from the Blue Pacific, Atlantic, Brancaster *and* Stonehenge *suites.*

wine glasses—sherry, white wine, red wine and champagne. These were designed with a tulip-shaped bowl on a heavy open foot for stability. They were sold exclusively through Halcyon Days of Brooks Street, London.

Plans to co-ordinate tableware and inexpensive glass were quickly achieved. By 1971, as well as the designs 'Tower' (in clear, smoky blue and topaz) and 'Brancaster' (clear) in stemware, decanters and jugs, chunky, multi-purpose tumbler designs included 'Atlantic' (clear), 'Blue Pacific' (smoky blue) and 'Sterling' (topaz). According to a report in *Counterpoint,* 1972, these complemented the Company's oven to tableware.

Where the three colours, smoky blue, topaz and amethyst, as well as clear glass were used most frequently and continually from 1969 to the early 1980s, between 1969 and about 1973 vases and dishes/bowls came in several other single colours and colour combinations. *(Figs 1 & 2)* The single colours were cranberry, orange (which was distinctly different from topaz, the former being opaque, the latter transparent), and white opal which were used for vases and dishes/bowls. The colour combinations were rose/rose, blue/blue, green/green and orange/yellow which were used for vases in a variety of shapes and sizes. By 1974, transparent green was added to the colours in regular use for candlesticks. Tortoiseshell was used for several years for vases and lanterns.

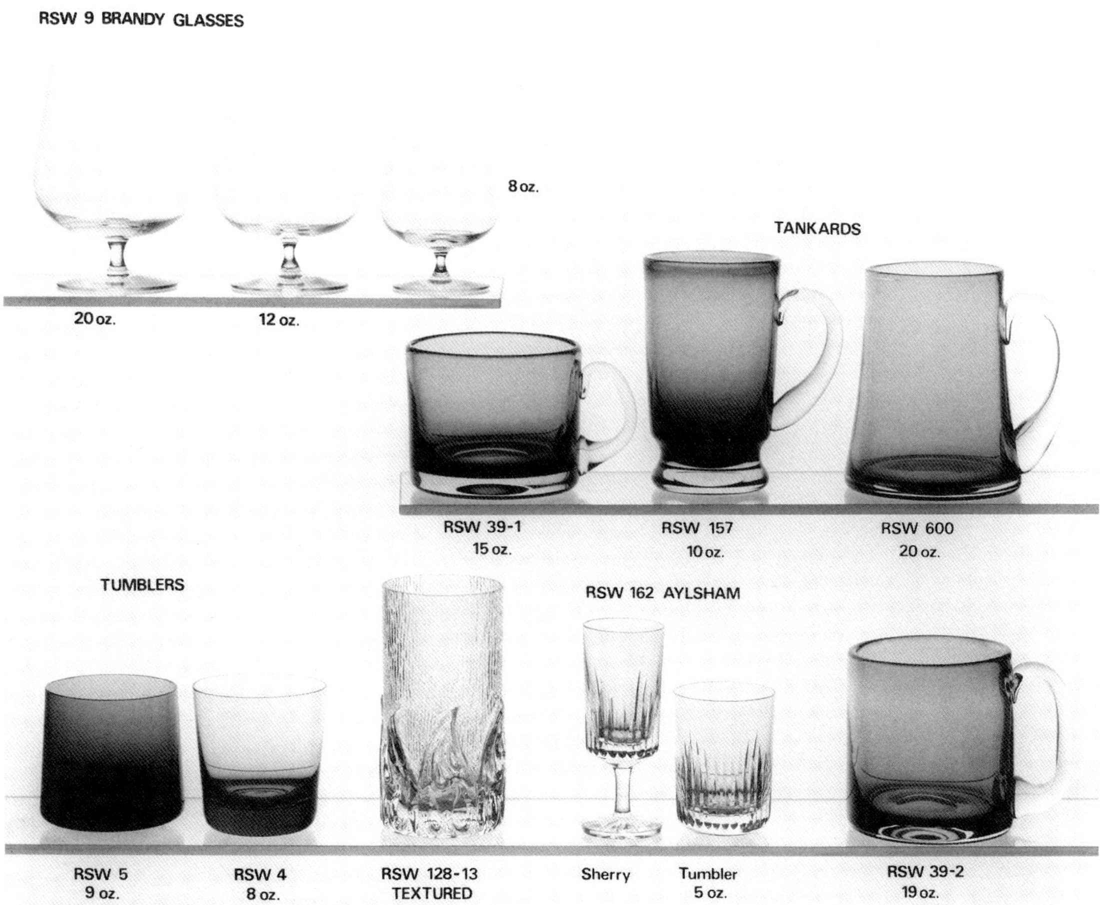

A range of stemware, tumbers and tankards.

The first specific foray into the Christmas gift market was not directly related to traditional Christmas themes. It was a cameo tankard. White on light blue jasper cameos were attached to smoky blue pint (57 cl) tankards, shape RSW39/1. The cameo choice was from Caesar's Head, Stubbs's Horse, and the *Golden Hind*. Brian Greatbatch, in a memo of 28th September, 1971, wrote to inform dealers that 'sufficient tankards are being made up to provide the home market with pre-Christmas deliveries, therefore there should be no hesitation in accepting orders for the Christmas season'. Later the selection of cameos on the blue tankards was widened to include an American Eagle, Shakespeare's head, and several different studies of horses from the designs of George Stubbs. The range of gift tankards was also expanded to include topaz tankards on which white on black jasper cameos were attached. The motifs were Caesar's Head, an American Eagle, and the choice of horse studies. The pint (57 cl) tankard, Shape RSW39/1, was the one most widely produced. It was used regularly not only for general giftware but also for many special commemorative items.

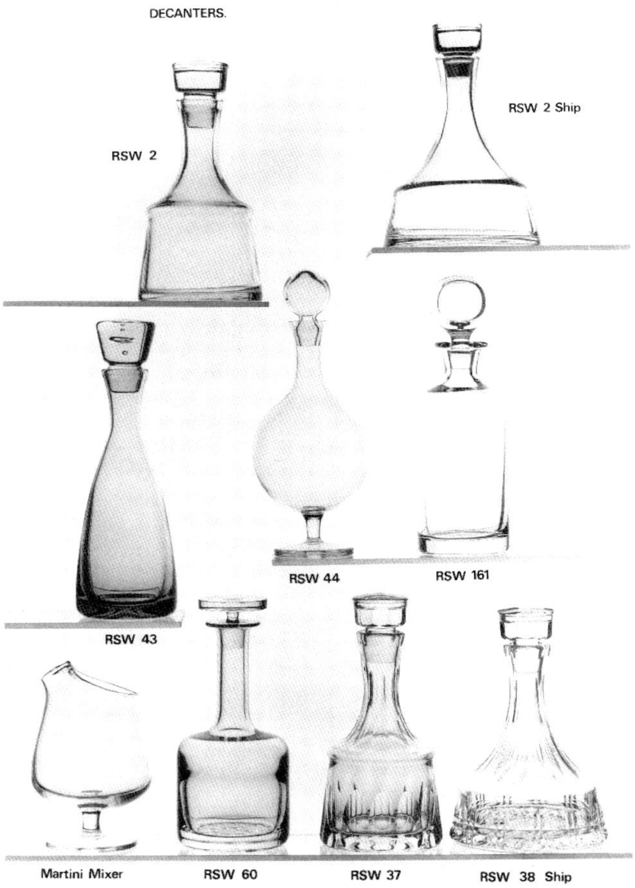

Plain and cut decanters and a martini mixer.

Several years later, other general giftware included bells. Plain *Town Crier* bells came in smoky blue, amethyst, topaz, and green with a clear glass handle. Each stood five-and-a-half inches (13.5 cm) high and was sold in a presentation box. Cameo bells were either smoky blue or topaz also with clear glass handles. The blue bells bore a white on light blue jasper cameo, the topaz bells, a white on black jasper cameo. The choice of cameos was the *Golden Hind* or a Stubbs's horse. These were set in a circular seal on the exterior wall of the bell. The bells were six inches (15.5 cm) high and were also boxed.

As part of its giftware selection, Wedgwood also produced tear-drop pendants *(Fig. 3)*. They came in clear crystal and the choice of colour was the usual blue, amethyst, topaz and green, the last four being enclosed in clear crystal. The edge of each was faceted. They originally cost three pounds and twenty-five pence for the clear crystal and three pounds and thirty-eight pence for encased coloured ones.

Giftware was made during the early years, but much more tableware was produced as is clear from lists recorded in the price books. These show the patterns produced from 1971 to

1973 were 'Tower' (clear, smoky blue and topaz), 'Brancaster', (clear), 'Atlantic' (clear), 'Blue Pacific', (smoky blue), 'Sterling', (topaz), 'Blakeney', and 'Norfolk', (both lead crystal). Items produced included plain and hand-cut drinkware — liqueur, sherry, cocktail/port, claret, champagne (both tall and bowl), goblets, beer goblets, brandy balloons in two sizes (5oz/14 cl and 20 oz/57 cl), a highball glass and tumblers. There were also a decanter, a ship's decanter and a jug. Not all items were made in all designs.

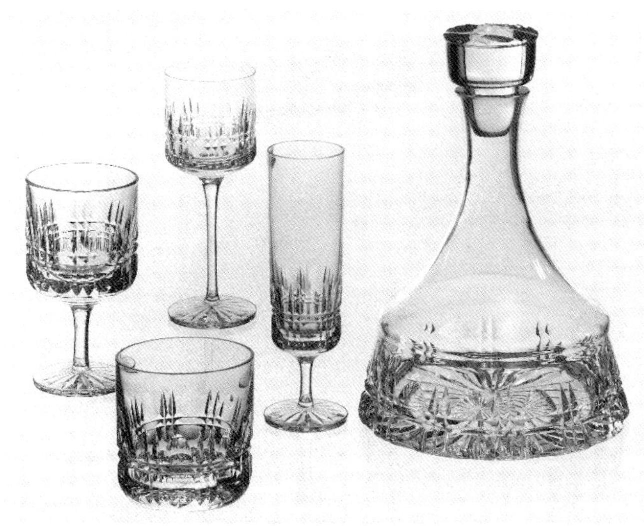

Blakeney *suite – claret, hock and tall champagne glasses, 10 oz/28.5 cl tumbler, and a ship's decanter.*

Hand-blown and hand-cut, glasses with matching decanters and jugs in 'Brancaster' and 'Norfolk' were identical in shape but different in cut. The former was plain, the latter faceted with a simple arched cut. At the same time, 'Blakeney' was cut with an exploding star pattern.

The least expensive item in the ranges available in October, 1971, was the 'Tower' suite liqueur glass which retailed at forty-five pence, while most expensive was the 'Blakeney' lead crystal decanter. This came boxed and cost eight pounds and eighty pence. By August, 1972, the 'Blakeney' fluted-necked ship's decanter retailed for seventeen pounds and sixty-five pence.

In 1973, there were deletions from and additions to the range. 'Sterling' was out of production while new patterns were 'Aylsham', 'Downham', 'Stonehenge', and 'Thornham'. 'Stonehenge' was made in clear, blue and green soda glass. Prices, too, changed with the least expensive still being a 'Tower' item, the sherry glass at sixty pence. The 'Blakeney' ship's decanter remained the dearest at nineteen pounds.

The April, 1975, price book lists the patterns as 'Blakeney', 'Brandon', 'Burnham', 'Dereham', 'Ely', 'Norfolk', and 'Norwich', all in lead crystal, and 'Brancaster' in soda glass. In 1975, the least expensive piece was the 'Norfolk' liqueur glass while the

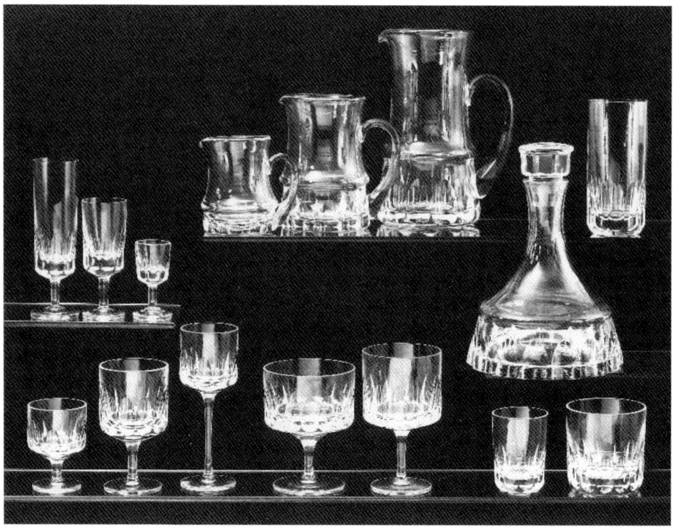

Norfolk *suite — Top row: Half pint/28cl jug, 1 pint/57cl jug, 2 pint/1.2 litre jug, highball glass;*
Middle row: Tall Champagne, sherry, liqueur glasses, and ship's decanter;
Bottom row: Port, claret, hock, bowl champagne, goblet, 5 oz/14 cl tumbler, 10 oz/28.5 cl tumbler .

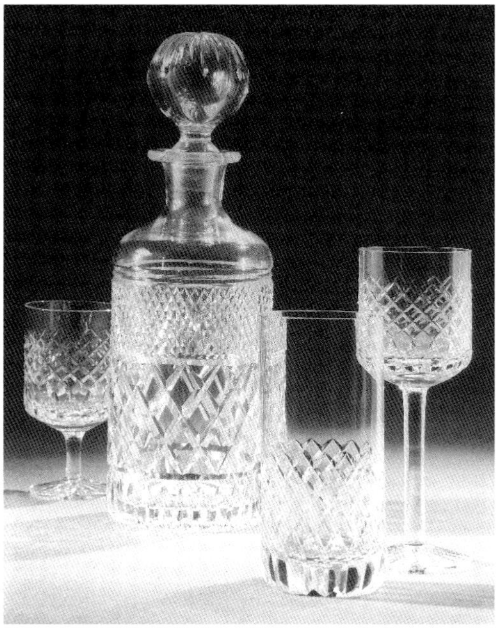

Alton *suite—claret, spirit decanter, highball and hock.*

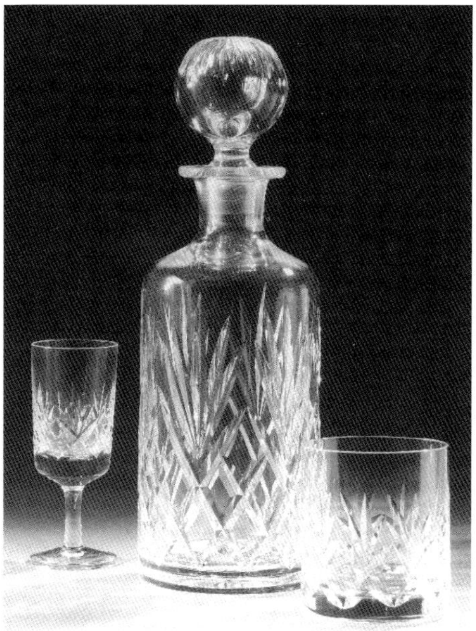

Ashbourne *suite—sherry, spirit decanter and 10 oz/28.5 cl tumbler.*

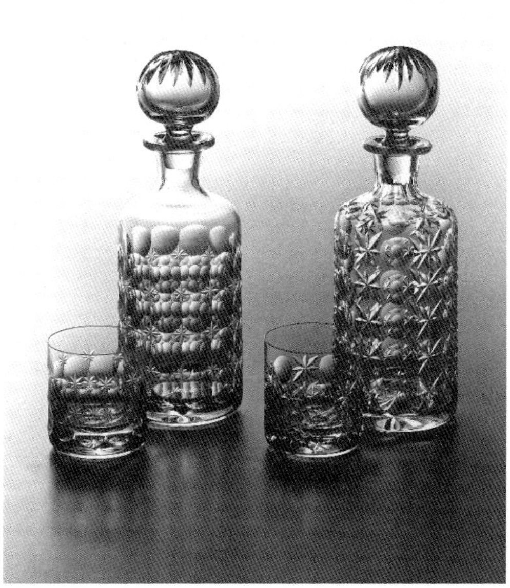

Dove *and* Derwent *suites—10 oz/28.5 cl tumbler and spirit decanter.*

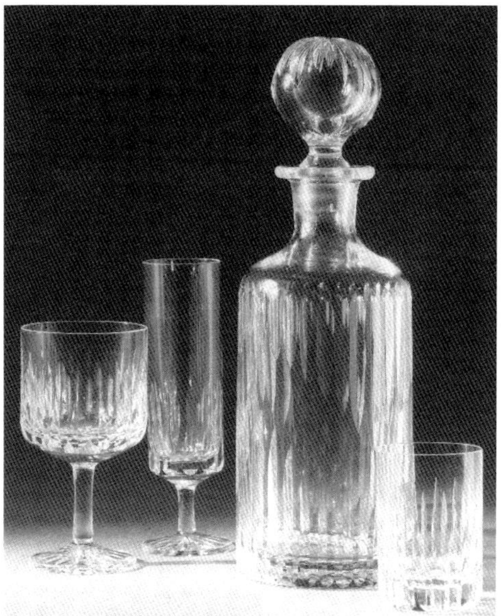

Rushton *suite—claret, tall champagne, spirit decanter, 10 oz/28.5 cl tumbler.*

'Blakeney' decanter had risen in price to thirty pounds forty-five pence. The range in August 1976 was 'Alton', 'Ashbourne', 'Blakeney', 'Denford', 'Derwent', 'Dove', 'Norfolk', and 'Rushton'—all lead crystal, with 'Brancaster' the only suite still in soda glass. Of these, 'Alton', 'Ashbourne', 'Blakeney', 'Derwent', 'Dove', and 'Rushton' were marketed on retail fliers as the Linden Range, describing the suites as combining 'elegant straight-sided shapes with intricate hand cutting in

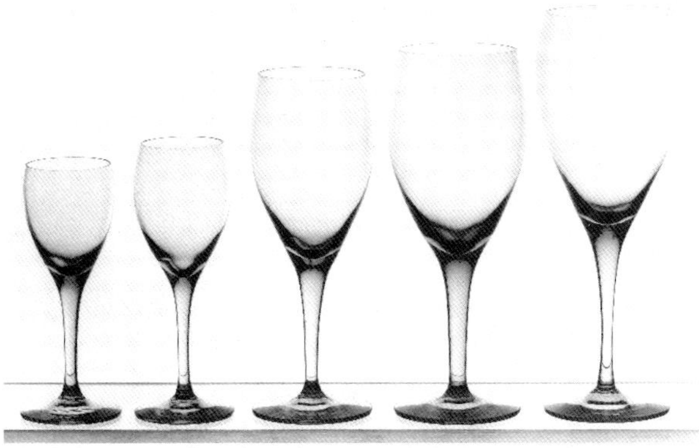

Fenland *suite—small sherry, large sherry, white wine, red wine, goblet.*

six patterns. The result—sparkling, timeless beautiful glasses and decanters that look equally at home with traditional or modern tableware'. This range continued into 1976 with the addition of 'Fenland', where the capacity of all glasses in this range was different from that in most other ranges. At this time the liqueur glass in the suites 'Ashbourne', 'Denford' and 'Norfolk' retailed at three pounds fifteen pence, and the 'Blakeney' decanter's price rose to thirty-nine pounds and ninety-five pence. The 'Derwent' spirit decanter was even more expensive at forty-three pounds and seventy-five pence. (It is interesting to note that many of the names given to glass patterns from King's Lynn were those of towns, villages and districts of Norfolk.) (Full details of items in all suites are listed in Appendix 1).

In 1976, additional to the suites for the table was a large range of boxed giftware, some pieces in lead crystal and others in soda glass. There were bowls, dishes, ashtrays, cake stands, candlesticks and candleholders, sugar bowls, creamers, decanters, ice buckets, Martini mixers with stirrers, and vases. Price of the items reflected the size and type of glass. The essential difference between the two types of glass is that lead crystal contains a greater per cent lead oxide. A reduction in the amount of lead reduces the finished brilliance of the item.

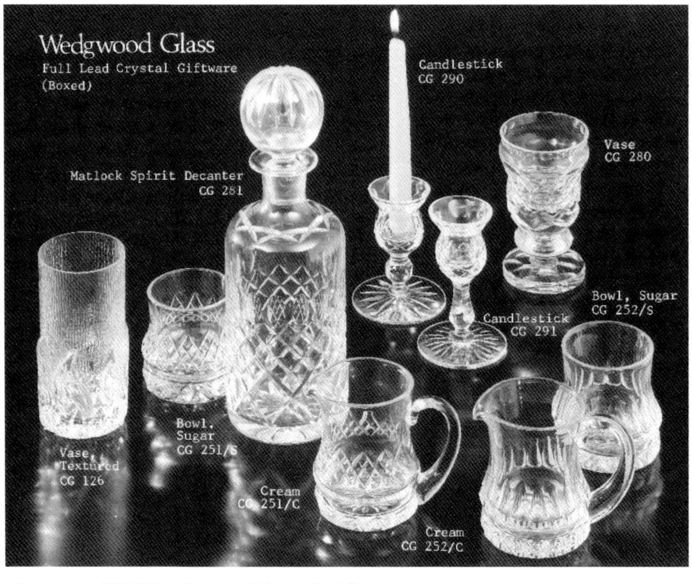

A range of full lead crystal boxed giftware.

Some of the drinkware patterns had complementary accessories, for example small tea and larger dinner bells in 'Ashbourne' and 'Denford'. Other designs for tea bells included 'Bakewell', 'Balmoral', 'Buckingham', and 'Windsor', while the only other dinner bell design was 'Matlock'. Other crystal items were honey pots, marmalade pots, pairs of brandy balloons, pairs of old fashioned tumblers, beer tankards, lager tankards, posy, bottle, stem and bud vases and ring stands.

By the end of the 1970s and into the early 1980s, Wedgwood Glass was advertised regularly in magazines and periodicals. These were as varied as *Readers' Digest*, *Woman's Journal*, *Gifts*, the *Observer* Colour Magazine supplement, *Management Today*, the *Bedford Journal*, *Brides*, *Good Housekeeping*, *House and Garden*, *Ideal Home*, *Homes and Gardens* and

HM Consul's List Supplement. All featured an illustrated article. Readers were informed of the quality of the product:

> *'Wedgwood is famous for the finest china in the world. But they also make glass to the same high standards of quality and design at their factory in King's Lynn.'*
>
> *'Like the selection below, all are hand-made and individually gift-boxed, so beautiful they are collectors' items.'*
>
> *'Each requires an extraordinary amount of skill to make. A craftsman of great ability who works to a predetermined design yet creates these works of art one at a time.'*
>
> *'It means that no two of one item are exactly alike. Every one is an original. And like all originals, something to treasure forever.'*

Specific items and the current price were frequently featured as the focus of the advertisements. Some of these were the Anniversary Goblets, most appropriately, in *Brides*, (as well as other publications), the 'Sandringham' candlesticks, the leaping dolphin, and a marmalade pot. The advertisements appeared between 1979 and 1982.

Retailers were provided with full-colour showcards showing a few of the range of both tableware and decorative items. Both black and white and full colour advertising fliers were also distributed through Wedgwood Rooms and other sales outlets. The fliers, similar to those produced for bone china tableware, illustrated in photographs and line drawings the items available. Current price lists were also distributed to accompany the fliers. For the export market, there was the flier that advertised 'British Craftsmanship direct to you'. Wedgwood organised packaging and air freight for its glassware to the United States *(Fig. 4)*. To boost sales, quotes were done in United States' dollars and included all shipping and duty costs at a competitive rate.

Direct advertising was not the only way that Wedgwood was able to bring its product to the attention of the public. Wedgwood featured as the tableware chosen for presentation of meals by competition finalists in the *Cook of the Realm* contest promoted by the magazine *Women's Realm* and broadcast on *Nationwide* on 28th April, 1971. It included 'Turquoise Florentine' (bone china), 'Blue Pacific' (oven to tableware) and 'Norfolk' and 'Brancaster' glasses and decanters. Quite different but equally effective in promoting the place of glass in the range of Wedgwood products available at the time was the documentary, *Glass Conscious*. It was a thirty minute telecast by Anglia TV in 1972 showing the skills of the craftsmen at King's Lynn. In the film *Just Tell Me What You Want*, Galway crystal with Coalport china was used for dining scene settings.

To represent England at the display of fine British products at Mons, Belgium, in 1979, only Wedgwood tableware, decorative items and glass were chosen. The reception held by the United Kingdom support unit of SHAPE (Supreme Headquarters, Allied Powers in Europe) in honour of Queen Elizabeth's birthday was attended by eleven hundred guests. (*Wedgwood Review*, August, 1979).

4

PAPERWEIGHTS

Utilitarian or works of art? The paperweight has been put to its practical use in many instances, but highly crafted weights have found their way in to specialised collections worldwide. Weights have been created in clear or coloured glass. The glass may enclose coloured canes in a range of patterns, (as in millefiore weights), glass flowers, simple or complicated coloured glass patterns, controlled or random air patterns, or small animals, for example, insects. There is practically no limit to the range of shapes in which the paperweights can be made.

The first of the paperweights designed for Wedgwood by Ronald Stennett-Willson appeared in 1970. These were domed paperweights some in clear glass and others with two or three balls of internal colour. All contained controlled air patterns *(Fig 5)*. Similar in internal form was hand-blown, multi-faceted 'Galaxy' paperweights which only ever contained two balls of colour (*Counterpoint,* 1971) *(Fig 6)*. The earliest colours encased in clear glass for both these shapes were opaque powder colours yellow, strawberry pink, green, white opal and several shades of blue. These colours were discontinued by 1973 as was 'Galaxy'. Simultaneously used were the transparent blue, amethyst and topaz and by 1974, green. To these were added speckled colours—pink and turquoise.

Was it a paperweight or a doorstopper? For a short period in the early 1970s weights large and heavy enough to be used as door-stoppers were also produced. These were domed clear glass enclosing colour and controlled air patterns.

Through the mid-1970s there was 'Spindrift', random patterns of assorted colours within clear flat-based spherical glass. At the end of the decade 'Seafern', in a choice of topaz, pink, blue, amethyst, brown or green with swirls of white and turquoise with swirls of green, and 'Stardance', in topaz, pink, blue, or green with amethyst, and pink or green with blue, were produced. *Counterpoint,* 1979, on page 8 described them as 'a three-dimensional design within clear glass; both heavy paperweights are globular and 7 cm high'. 'Spindrift' was produced for a much greater time than either 'Seafern' or 'Stardance'.

In 1980, 'Maypole' and 'Harlequin' were added to the selection of paperweights. Three-and-a-quarter inches (8.5 cm) high, the former 'captures ribbons of pink, blue, green, or yellow glass within a clear casing' as stated in *Counterpoint,* 1980, on page 15. The latter was two-and-a-quarter inches (5.75 cm) high and featured bubbles and colour, in blue, pink, yellow, or white, or two colours combined—mingled with clear glass *(Fig 7)*. The last globular paperweight was 'Galactic'. Clear glass encased a globe of a single colour—blue, green, or amethyst over which was clear moulded glass sprinkled with fine glass powder. 'Galactic' was two-and-a-half inches (6 cm) high.

Through the 'Andromeda Collection', Ronald Stennett-Willson's hand-made paperweights captured the fascination of space. Because of man's exploration of the space and a greater interest in the solar system—planets, stars, and galaxies, the coloured globe motif, apparently suspended within clear glass, formed the theme for the collection. These weights were quite difficult to make. When the prototypes were made, the central ball of colour deformed when encased in clear glass. Glass master Paul Miller's experimentation resulted in success. To produce a sphere, the coloured shape had initially to be oval. When encased in clear glass this was compressed, forming the desired sphere. The weight was then faceted. One thousand weights were to be produced in each of four shapes and each set was made in four colours—green, red, yellow and blue. The shapes were titled 'Dorado', 'Eridanus', 'Tucana', and 'Capella'.

Creation of items such as these enables the 'ability, knowledge and technique' to be extended beyond daily tasks. 'This in turn has an effect on the general quality of glass making in a factory, because new ways of working discovered in response to the demands of an adventurous designer can be applied to general production' (Stennett-Willson, *Modern Glass,* p. 111).

There were also the 'Apollo' paperweights. They consisted of different sized clear crystal pieces with controlled internal air decorations and produced in a limited edition.

Where the 'Andromeda Collection' *(Fig. 8)* was the most complex, probably the simplest paperweight produced by Wedgwood Glass was the clear disc used for commemorative events. As well as the three-and-a-half inch (9 cm) diameter disc there was the smaller one with a three-inch (7.75 cm) diameter. The clear disc was used for two basic Company designs in the mid- to late 1970s. The former size was etched with the signs of the zodiac. The full set consisted of twelve paperweights. On each a stylised sign and its title were etched in the centre of the disc. Around the outer circle were the twelve symbols of the zodiac. This shape was regularly used for commemorative events and commissions. The latter size had attached to the centre a press moulded heart shape. One design was a clear heart. The others were a colour choice of blue, amethyst, topaz, or green *(Fig. 9)*.

There was also a range of cut crystal drum and pumpkin shaped paperweights. In the centre of the top were white on light blue jasper medallions. Those for general sale included Caesar's head, Cupid stringing his bow, the *Golden Hind* and several dif-

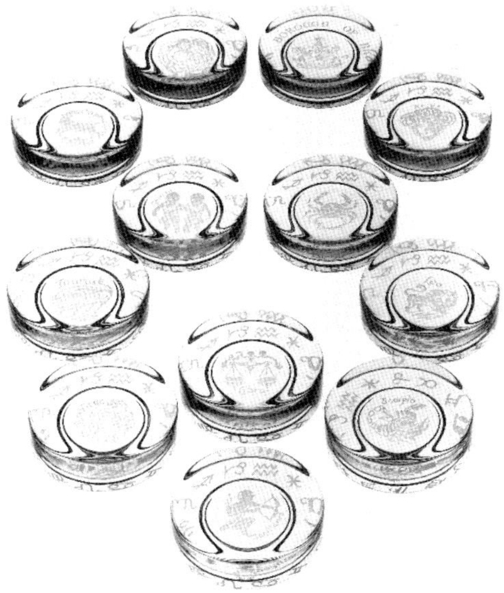

Eleven Zodiac disc paperweights (no Pisces). Top right—'London Borough of Bromley'.

ferent designs of horses after those of George Stubbs *(Fig. 10)*. There were others on which were floral decorated bone china medallions. The most complicated to make were those within which were hand-painted bone china Coalport flowers.

Animals and Plants

Throughout the decade of the 1970s, Wedgwood produced a menagerie of animal, as well as fruit and mushroom paperweights in jewel-like colours *(Figs 11–38)*. When first issued they were inexpensive, but displayed all the creative design skills of the glass artist, Ronald Stennett-Willson, and towards the end of the 1970s, Paul Miller, and the craftsmen. The first items to be released were a small bird (RSW 70), a large bird (RSW 71), a penguin (RSW 72), a long-tailed bird (RSW 73), and a fish (RSW 74) sometimes referred to as a trout. Originally the small birds were produced in clear glass, blue, topaz and amethyst, and speckled colours. The large birds were produced in cased yellow, pink, light blue and green, and assorted speckled finishes including cream and brown, and dark and blue. The outer casing on the early speckled birds was quite thick and obvious. On later examples of all shapes, the casing was thin and much less obvious, reflecting the increased skill of the maker. Penguins came only in blue, amethyst (dark enough to appear black) and topaz. Long-tailed birds were in only one single colour—blue, and three speckled colour combinations—cream and brown, dark and white, and pink and white. These birds were very delicate because of the fineness of both their long necks and tails. Fish were speckled turquoise, speckled brown, and speckled cream and brown. All items could be bought individually gift boxed. Birds in both sizes and the fish were also sold as boxed sets of four. In each box were assorted speckled finishes in four basic variations.

A full-colour advertising flier of the time described the pieces as 'Studies in hand made glass ... individually produced by craftsmen. Great ability is necessary to work to a predetermined design yet create these works of art one at a time. This means no two are exactly alike—each one is an original'. This is evident when examining a range of any of the items. Colour was consistent, but sizes often varied quite markedly. One specimen was produced as quite a large piece. A similar specimen was quite small, comparatively. The latter should not be confused with a similar item which belongs to the later Lilliput series. The difference was never reflected in the price of larger versus smaller item. The difference was the result of different craftsmen using slightly different amounts of glass at different times to produce the items. Depending on the complexity of the figurine, a team could make between seventy and one hundred and forty items in one day, while some glassmakers could make up to five hundred small birds in that time.

To the original birds, penguin and fish were gradually added many more shapes in the next ten years. These were an owl, a seal, duck, mouse, egg, cat, elephant (either with trunk up or trunk down), baby elephant, frog, hedgehog, polar bear, snail, squirrel, whale, fledgling, duckling, partridge, robin, Scotty dog/terrier, seated dog/puppy, dolphin, hippo, rabbit (in two sizes), hare, panda, pig, parrot, rhino, otter, stoat, and Jumbo, a large elephant. A second size of penguin was also added to the list. There were also an apple, pear, mushroom, seashell, a Cornucopia vase, and a teddy bear.

Many of the pieces were produced in a single solid colour, e.g. topaz, lilac, sapphire, green, and in clear glass. Others were in coloured glass encased in clear glass, e.g. powder blue, yellow, grey, or white. Some were speckled in a single colour—topaz, green, pink, amethyst, white, or brown. Others were speckled in two colours—blue and green, i.e. turquoise, cream and brown, red and brown, blue and yellow, blue and pink, blue and green, white and brown, white and pink, white and cream, white and turquoise, blue and dark, or yellow and brown. In all these examples of speckling there was a clear glass core and a layer of coloured granules, in some cases coloured powder, and in other cases both, over which was an outer casing of clear glass. The grey speckling through the use of powder on some animals was so fine as to resemble fur. Two weights were produced in crystal—a three-headed elephant ring stand and a leaping dolphin*(See Appendix 5)*. The range of colours and colour combinations for figurines was greatly expanded by the last years of the decade, but there was never a year when figurines in all colours and all colour combinations were produced.

While the range of colours was extensive, no items were made in the full colour range. The most frequently used single colours were topaz, sapphire and lilac (amethyst so pale as to appear pink). The most frequently used speckled colours were pink and turquoise, while several items came in one colour combination only. For example, the robin was only made in red and brown while the panda was only in what was called dark and white. ('Dark' was the deepest amethyst or blue which, because of the thickness of the glass, appeared almost black). Some colour combinations were used only once. These included blue and yellow, blue and pink, and blue and green used for parrots, white and turquoise for a seashell, white and cream, yellow and brown, and speckled grey for an owl, and speckled amethyst for a Scotty dog.

Natural colour was used for many items. This most specifically occurred with grey for the elephant, otter, seal, squirrel, and mouse; the speckled green and speckled brown for the frog; the cream and brown, yellow and brown, speckled grey, and white and cream for the owl; topaz for the squirrel, or white for the polar bear and rabbit. Colour used for parrots—blue and yellow, blue and pink and blue and green, exemplified their natural plumage, as did that for ducks, particularly wild ducks from various regions of the world, in speckled green, speckled turquoise and speckled brown. Penguins and the panda in dark and white were true to life. When produced in sapphire, speckled green or speckled turquoise dolphins and whales depicted the colour of the sea. Speckled green, speckled pink or speckled brown apples could have come straight off the tree. Mushrooms in sapphire, topaz, white and brown, cream and brown, or white and pink would look in place on the forest or jungle floor.

At the same time there was great artistic creativity in the use of colour. This is evident in many pieces through the use of such colours as sapphire or topaz for otters, hippos, seals, and penguins, lilac for hedgehogs, speckled turquoise for elephants and dogs, or speckled pink for stoats, hares and rabbits. When viewed together, this range of colours provides quite an unlikely menagerie for Noah's Ark.

As with all hand-made items, no two of the paperweights were identical. In the early years of production, several colours and styles were used for a relatively short period. This colour was produced by the use of powder rather than of granules, and included a brilliant yellow, white opal, strawberry pink and dense blue to colour domed and 'Galaxy' paperweights, and with the exception of opal white, birds. Yellow, in the form of granules, was used later in the 'Andromeda Collection'.

During the rest of the period of production, the main powder to be used was grey, which when melted at the correct temperature, gave the finished item the appearance of having fur. Blue powder was also used on the backs of the parrots. All other speckling was achieved through the use of coloured granules.

Although the majority of the paperweights were finished with a shiny surface, there were several, for example the apple, pear, snail, and elephant, that were produced with a matt surface. The rhino had a clear shiny head (enclosing a bubble of topaz) and a clear matt body. They are recognisable by colour and shape as coming from the Wedgwood factory. More importantly they are stamped, though on the matt surface the finely etched mark is sometimes difficult to see. During the years of production, all first quality figures were etched with 'Wedgwood England' and a paper or foil label was attached.

Production of the coloured animal and plant paperweights continued into the early 1980s as is evident from price lists and home sales invoices. From 1982, many of the tableware and ornamental items were made in midnight, a transparent grey colour used to produce several of the animal figures including an owl, a snail, a pig and a teddy bear. The etched base mark is different from that previously used. So are the labels. (Full details in Chapter 13 Marks and Labels)

As well as the large animal, fruit and mushroom paperweights, a collection of smaller ones was introduced in 1979. They were the handmade items of the crystal Lilliput Collection. The range of shapes was not quite as extensive, nor was the range of colours as those of the larger series. The first twelve were an apple, a dolphin, duck, duckling, elephant, mushroom, owl, penguin, polar bear, shell, snail, and whale. Two years later, *Counterpoint*, 1981,on p.8 stated that as the 'Lilliput Collection of miniature sculptures in sparkling lead crystal celebrates its second birthday', the range was expanded with the addition of a pear, hippopotamus, hare, and a Norfolk pig. This collection was further expanded with the addition of a squirrel, frog, hedgehog, long-tailed bird, a teddy bear and a miniature leaping dolphin. All came in clear crystal, but some came in colours including topaz, sapphire and lilac, and even a few were speckled in turquoise or pink*(See Appendix 6)*.

5

CANDLESTICKS AND CANDLEHOLDERS

Four major candlestick and candleholder designs by Ronald Stennett-Willson made at King's Lynn in the 1970s were 'Sandringham', 'Brancaster', 'Cromer' and 'Sheringham'. If any of these designs could be said to be 'simple', it was 'Sandringham', the delicate, fine-drawn stem candlestick. It came in four heights—three-and-a-half inches (9 cm), six-and-a-half inches (16.5 cm), seven-and three-quarter inches (17.25 cm), and nine-and-a-half inches (24.25 cm). More complexity occurred in 'Brancaster'. It was straw-stemmed, that is, the stems were hollow. Only three heights were made—five-and-a-half inches (14 cm), eight inches (20.5 cm), and eleven inches (28 cm). 'Cromer' held either a round candle or one with a two-inch (5 cm) diameter flat base. The design had a drawn stem and came in three heights, four-and-a-quarter inches, (12 cm) six inches (15.5 cm), and eight-and-a-quarter inches (21 cm). The last, 'Sheringham', was quite complex, requiring skilful work in combining various numbers of pieces of glass to create candleholders of six commercial heights. They included one ring, two rings, three rings, five rings, and until the mid-1970s, seven rings and nine rings. These last two sizes were relatively difficult to make as an error in attaching the final rings or the foot meant the candleholder was ruined.

During the period the candlesticks and candleholders were made, initially they were in clear and three colours—topaz, blue, and amethyst, and from 1974, in clear and four colours when transparent green was introduced. The exception was 'Cromer' which did not come in green. The Wedgwood price book from 1971 records the cost of 'Sandringham' candlesticks ranged from one pound to three pounds and thirty pence, that of 'Brancaster' from ninety pence to seven pounds and thirty pence, while 'Sheringham' because of the complexity ranged from one pound and ninety pence for a one-ring to fourteen pounds and ten pence for a nine-ring candleholder *(Figs 39–41)*.

Candles were sold to match the candlesticks and candleholders. For 'Sandringham' the colour choice was white, blue, orange, and purple, while for 'Brancaster', 'Cromer' and 'Sheringham' it was white, red, blue, orange, amethyst and pink. Not only did Wedgwood produce this range of candlesticks and candleholders and provide candles, but also in the early 1980s, it introduced its own decorations for them, according to a report in *Counterpoint*, 1982, on p. 7 'the fireproof, washable flower, mounted on an expanding ring' in a choice of co-ordinated colours. They were designed in two sizes, one to fit the narrow 'Sandringham' candlestick, and another to fit the broad 'Brancaster' and 'Sheringham' candleholders. When fresh flowers were not available or too dear, the life-like multi-petalled, artificial option was white, sapphire, lilac, topaz or green to co-ordinate with the colours of the candlesticks or candleholders. The combination of candlestick or candleholder and floral arrangement was sold as a boxed set. Although the information in *Counterpoint* referred to the floral decoration as 'fireproof', each box bore the clear warning 'These candle rings are inflammable. They must be removed before the candle is lit'.

Other coded but unnamed candlestick, candleholder and table lantern designs were also produced. Several of these designs were able to accommodate at least two candle sizes—standard and broad-based. A couple of these wider candleholders could also be used as posy vases. These last had matching candles in white, blue, orange, and purple.

A further design from Ronald Stennett-Willson was a wind-light, a two piece lantern-like candleholder. It was produced in textured clear glass. The base could double as a posy vase.

Among the later candlestick designs were 'Whorl' and 'Helix'. The former came in the standard clear and four colours but in only one height—three-and-a-half inches (9 cm). The latter came in the same clear and colour range but there were three heights—four inches (10.25 cm), five-and-a-half inches (14 cm) and seven inches (18 cm). The regular clear and colour range was used for most candlestick and candleholder shapes, but a few were also made in tortoise-shell.

In 1975, the Design and Industries Association celebrated its diamond jubilee with a competition. Ten thousand items were submitted. Four hundred were personally selected by Professor Sir Misha Black, president of the Association, as meeting the Design Index for the 'Fitness for Purpose'. Exhibitions to display them were held in London and Glasgow in January and February. True to the philosophy of Josiah I who was a firm believer in well-designed functional goods and the need to display and promote them to the public, Wedgwood Glass was among the eleven designs which were submitted by Wedgwood (they included Midwinter and Royal Tuscan hotelware). Wedgwood glass was an innovation of the twentieth century and its inclusion in the prestigious selection for the Design Index reinforced the Wedgwood tradition—all items must conform to principles of good design.

6

ROYAL COMMEMORATIVES

It has been a centuries old custom to commemorate a significant event on glassware. Victorious Roman gladiators received engraved trophies. Examples of these are still held in several Italian museums. Old armorial Venetian, Bohemian and Dutch glass bears decoration in coloured enamel, and craftsmen of the last two countries were expert in the technique of engraving with the wheel and diamond point. One of the earliest specimens of etched English glass seems to be the Exeter Flute currently held in the Royal Albert Museum, Exeter. (There is no record of its use in Exeter.) Its alleged production in London was for many years attributed to the Savoy Glasshouse of the Duke of Buckingham. More recent research suggests it was probably made and decorated in the Netherlands for the coronation of King Charles II in 1661. It bears a strong resemblance to similar glasses of the period also made on the Continent. The tall narrow flute is diamond point etched with a bust of the king in a medallion. It also bears the stump of an oak tree and the words 'God Bless King Charles the Second'.

The period after the Restoration in 1660 saw the experimentation in and development of the first full lead crystal glass in England by George Ravenscroft about 1676. His discovery had a positive impact on glass production in England with small glassworks opening in many centres across the country, including, as previously mentioned, at King's Lynn. From the coronation of Queen Anne in 1702, every subsequent coronation of a British monarch has been commemorated in glass. The extant specimens clearly show the growing mastery not only of the glassmakers but also of the decorators. Each generation utilised the advances of technology to improve its product.

Wedgwood Glass played its role in commemorating royal events but not of a monarch's coronation. The first glass commemorative item made by Wedgwood Glass at the King's Lynn factory was an amethyst tankard for the Investiture of His Royal Highness, Prince Charles, as Prince of Wales at Carnarvon 1st July 1969 *(Fig. 42)*. It bore the Welsh Dragon pressed as a seal on the front. This first edition was five hundred. The following decade was a boom period for further royal and other commemoratives with many produced in glass.

The Silver Wedding on 20th November, 1972, of Her Majesty Queen Elizabeth II and His Royal Highness Prince Philip, Duke of Edinburgh was the first major production event of the decade. The glass products were two sets of goblets *(Fig. 43)*. One set was smoky blue. Within a hand-cut laurel wreath, was a white on light blue jasper portrait cameo medallion of the Queen on one goblet and of Prince Philip on the other. The cameos were applied to the exterior as a seal. The design used on the cameos was that of Arnold Machin. (It was also used on the full sized royal family portrait medallions issued in light blue and white jasper. The Queen's profile had previously been introduced for use on British stamps and coins). The limited edition consisted of five hundred pairs of goblets accompanied by signed, numbered certificates and a descriptive folder within a presentation box. The original price for the pair was twenty-five pounds.

The other set of goblets was topaz. These were identical in shape and decoration with the exception that the cameos were white on black jasper. They were not numbered and did not have a commemorative certificate. The edition was also five hundred pairs originally sold mainly in Britain but with a limited number going to the Canadian market.

To commemorate the wedding of Her Royal Highness, Princess Anne to Captain Mark Phillips on the 14th November, 1973, a similar blue glass hand-cut goblet with a clear stem and base was produced. For this item, within the hand-cut laurel wreath, a white on light blue jasper portrait cameo medallion of the Princess, designed by Arnold Machin from a photograph by the Earl of Lichfield, was set as a seal to the exterior of the bowl. This edition, too, was five hundred.

To complete the set of the Royal Family, a similar blue goblet with the white on light blue jasper portrait cameo medallion, designed by Arnold Machin, of Prince Charles, Prince of Wales, was produced in an edition of three thousand. All goblets stood approximately five inches (12.75 cm) high.

In 1977, for the Silver Jubilee of Queen Elizabeth's accession to the throne there were several completely different items produced. They were extremely popular to such an extent that the King's Lynn factory was working to full capacity. Limited editions quickly sold out. Unlimited editions were made during the whole year. A national committee, chaired by the Prince of Wales, was set up to comment on the range of items produced for the Silver Jubilee. It selected from the five items in the field of glass which met the standards, three made by Wedgwood Glass – the decanter, the clear goblet and the disc paperweight. Ronald Stennett-Willson led the successful design team which included the complementary abilities of technologists, salesmen and accountants *(Fig. 44)*.

The range for the British market included:

- The simplest, a three-and-a-quarter inch (8 cm) diameter, clear glass, disc paperweight etched with the Queen's cypher and a commemorative inscription, 'THE SILVER JUBILEE 1952–77 … H. M. QUEEN ELIZABETH II'. It sold for four pounds and eighty-five pence.
- A second paperweight, an orb-shaped, hand-cut lead crystal, two-and-a-half inches (6.5 cm) in diameter. The orb shape was one emblem of the monarch's regalia. A one-and-seven-eighth inch (3.5 cm) white on royal blue jasper portrait cameo medallion of the Queen was inserted on the top and the commemorative inscription, 'SILVER JUBILEE OF HER MAJESTY QUEEN ELIZABETH II * 1952–1977 *', was engraved round the centre. Its original price was fifteen pounds and thirty pence. This paperweight was also produced with the commemorative inscription replaced by twenty-five hand-cut six-point stars and '1977'.
- A round eleven-and-a-half inch (29.5 cm) high spirit decanter on which were etched in a banner the Royal Coat of Arms and below it the commemorative inscription, '1952–1977 SILVER JUBILEE'. It had an air-filled spherical stopper. The decanter was produced in a limited edition of one thousand, came with a signed, numbered certificate, and sold for fourteen pounds and ninety-five pence.

- A six-and-a-half inch (16.75 cm) high clear glass goblet etched on which were the Royal Coat of Arms and same inscription. It was produced in an unlimited edition and sold for ten pounds and ninety-five pence.
- A cased amethyst four-inch (10.25 cm) high tankard which was finely etched with Arnold Machin's portrait of the Queen above a garland of British national emblems – the rose, thistle, leek and shamrock – and a commemorative inscription within a banner 'EIIR THE SILVER JUBILEE 1952–1977'. The tankard sold for eight pounds and eighty pence.
- A hand bell which was in amethyst glass with a clear glass handle. The bell stood five-and-three-quarters inches (14.75 cm) high and had a clapper of royal blue jasper. Set into an exterior seal was a three-quarter inch (2 cm) white on royal blue jasper portrait cameo medallion of the Queen. It sold for thirteen pounds and ninety-five pence.
- Two five-inch (12.75 cm) high goblets, set into an exterior seal was a three-quarter inch (2 cm) white on royal blue jasper portrait cameo medallion. It was framed by a hand-cut laurel leaf decoration on the amethyst bowl. The stem of the goblets was clear glass. An edition of one thousand was produced with the cameo of the Queen. For Prince Philip, the edition was two hundred and fifty. Both goblets retailed for fifteen pounds and seventy-five pence.
- One glass item the decoration of which was further enhanced by the addition of a sterling silver frame. It was a three-inch (7.75 cm) diameter lead crystal drum paperweight which bore the white on royal blue portrait cameo medallion of the Queen set as a seal in the top etched around which was 'H.M. QUEEN ELIZABETH II 1952 SILVER JUBILEE 1977'. There were five impression marks struck into the frame: the leopard of the London Assay Office; the lion denoting sterling silver; the date letter; the Wedgwood manufacturer's mark, JW, and a special Silver Jubilee mark, the Queen's profile. One thousand of these items were issued with a special certificate folder in a dark blue box lined with blue satin.

Most commemorative items were sold in the standard Company box on which was a special label bearing the Machin designed profile of the Queen encircled by 'ROYAL SILVER JUBILEE 1953–1977'. On the silver-edged certificate inserted within each presentation box was a description of the particular item. The box also contained a small folder illustrating all items available in the series and a card on which was a short explanation of the role of monarch and her place in the history of the United Kingdom:

> *'The 25th anniversary of Her Most Excellent Majesty Elizabeth the Second's succession (sic) to the throne is celebrated in 1977.*
>
> *'Born at 17 Bruton Street, London W1 on April 21, 1926, Her Majesty was crowned in Westminster Abbey (where she had married Philip Mountbatten RN in 1947) on June 2, 1953, following the death of her father, King George VI on February 6 in the previous year.*
>
> *'The monarchy is the United Kingdom's oldest secular institution; its continuity has been broken only once (1649–1660) and the hereditary principle upon which it was founded survives. The Queen personifies the State, being in law, head of the executive, an integral part of the legislature and head of the judiciary. She is also commander-in-chief of the armed forces of the Crown and temporal governor of the established Church of England. The United Kingdom is governed by Her Majesty's Government and the Prime Minister is appointed by her.*
>
> *'The title to the Crown derives from statute and common law rules descent; only common consent by all 36 Commonwealth nations (of which Elizabeth II is Sovereign) could alter succession. The heir to the throne is the Prince of Wales, born at Buckingham Palace on*

November 14, 1948 and eldest of the four children of HM The Queen and HRH The Duke of Edinburgh RN.'

Special variations to the editions were ordered by stores in Britain, for example, the amethyst bell produced for general sale was commissioned in an edition of seven hundred and fifty for John Sinclair. This bell differed from the former in that the portrait cameo medallion of the Queen was white on lilac jasper and the clapper was lilac jasper. On the reverse was etched the Royal cypher. It sold for the higher price of nineteen pounds and fifty pence. For Harrods of Knightsbridge, the bell was in smoky blue glass and bore a white on royal blue portrait cameo medallion of the Queen. The clapper was royal blue jasper. On the reverse was etched 'Silver Jubilee of Her Majesty Queen Elizabeth II 1952-1977'. This bell differed from the others in that the Royal cypher was etched into the flat top of the clear glass handle. The edition was one hundred and seventy-five.

Amethyst tankards with clear handles and bearing white on royal blue jasper portrait cameo medallions, one of the Queen and one of the Duke of Edinburgh, were included in the Silver Jubilee commemorative items. The back of the former was etched 'In celebration of the SILVER JUBILEE of HER MAJESTY QUEEN ELIZABETH II 1952-1977', while the back of the latter bore 'HRH PRINCE PHILIP DUKE OF EDINBURGH'. The edition was two thousand five hundred for each tankard. Individual tankards originally sold for fourteen pounds and ninety-five pence.

There was also a one-ring amethyst 'Sheringham' candleholder to which a white on royal blue three-quarter inch (2 cm) portrait cameo medallion of the Queen was attached as a seal. It was produced in an edition of three thousand and retailed for eight pounds and seventy-five pence.

The profile of the Queen and the inscription 'THE SILVER JUBILEE 1952–1977' in a banner, and which incorporated the design of the four national flowers and emblems were etched on the bowl of a six-and-a-half inch (16.75 cm) high clear glass goblet with a traditionally shaped stem and foot. The edition was unlimited, but only available through mail order. The design was exclusive to Gratton Warehouses Limited of Bradford, Yorkshire. The goblet retailed for eleven pounds and ninety-five pence.

Special editions also went to British Commonwealth countries including Australia and Canada. Without the etched cypher the amethyst bell bearing the white on lilac jasper portrait cameo medallion of the Queen was used to commemorate the Royal visit to Australia in 1977. The edition was two hundred and fifty and its original price was thirteen pounds and ninety-five pence. (In Australia it retailed for fifty-nine dollars and ninety-five cents).

As well there was a five-inch (12.75 cm) high amethyst goblet on a clear stem and base (identical in shape and ornamentation to that for sale in Britain), but for the Commonwealth countries, the portrait cameo medallion of the Queen was white on lilac jasper. This goblet served several purposes. It was a Silver Jubilee commemorative and used for special Royal events of that year. It was sold in Australia with an inscription on the back that read: 'To celebrate the Silver Jubilee of Her Majesty Queen Elizabeth II 1952–1977 and to mark the visit to Australia by Her Majesty and HRH the Duke of Edinburgh in the Jubilee year'. The Australian edition numbered five hundred.

In Canada, as well as the amethyst goblet bearing the white on lilac jasper portrait cameo medallion of the Queen, there was a one bearing a similarly coloured portrait cameo medallion of the Duke of Edinburgh. The former goblet was produced in an edition of five hundred, the latter in and edition of two hundred and fifty. Neither bore any inscription.

The following year, 1978, the Silver Jubilee of Queen Elizabeth's coronation was also celebrated with glass items *(Fig. 45)*:

- The simplest of these was a clear glass disc paperweight three-and-a-quarter inches (9.5 cm) in diameter. The centre was finely etched with the Coronation Chair. Surrounding it was the commemorative inscription, (in Old English font)—'Coronation Anniversary 1953–1978'. Produced as an unlimited edition, the paperweight sold for six pounds and eighty-five pence.
- There was a smoky blue tankard, four inches (10.25 cm) high. Etched on the front was the western façade of Westminster Abbey, and on the base the circular commemorative inscription 'Coronation Anniversary 1953–1978'. It retailed for twelve pounds and ninety-five pence.
- The same scene was etched on the spirit decanter. This eleven-and-a-half inch (29.5 cm) high spirit decanter with a spherical air filled stopper was hand-blown in clear glass. It bore the same commemorative inscription on the base. The edition was one thousand, it sold for twenty-four pounds and ninety-five pence.
- Again there were two goblets, one in amethyst and the other in smoky blue glass. The shapes differed from those for the Royal Silver Wedding and the accession jubilee. Both editions were five inches (12.75 cm) high, but there were differences other than colour. The amethyst goblet was described in correspondence to retailers as 'carrying a hand-cut lozenge incorporating a ¾' round light blue and white Wedgwood Jasper cameo of the Queen surrounded by hand-cut laurels. The cased amethyst goblet bowl is formed on a clear hand-cut stem and the foot carries an etched inscription'. It read 'CORONATION ANNIVERSARY 1953–1978'. There were fifteen hundred amethyst goblets, which sold for twenty-eight pounds and twenty-five pence.
- The 'simple blue cased hand-made royal goblet with a clear stem and foot' also bore the three-quarter inch (2 cm) white on light blue jasper portrait cameo medallion of the Queen set as a seal and the coronation commemorative base inscription. The goblet was sold in what was called a commemorative edition and originally cost twelve pounds and ninety-five pence.

As with the accession jubilee, colour variations of some items were produced for British Commonwealth countries. A specific example of this was a commemorative item was made for exclusive sale in Australia. Similar in most details to the blue goblet sold in Britain, it was a simple amethyst five-inch (12.75 cm) high cased goblet with a clear stem and foot. The three-quarter inch (2 cm) portrait cameo medallion of the Queen was white on lilac jasper set as a seal. There was no hand-cut decoration. It bore the commemorative base stamp with the addition of 'AUSTRALIA'. The edition was three hundred.

There was also an olive cut drum paperweight which appears not to have been made for a particular royal event. It bore a one-and-three-quarter inch (4.5 cm) white on royal blue jasper portrait cameo of the Queen. It differed from all those previously mentioned as the edge of the cameo is impressed with an acorn and oak leaf border.

Queen Elizabeth the Queen Mother, recipient of gifts from the factory at King's Lynn was herself commemorated in 1980 with an amethyst goblet on a cut clear glass stem and foot. Encircled by hand-cut laurel leaves on the bowl of the goblet was a white on pale blue jasper cameo medallion of the Queen Mother set as a seal *(Fig. 46)*. Around the foot was etched 'TO CELEBRATE THE 80TH BIRTHDAY OF HER MAJESTY THE QUEEN MOTHER'.

Glass items were designed and produced for the wedding on 29th July 1981 of the Prince of Wales to Lady Diana Spencer *(Figs 47–49)*:

- The simplest was a clear, three-and-a-quarter inch (8.5 cm) glass disc paperweight. The centre was etched with the year, 1981, and the Prince of Wales's Badge of Ostrich Feathers around which was inscribed in Italic font, '*Royal Wedding HRH Prince of Wales Lady Diana Spencer*'.

- A second clear glass paperweight bore a two-and three-quarter inch (7 cm) diameter double portrait cameo in white on light blue jasper. On the banner below the couple was written 'ROYAL WEDDING JULY 1981'. The side was engraved '*To Celebrate Marriage H.R.H.Prince of Wales Lady Diana Spencer St Paul's Cathedral*'. The base was star cut.
- The third paperweight, a hand-cut crystal drum, also carried the double portrait cameo in white on light blue jasper. The cameo differed from the previous one in size, this time being one-and-a-half inches (4 cm) in diameter. The side of the weight was etched 'Royal Wedding HRH Prince of Wales Lady Diana Spencer 29 July 1981'. The base was also star cut.
- Three full lead crystal bells were an addition to previous collections. The main etching on one of the 'Ashbourne' tea bells was the Prince of Wales's Ostrich Feathers and the year, above which was 'Royal Wedding' and below, 'Prince of Wales * Lady Diana'. Three seven-point stars were cut into the back. The central etched feature of the second 'Ashbourne' tea bell was St Paul's Cathedral. Above it was written ST. PAUL'S and below in a banner ROYAL WEDDING JULY 1981. The back was also cut with the three seven-point stars. This bell was exclusive to John Sinclair. On the 'Matlock' dinner bell the focus was the etched double portrait above which was '*St. Paul's Cathedral*' while below was 'ROYAL WEDDING July 1981' inscribed within a banner. The back was cut with four crosses and olives.
- The clear glass spirit decanter, in an edition of one thousand, was identical in style to those produced for both the 1977 and 1978 Jubilees with the difference being that the central etching was the façade of St Paul's Cathedral where the Wedding took place. On either side of the cathedral were etched the portraits of the couple. In a banner above it was 'ST.PAUL'S CATHEDRAL' and below 'ROYAL WEDDING'. In a cartouche framing the central motif were the words 'JULY 29TH TO CELEBRATE THE WEDDING OF HRH PRINCE CHARLES AND LADY DIANA SPENCER'.
- There were two goblets. The clear crystal goblet was etched on the front with the Prince of Wales's Ostrich Feathers. On the back was 'Royal Wedding H.R.H Prince of Wales Lady Diana Spencer St. Paul's Cathedral 29 July 1981'. The amethyst goblet was similar to that produced for the Silver Jubilee of the accession, having etched laurel leaves and a hand-cut clear glass stem and foot. It bore the white on light blue jasper double portrait cameo medallion set as a seal. The clear base was etched with a miniature of St Paul's, a miniature of the Prince of Wales's Feathers, and the commemoration 'St Paul's Cathedral 29 July 1981'. The edition was one thousand.
- The only item unique to the collection was the first and only two-handled loving cup made by Wedgwood Glass. It was amethyst with clear glass handles. It, too, was etched with the Ostrich Feathers. Of the limited editions it was the largest, being fifteen hundred.

With these pieces was a special 'The Royal Wedding Chalice'. The certificate 'issued May 1981' contained within the crimson silk lined box described the chalice as a 'full Lead-cut crystal hand made 9' goblet of Antique proportions, made in celebration of the marriage of H.R.H. Prince of Wales and Lady Diana Spencer on 29th July 1981. The Royal Emblem and Commemorative inscription are copper wheel engraved by hand.' The inscription read 'ROYAL WEDDING ST PAUL'S CATHEDRAL 29 JULY 1981'. Both the bowl and underside of the base were olive cut. The edition, the smallest of any produced in glass, was one hundred. It originally sold for one hundred pounds.

Special crimson boxes (some being gilt edged) for these commemorative items bore a label, the central symbol being the Prince of Wales's Feathers encircled by 'ROYAL WEDDING JULY 1981' all being printed in gold.

Gifts from Wedgwood Glass

As well as Royal commemoratives there were Royal gifts. There was the previously mentioned pair of specially engraved decanters which was presented to Princess Margaret at the opening of the new King's Lynn factory in June 1974. In 1979, Charter Trustees of the town of King's Lynn commissioned two specially etched decanters and eight tumblers to mark the Queen Mother's 25th anniversary as a Freeman of King's Lynn. On one decanter is the Queen Mother's Coat of Arms, while on the other were the arms of King's Lynn and a message of loyal greetings. The Duchess of Kent was also the recipient of several gifts. One was a decanter presented in July 1980 at the opening of the Queen Elizabeth Hospital. Another was a rose bowl presented in December of the same year by Buckland DC.

Pope John Paul II was also the recipient of a gift though not from King's Lynn. In his case it was a hand-cut eighteen-inch (46 cm), traditional Grecian shaped Galway Crystal vase. It commemorated his visit to Galway in September 1979. The vase was cut by craftsmen John Connelly and Eddie Doyle, both of whom were with Bishop Eammonn Casey when it was presented to the Pope. On one side it was inscribed with a view of the Galway Cathedral, and on the other 'Presented to His Holiness Pope John Paul II by the Diocese of Galway Kilmacdaugh and Kilpenora 30th Sept 1979' (and in Gaelic—'buioc as le dia').

7

OTHER COMMEMORATIVES

The centenary in 1974 of the birth of Winston Churchill saw the production of a smoky blue goblet similar to those produced for the royal commemoratives. The white on light blue jasper portrait cameo medallion of Churchill designed by Arnold Machin was set as a seal and the laurel leaves hand-cut around it. The edition was one thousand. As well, there was a topaz tankard with a white on black jasper portrait cameo medallion set within a seal. This edition was seven hundred and fifty. In a letter dated August, 1974, to sales outlets William U. Lydeard, Sales Director of the Marketing Division, informed retailers that 'demand for these pieces has been so great' that orders were not accepted unless accompanied by full payment. Finally, there was a three-and-a-half-inch (9 cm) lead crystal, hand-cut, drum-shaped paperweight on the top of which was inserted a white on light blue jasper portrait cameo medallion. Round the circumference it was inscribed 'GIVE US THE TOOLS AND WE WILL FINISH THE JOB' SIR WINSTON CHURCHILL.

Similar sized drum-shaped, hand-cut crystal paperweights were produced for two British naval heroes, in the centre top of which were inserted white on light blue jasper portrait cameo medallions. One was of Horatio Lord Nelson, a reproduction of that modelled in 1798 by John De Vaere. It was inscribed LORD NELSON 'THANK GOD I'VE DONE MY DUTY'. The other was of Lord Louis Mountbatten of Burma. It was inscribed LORD MOUNTBATTEN OF BURMA 'IN HONOUR BOUND'. The sides of both were hand-cut in a simple diamond pattern. The top and bottom edges were incised. On the base of both was a hand-cut star pattern. Each was produced in an edition of one thousand. Both originally sold for thirty-two pounds.

A similar drum-shaped cameo paperweight was produced on which was inserted a white on light blue jasper portrait cameo medallion of Charles Dickens. The edition was seven thousand five hundred.

The only Olympic Games to be commemorated in Wedgwood glass were those held in Montreal in 1976. Several items were made for exclusive sale in Canada *(Fig. 50)*. For this event the cameo depicted was the Olympic Torch Runner. The first piece was a five-inch (12.75 cm) high smoky blue goblet, on which a white on light blue jasper cameo of the Torch Runner was set as a seal. The goblet was identical in design to those produced for the Silver Wedding Anniversary of Queen Elizabeth and Prince Philip, with the exception of the cameo. The edition was five hundred. The second was a topaz tankard embossed with a white on black jasper cameo of the Torch Runner. It was issued in an edition of seven hundred and fifty. The third item was a smoky blue tankard on which the Torch Runner and 'OLYMPIAD XXI MONTREAL' were finely etched. This edition was unlimited. The last item was a smoky blue bell bearing a white on light blue jasper cameo of the Torch Runner set in a seal and produced in an edition of five hundred.

Eighteenth and nineteenth century transport provided significant events and inventions of particular noteworthiness. In 1777, there was the completion and opening of the Trent and Mersey Canal, in 1825, the first rail service from Stockton to Darlington, and in 1830 the opening of the Liverpool to Manchester railway. Of the three events, the first was the most important to Wedgwood as the canal passed its new factory at Etruria. The bi-centenary of opening of the Trent and Mersey Canal was marked by three boxed, commemorative items, each of which came with a certificate. Two were issued directly by Wedgwood. One was specially commissioned by the Trent and Mersey Canal Society. The certificate in each box described the importance of Josiah Wedgwood (1730-95) to the construction of the canal. He 'was a prime mover in obtaining Parliamentary sanction for the construction of this canal—an engineering triumph which greatly benefited industry and the general public. Linking two rivers across the breadth of the Midlands it contained 75 locks, rose to a level of 326 feet and had navigation of just over 93 miles.

> *'An association for promoting the scheme was formed in 1765, the necessary Bill was passed in May 1766 and, as Honorary Treasurer of the Company of Proprietors of the Navigation from the Trent to the Mersey, Josiah cut the first sod at Brownhills, between Burslem and Tunstall, on July 26 in that year. The master potter had subscribed £1,000 in shares towards building costs and also given security of £10,000.*
>
> *'The canal progressed rapidly, passing through the Wedgwood estate at Etruria (a branch was constructed up to the factory occupied by the pottery company until it moved to Barlaston in 1938) and navigation was completed in May 1777, at a cost of some £300,000.'*

Each certificate also gave specific information about its item. The three-and-a-quarter inch (8.5 cm), clear glass paperweight was etched with a reproduction of the canal company's seal—and the motto 'IN PATRIAM POPLUMQUE FLUAT' (It flows for Country and People). The original seal is in the National Railway Museum in York. Round the circumference was etched 'COMPANY OF PROPRIETORS OF THE NAVIGATION FROM THE TRENT TO THE MERSEY'.

The four-inch (10.25 cm) high smoky blue tankard, issued in a limited edition of one thousand, was etched with a view of the Etruria factory and the canal on one side, and a portrait of Josiah Wedgwood on the other. 'BICENTENARY OF THE TRENT & MERSEY CANAL 1777–1977' was written above the etching of the factory, while below it was 'ETRURIA WORKS OF JOSIAH WEDGWOOD I'.

The third item was a six-and-a-half inch (16.5 cm) high goblet. On the front of the bowl was etched the same scene as on the paperweight—the canal company's seal—above which was 'TRENT AND MERSEY 1777 1977'. On the back was 'SPECIALLY COMMISSIONED BY THE TRENT AND MERSEY CANAL SOCIETY to celebrate the bi-centenary of the completion of the Navigation'. The numbered edition was seven hundred and fifty.

For the first in a series of travel tankards, the sesqui-centenary of the first rail service, the smoky blue tankard was again used. Finely etched onto one side was Stephenson's *Locomotion No 1* 'STOCKTON & DARLINGTON 1825–1975'. Stephenson was at the controls of 'Locomotion No 1' as it hauled the first passenger train on the 27th September, 1825. The twenty-six-and-a-half mile long, privately built railway was a further technical success for Stephenson.

For the second of the series in 1980, the *Rocket* was used on a smoky blue tankard for the sesqui-centenary of the first steam-drawn passenger service between Liverpool and Manchester. The *Rocket* and a first class passenger coach below which was 'LIVERPOOL & MANCHESTER RAILWAY 1830–1980' were etched on the front. On the back was etched the 'Rocket 150' emblem. It incorporated the British Rail motif, the shield from the City of Manchester Coat of Arms, the Liver Bird from the City of Liverpool Coat of Arms, and a Liverpool and Manchester 1830 first class coach encircled by the commemorative inscription 'LIVERPOOL AND MANCHESTER RAILWAY ANNIVERSARY 150 YEARS'. The tankard was issued in numbered edition of one thousand.

The certificate included a synopsis of events leading to the success of the *Rocket*. It had been one of three steam locomotives in competition for use on the new line. In 1829, trials on a level mile long track at Rainhill, a village outside Liverpool, saw *Rocket* outright winner over *Novelty* and *Sans Pariel*. The official opening day, 15th September, 1830, was also the day of the first rail fatality. President of the Board of Trade, William Huskisson MP, was struck by the locomotive and died later the same day from his injuries.

Evidence exists of a proposed additional commemorative item for the event, 'Version #1', which did not go into commercial production. The evidence is in the form of a 'Certificate of Authenticity Rainhill Trials 150th Anniversary' that would have been included in the gift box. Similarly etched with the *Rocket*, the item was a goblet but it was to have been in an edition of two thousand.

Though not directly part of the British transport series but complementing it, the fiftieth anniversary of the twenty-one day around the world flight of the pioneering German airship *Graf Zepplin* was commemorated on a smoky blue tankard. In an oval cartouche was etched an image of the airship in flight over a town and, on the reverse the inscription 'GRAF ZEPPLIN—50TH ANNIVERSARY of the AROUND THE WORLD FLIGHT—1929–1979'. This piece was made exclusively for Wedgwood Rooms in an edition of two hundred and fifty *(Fig. 51)*.

In 1981, *Locomotion No 1* was the focus for a clear 'County' goblet to commemorate the bi-centenary of George Stephenson's birth. It was etched on the front, while the etching on the back was the Stephenson family crest and motto 'Never Give Up', and under the crest 'BI-CENTENARY GEORGE STEPHENSON 1781–1981'.

An amethyst goblet on a clear glass stem commemorated the twenty-fifth anniversary of the Conquest of Everest, the world's highest mountain *(Fig. 52)*. This occurred on the 29th May, 1953, four days before the Coronation of Queen Elizabeth II. The two members of the team to reach the peak were New Zealander, Edmund Hillary, and Sherpa guide, Tenzing Norgay. On the front is the victorious climber planting the national flag of the United Kingdom on the summit. On either side of him are the years, 1953 and 1978. The etching on the back depicts the South Col route taken by the British 1953 expedition. The inscription encircling the base of the bowl reads '25th ANNIVERSARY OF THE CONQUEST OF EVEREST SOUTH ROUTE TAKEN TO THE PEAK'. The goblet was six-and-a-half inches (16.5 cm) high and produced in a numbered limited edition of fifteen hundred, selling originally for twenty-one pounds and fifty pence.

The discovery in May 1999 of the body of an earlier climber, George Mallory, has not answered the question of whether his 1924 expedition reached the summit of Everest first. If it did, it does not detract from the success of the 1953 expedition, as members of the latter climb not only reached the peak, but also descended safely. (Mallory was accompanied in the final stages of the climb by Sandy Irvine whose body has not, to date, been found).

1978 was also the novo-centenary of the Tower of London. Work commenced on the 'White Tower', the oldest of the buildings which make up the London landmark, in 1078, under Gundulph, Bishop of Rochester, as a fortress for William I (the Conqueror). Completion took place in the reign of Henry I. During its nine hundred years, the Tower of London has been a fortress, a royal palace and starting point for coronation processions up to the reign of Charles I whose procession was the last. (Oliver Cromwell destroyed the royal apartments). Parts of the Tower were also used as a prison, the last prisoner being Rudolph Hess during World War II. It once housed the Royal Mint, the Record Office, and a menagerie, and is still used to house the Crown Jewels, is the home of the Yeoman Warders and guarded by the military from the same regiments which serve at Buckingham Palace and St James's Palace. Architecturally it shows evidence of the different periods during which the various parts were added from the original Norman White Tower to the Waterloo Barracks, built after the destruction by fire of the Grand Storehouse in 1841.

Two glass items commemorated the novo-centenary *(Fig. 53)*. The first was a smoky blue glass tankard on which was etched a modern view of the White Tower as seen from across the Thames River. The limited edition was fifteen hundred and it sold for thirteen pounds and ninety-five pence. The second piece was a three-and-a-quarter inch (8.5 cm) clear glass disc paperweight in the centre of which was etched the same view and which was encircled by the inscription 'THE TOWER OF LONDON 1078–1978'. This paperweight originally sold for six pounds and eighty-five pence.

In 1983 a circular crystal paperweight was produced. A white on light blue two-and-three-quarter inch (7 cm) diameter jasper cameo depicting the same view of the Tower encircled by a *bas relief* of oak leaves and acorns was inserted into the top. The edge of the weight was inscribed with a calendar for 1983 while the base was diamond cut.

In 1980 the two hundred and fiftieth anniversary of Josiah Wedgwood's birthday was commemorated with a smoky blue goblet. A three-quarter inch (2 cm) white on royal blue jasper portrait cameo medallion of the Company's founder was inserted as a seal on the bowl. The stem was cut clear glass and the inscription '250th ANNIVERSARY JOSIAH WEDGWOOD FRS * 1730–1980 *' was etched around the foot.

To commemorate the first visit to Great Britain in May 1982 by an incumbent Pope, His Holiness Pope John Paul II, as well as other Wedgwood souvenirs, boxed glass items were produced *(Fig. 54)*. There were two paperweights. The first was a disc paperweight on which was etched the figure of the Pope, the first non-Italian since Adrian IV, the only English Pope. The second was a crystal drum paperweight on which was inserted a two-and three-quarter inch (7 cm) white on light blue jasper portrait cameo medallion of the Pope below which were the words 'JOHANNES PAVLVS II' (John Paul II) on a banner in the form of a stole. The figure of the Pope was modelled by Michael Dillon, Wedgwood's chief modeller. Unlike crystal paperweights produced during the 1970s, this one had a diameter of three-and-a-half inches (9 cm) and was only one inch (2.5 cm) deep. Hand cutting on the side was a simple diamond pattern and on the base a star. The third item was a crystal tea bell which was etched with the figure of the Pope. The fourth piece was an amethyst goblet on a clear hand-cut stem. The goblet, identical to that produced for the Queen's Coronation Jubilee, carried a white on light blue jasper portrait cameo medallion of the Pope set as a seal and surrounded by hand-cut laurels. Etched on the foot was the inscription 'Visit of Pope John Paul II, Great Britain, 1982'. The edition was two hundred and fifty and was accompanied by a signed numbered certificate. Most papal commemoratives were sold in crimson presentation boxes on which were labels, the central motif of which was the triple papal tiara encircled by 'THE VISIT OF POPE JOHN PAUL II 1982'. All printing was in gold.

In the Victoria and Albert Museum is the 'Betley Window' from the now-demolished Betley Hall, Staffordshire. It depicts English May Games and Morris Dancers. The window is possibly the oldest surviving example of its kind. The figure of 'Tom the Piper' was depicted on a May Festival paperweight shaped like a Gothic stained glass window, and in an edition of seventeen hundred and fifty, it originally sold for fourteen pounds and twenty-five pence. In 1982, seven of these 'Tom the Piper' paperweights were used as awards for the 'Music Teachers' magazine.

8

COMMISSIONS

Of the many glass and crystal items produced at King's Lynn, certain shapes and colours were used for Wedgwood's selected events for special commemoration or celebration. At the same time some of the pieces were left as blanks. For individuals, organisations, and corporations both within Britain and abroad, Wedgwood Glass provided advertising literature with photographs from the special issues department illustrating what shapes and colours could be chosen for specific commissions. According to the information on an advertising flier, the items could be ordered to 'commemorate events in their histories, to promote the corporate image or products, or to provide an incentive gift which is a collector's piece and assured of appreciation by recipients'. There is reference earlier to major publications in which advertising was placed.

In the collection were a tear-drop shaped 'Valentine' and a disc paperweight. There were glass and crystal decanters, both spirit and 'Mallett' wine, as well as plain ship's decanters. Goblet shapes included 'Rutland', 'Oakham' with its air-twist stem, 'County', 'Norwich', and an untitled one with a ringed stem. Tankard shapes were available in a choice of amethyst, smoky blue and less frequently, sapphire blue, topaz, and clear glass. These items could be supplied in a special crimson and gold satin-lined presentation box with personalised certificates or greeting cards on request. They could also be supplied in standard boxes.

To meet customers' requirements, staff from the design centre advised customers on decoration of 'blanks'. This decoration included etching and hand engraving, or the supply of a logotyped bone china disc set as a seal on one side *(Fig. 55)*. Monograms or simple logotypes were etched on glass and crystal pieces. No full records exist of commissions undertaken by Wedgwood Glass at King's Lynn, but some of the special commissions and the details relating to the reason for their production for the British market included:

- A five-inch (12.75 cm) diameter heavy straight-sided topaz bowl (RSW27) for the '21ST KING'S LYNN FESTIVAL 1971'. Impressed into the centre of the base were string and brass instruments and a music book. This festival is held for two weeks beginning on February 14 each year in King's Lynn, Norfolk, United Kingdom. It historically began in 1537 as a Valentine's Day Trade Fair. In the early 1900s, it became a spectacular event where travelling showpeople could display their latest amusements. In 1950, the event officially became the 'King's Lynn Festival' and themed a Fun Fair of amusements, rides and musical attractions. The event continues to attract famous musicians and performers in Ballet, Opera, Orchestra, Jazz and Folk Music.

- A smoky blue tankard on the front of which was the Corps' insignia of the crown over the intertwined initials RAOC and motto 'SUA TELA TONANTI' (which has no true translation, but corpsmen once used 'To the Thunder His Arms', and more recently 'To the Warrior His Arms'). The back was etched 'TO COMMEMORATE THE VISIT OF THE COLONEL-IN-CHIEF HER MAJESTY QUEEN ELIZABETH II TO THE ROYAL ARMY ORDINANCE CORPS 9 JUNE 1972 *(Fig. 56)*'.
- A tall champagne glass etched with the Coat of Arms of the City of London 'DOMINE DIRIGE NOS' (Lord Direct Us). This glass bore the date 1972 and the artist's full name, John Finnie.
- A goblet for the City of Leicester. It bore the city's Coat of Arms, the etched date 1972 but only the initials 'J F' (for John Finnie).
- A goblet for *The Order of Saint John of Jerusalem* etched with its Coat of Arms, also 1972 and 'J F'.
- A goblet etched with the Coat of Arms of Barclay's Bank, and the same year and initials as the previous goblets.
- A goblet etched with a mediaeval knight in full armour and riding his galloping charger. It bore the same year and initials.
- A goblet etched with a cottage, 1972 and 'J F'.
- A goblet etched with a gliding swan with its wings fluffed above its back, the same year and initials.
- Crystal glasses with a matching decanter in the 'Blakeney' suite for exclusive use on British Airways' Concorde. All pieces had one panel of the cut pattern left blank then etched with a Concorde in flight.
- Cocktail or drink stirrers, which are also called 'swizzle sticks', again for the exclusive use of passengers on British Airways' Concorde flights. A stylised delta-winged supersonic plane with the nose drooping for take-off or landing was depicted at the top of the clear glass stirrer.
- 'Plant a Tree in '73' a clear glass goblet on an air-filled stem. On the bowl were engraved leafless trees of Britain, the Beech, Elm, Birch, Ash, Oak, and Lime under each of which were written the names. The issue was five hundred.
- A rummer commemorating eleven hundred years of Ely Cathedral. Etched on it was the cathedral's crest of three keys, on either side of which were 673 and 1973, while below was 'ELY CATHEDRAL'.
- A smoky blue glass goblet to celebrate in 1974 the 250th anniversary of the birth of George Stubbs, the artist who painted the portrait of the Wedgwood family which hung in the long gallery at Barlaston Museum. His self-portrait was depicted on the white on light blue jasper portrait cameo medallion which was set as a seal on the exterior wall. As with similar goblets there was the hand-cut laurel wreath. The edition was limited to five hundred and sold for fifteen pounds and seventy-five pence.

- A goblet for the centenary of 'J & W TOMLINSON LTD 1875–1975'. The words were etched in an oval round the company logo 'J & W T LTD' *(Fig. 57)*.
- A disc paperweight in the centre of which was etched Norwich Cathedral.
- A smoky blue tankard in an edition of five hundred depicting Canterbury Cathedral viewed from the north-west and made for the Wedgwood Rooms at Riceman's of Canterbury.
- A chalice on which was etched King's College Chapel, Cambridge, and the Coat of Arms of the college.
- A goblet on which was etched the Coat of Arms of the British House of Commons.
- A smoky blue tankard on which was etched the crest of the 'Association of Public Lighting Engineers'.
- A pair of topaz Egyptian theme goblets depicting King Tutankhamun and Queen Ankhsenamun. The commission for five hundred pairs was made by John Sinclair.
- A goblet around the top of which was 'Let's drink together friendly and embrace'. The focus was the etched profile of William Shakespeare (the same design as on the portrait medallion) encircled by laurel leaves. Above the profile was 'Henry VI part 2—act 4 scene 2' (from which the quote came), while below was '1564–1616 Stratford upon Avon'.
- '+ Me Spede' ('with hope in me') phoenix goblet.
- 'County' goblets on which were etched birds of Britain including a woodpecker, pheasant, magpie, swift, barn owl, falcon, and snipe.
- A Masonic firing-glass.
- Lights for the garden of Sandringham House. These were extremely large and heavy to make. Each had to be made by an extended team with several men taking turns to blow the large light covers. They were features of the garden for many years, but towards the end of the twentieth century were replaced.
- A 'County' Goblet for Mr Norman Graham in an edition of one hundred and fifty. On it was etched a rearing horse encircled by 'KENT COUNTY CRICKET CLUB NORMAN GRAHAM BENEFIT YEAR 1977'.
- A souvenir drum paperweight for the Leeds Castle gift shop—an unlimited edition.
- An etched crystal bowl for the 'Hatfield House Festival of Gardening'. The etching included a gardener on the front, and a hat, gardening implements, flowers, foliage and butterflies on the back.
- A goblet produced for Bolingbroke & Wenley Ltd, Chelmsford, depicting Willy Lott's cottage, East Bergholt, Suffolk. It was to have been first in a series of East Anglian Scenes. The cottage was situated near the millstream of Flatford Mill, Suffolk, painted by John Constable (1776-1837) in 'The Hay Wain'.
- 'To celebrate the occasion of Hall Thermotank's One Hundred Years involvement in the refrig eration industry, we would like you to accept the Centenary Tankard with our thanks and best wishes for the future' was written on the gift card included in the box. The tankard was engraved with the company's snowflake logo while the monogram was encircled by 'ONE HUNDRED YEARS OF REFRIGERATION 1877-1977'.
- A clear goblet on which was etched below the lip 'ROUND TABLE GOLDEN JUBILEE 1927 1977'. The central focus was the Round Table logo and below it was 'Founded by Louis Marchesi' and the motto 'ADOPT ADAPT IMPROVE'.

- A goblet for the Sandringham Estate, Norfolk, on which was engraved the west front of Sandringham House, in the foreground of which was Queen Elizabeth II mounted on her horse, 'Cossack'.
- A disc weight for King's Lynn. Round the circumference was 'A PORT OF A THOUSAND YEARS'. In the centre were the arms of the city below which was 'KING'S LYNN'.
- A disc weight on which was etched Balmoral Castle. Thistles were etched round the circumference.
- A second disc weight in the centre of which were etched the intertwined initials V and A and a single thistle while round the bottom was 'BALMORAL CASTLE' and around the top were entwined thistles.
- A disc paperweight bearing as the central motif the Coat of Arms of and encircled by 'LONDON BOROUGH OF BROMLEY'.
- A smoky blue tankard for the Royal Air Force XIII (PR) Squadron on which was etched its insignia and the reason for the commission—'Proceeded Overseas 17th November 1942 Returned to England 3rd October 1978'.
- A sapphire blue tankard for the same squadron, but commemorating a different event. The central figure was PR9 Canberra photographic reconnaissance bomber. To the left of which was 'XIII (PR) SQUADRON' and to the right 'ADJUVAMUS TUENDO' (We Assist by Watching), while below was '10TH JANUARY 1915–5TH JANUARY 1982', the dates of the formation and disbandment of the squadron. It had seen overseas service during two World Wars and performed reconnaissance duties in peacetime. What makes this tankard different from most others produced is the position of the etching—opposite the handle. On the others the motif is to the left of the handle in such a way that it faces the holder should the tankard actually be used (by a right-handed person).
- A disc paperweight around the edge of which was etched 'DRG Flexible Packaging THE ROBINSON WAXED PAPER COMPANY LIMITED'. In the centre was 'DRG 50th Anniversary 1928–1978'.
- A goblet celebrating the life of Robert Burns, 1759-1796. It bore an etched three-quarter portrait and shoulders of the Scottish poet.
- A challenge for glass blowers and investors was the prize glass piggy bank. The BBC Radio 4 programme, 'Money Box', held a competition for listeners to invest an imaginary one thousand pounds into a choice of unit trusts (mutual funds) over a period of a year. The winner, who achieved the best return on investment, won the prize. The clear glass piggy bank was wheel-etched 'UNIT TRUST INVESTOR OF THE YEAR' on one side and 'MONEY BOX 1979-1980' on the other.

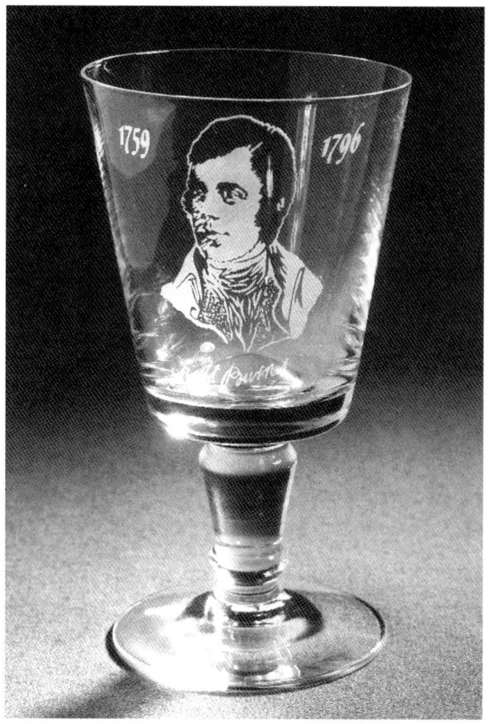

Etched goblet to celebrate the life of Scottish poet, Robert Burns.

This was to be an annual event, but there is no mention of Wedgwood's involvement in the competition the next year. The manufacture of the glass money box posed problems for the master craftsmen—firstly getting the pig shape right, secondly adding the separately formed ears and tail, and lastly adding the coin slot. They succeeded admirably in making this piece. (Similar piggy banks were on general sale but they were not numerous because of the difficulty in making them. They were not etched).

- A decanter with an air-filled stopper presented to the winner by 'FRIENDS' PROVIDENT MASTERS'. In a cartouche encircling the Badminton logo and 1979 was etched 'THE WORLD'S FIRST BADMINTON TOURNAMENT ROYAL ALBERT HALL LONDON'.
- A squash trophy, also 1979.
- A disc paperweight to commemorate 'The 200th Running of the Derby'. The centre was etched with a three-quarter face of the '12TH EARL OF DERBY' while round the edge was '200TH RUNNING THE DERBY STAKES' and two galloping racehorses. The certificate informed purchasers 'The Paperweight is hand made, the design a special commission for John Sinclair, in a limited edition of 2000' *(Fig. 58)*.
- A footed bowl presented to the Mercantile and General Re-insurance Company PLC on the 75th anniversary of Friends' Provident Life Office.
- A disc weight for DORNAY FOODS * JANUARY 1979. In the centre was etched a delivery van.
- A disc weight for the 'THE CENTRAL NURSING COUNCIL FOR ENGLAND AND WALES'. These words were etched to encircle the logo for the Council and the date AD 1919.
- A disc weight around the circumference of which was 'THE INSTITUTE OF SALES AND MARKETING MANAGEMENT'. In the centre was association's crest and motto 'PROFITABILITY THROUGH PROFICIENCY'. The paperweight was given to full members of the association.
- A goblet, decanter, drum paperweight and tankard for the 25th Anniversary of ITN. The company logo was surrounded by '*Twenty-fifth anniversary* 1955–1980'. (This commission was used in advertisements as an example of what was available from Wedgwood Glass in *Management Today*, October 1980).
- A decanter for the Eastern Gas gem awards in 1980.
- A decanter for the East Anglian Management 1980 Games.
- A goblet for the Golf Society, Surrey, given to Mr Moffatt in 1980.
- A lidded mustard pot and spoon in an edition of two hundred and fifty commissioned for exclusive sale by the Mustard Shop to commemorate the wedding of the Prince and Princess of Wales in 1981. Situated in an attractive alleyway in the centre of old Norwich, Coleman's Mustard Shop opened in 1973 to commemorate the 150th anniversary of the company. As well as selling a variety of mustard, it had a museum which traced the company's history in the manufacture of mustard.
- A sapphire blue tankard to mark the official opening of the Humber Bridge by Queen Elizabeth II. The bridge under which HUMBER BRIDGE THE LONGEST SINGLE SPAN BRIDGE IN THE WORLD was etched on one side. The tankard was included in souvenirs on display and sale in Hull during its civic week for the opening in 1981.

- A disc paperweight around the circumference of which was etched 'XI INTERNATIONAL CONGRESS OF ALLERGOLOGY & CLINICAL IMMUNOLOGY'. It encircled LONDON '82 ICACI.
- A disc weight for Fairclough Engineering to celebrate the firm's centenary 1983–1983—impressed 'FAIRCLOUGH 100 YEARS OF PROGRESS'.
- A disc weight etched around the top of which was etched 'Grimsby Cleethropes Lions Club', in the centre the crest of the International Lions Club, and around the bottom 'Market Rasen 1985'.
- Plaques into which were pressed animal shapes which included a walrus, elephant and eagle. (The pressed definition of the animals was not as precise as that of the etched birds or stag).
- Souvenir plaques sold from specific places of historic interest, for example, Winchester Cathedral, or special events such as birthdays and weddings.
- *Wedgwood Bird Crystals* were created for Danbury Mint for its mail order customers. A letter to customers described the crystals as reflecting 'the wonderful characteristics of each bird'. The birds, deeply but delicately sand etched into the plaques were the heron, goose, swan, woodpecker, owl, kingfisher, eagle, snipe, seagull, duck, falcon and chick, and pheasant. Characteristics of each bird were precisely depicted in the 'soft' surface etching, while the eye(s) was/were polished to piercing clarity. One curved edge of each crystal was impressed with foliage, while opposite it the impression was that of rock. Near each bird was additional foliage, twigs, a branch or rocks specific to its natural environment. These plaques proved difficult to produce as they tended to stick to the moulds and would not come out easily *(Figs 59–61)*.
- A Stag crystal for the Danbury Mint similar in design and manufacture to the birds *(Fig. 62)*.

Wedgwood produced items to commemorate historical events of countries other than the United Kingdom. In several of these situations there was or had been a colonial or Commonwealth link between the particular country and Britain. In other cases the commission came directly from a town, organisation, or business for which an event was important and which wanted a significant souvenir item either to sell to the public or present to people who had contributed to its advancement or welfare. Some of these included:

- The first set of three glass souvenirs for the foreign market being the 350th anniversary of the voyage of the Mayflower. It commemorated the voyage from Leyden, Holland of the Pilgrim Fathers and their families to the New World. Their last port for repairs and revictualling was Plymouth (UK) which they left on 6th September, 1620. Landfall was made at Plymouth Rock in North America on 21st December the same year. The commemorative certificate stated that 'on 1st June 1621 the settlement they had established six months earlier at Plymouth was legalised by a patent from the Council in New England. The endurance and the eventual success of the few men, women and children established them as the fore-runners of the American way of life'.

  The commemorative items were, firstly, a clear glass tankard on which was set a pressed topaz glass seal. The seal comprised an image of a ship above which was 'Mayflower 350' while below was '1620–1970'. The numbered edition was two thousand. Secondly there was a clear goblet with a similar clear seal and produced in a numbered edition of two thousand. Lastly there was a five-inch (13 cm) diameter sweets' dish into the base of which was pressed the commemorative seal. The dish was available in an unlimited edition in either clear or topaz glass.
- For the centenary of the Royal Canadian Mounted Police, a uniformed Mountie on horseback

and the years 1873–1973 were etched on a smoky blue tankard.

- A 'sparkling ice blue mug'—tankard—for the Winnipeg centenary of the city's incorporation. The trading post of Winnipeg was established over 200 years ago. The name came from the Cree words, 'Win'—muddy, and 'Nippee'—waters. The centennial crest was formed by joining four 'Ws'. These created a perimeter to express the unity of the city created by the joining of the original thirteen municipalities. The lines between the 'Ws' represented the roadways—water, land, rail, air—that contributed to the city's growth. The joined dates—1874–1974—symbolised links with the past. On the outer part of the symbol, the arrows pointing in all directions depicted continuing growth of the former trading post. The descriptive folder contained in the presentation box informed the owner 'your Wedgwood commemorative mug has been created in keeping with a superb tradition of quality and prestige. It is an investment that will delight you now, and will reward you and your heirs as it grows in value. Your mug is one of a total limited edition of 300'.
- An amethyst tankard on which was etched the Houses of the Canadian Parliament in Ottawa. On the base was a special additional mark—'EXCLUSIVE TO McINTOSH & WATTS, OTTAWA CANADA'.
- A clear glass 'County' goblet on which was etched the Coat of Arms of Belleville, Ontario, Canada. This was for the town's centenary.
- In 1976 several special editions produced for the bi-centenary of American Independence. There was an amethyst bell bearing a white on royal blue jasper portrait cameo medallion of George Washington. The edition was seven hundred and fifty. There was a crystal drum paperweight bearing a white on light blue jasper portrait cameo medallion of George Washington. The top bore the inscription 'UNITED STATES OF AMERICA 1776–1976' and six five-point stars. The side was diamond cut. The edition was four hundred. A blue glass bell bore a white on light blue jasper cameo of the Liberty Bell *(Fig. 63)*.

  Two five-inch (12.75 cm) high smoky blue goblets also for the bi-centenary of American Independence. One goblet bore a white on light blue jasper portrait cameo medallion of George Washington, the other a similar cameo medallion of Martha Washington. Within a hand-cut laurel wreath each cameo was set as a seal onto the exterior of the goblet. They were commissioned by the Wedgwood Collectors' Society and each base was etched with the Society's logo. The issue price for each goblet was one hundred and fifty United States dollars.

  A straight-sided smoky blue goblet/chalice bearing a one-and-a-half inch (4 cm) white on light blue jasper cameo of the American bald eagle. The goblet is similar in shape to the prestige goblets but is not cut with laurel leaves.
- A smoky blue goblet to commemorate the twenty-fifth Season of the Stratford Festival in Ontario, 1953–1977. The goblet carried a white on light blue jasper cameo portrait medallion of William Shakespeare being a reproduction of that originally modelled in 1777 by William Hackwood. The medallion was set in a hand-cut circular lozenge and framed by hand-cut laurel leaves. The blue goblet was formed on a clear glass stem and foot. The edition of two hundred and fifty was commissioned by J. L.Bradshaw. The idea for a festival in the Canadian town bearing the same name as that of the poet's birthplace came from a local journalist, Tom Patterson. The first performance was held on July 13, 1953 in a tent theatre in which was a thrust stage open on three sides to the audience.Tanya Moiseiwitsch designed the stage, an adaptation of an Elizabethan stage. She worked in collaboration with director Tyrone Guthrie. Dur-

ing that first season *Richard III* and *All's Well that Ends Well* were performed. Alec Guinness was a starring performer. The tent was dismantled for the final time in 1956 and replaced by a permanent 2,258-seat auditorium which retained the thrust stage. The theatre became home not only to the Stratford Festival but also to major works of classic and contemporary theatre, to operetta, opera and to New Canadian plays.

- A disc paperweight bearing in full colour the Seal of the Department of the Air Force of the United States of America.
- A disc paperweight bearing in full colour the Seal of the Department of the Army of the United States of America.
- A disc paperweight bearing in full colour the insignia of the Berlin Brigade (United States Army)
- A disc paperweight in the centre of which was etched the head of Queen Victoria and around it was inscribed 'TO CELEBRATE THE CENTENARY OF THE EXHIBITION BUILDING OPENED OCTOBER 1st 1880', in Melbourne, Australia. It was commissioned by and made exclusively for the department store, Buckley & Nunn Limited in an edition of two hundred and fifty. The Melbourne International Centenary Exhibition recreated the spirit of the international exhibition of 1880-1881. Wedgwood, in association with the department store, organised a representative display of the company's products and featured the 250th anniversary collection.
- A Wild Turkey Crystal Decanter for Austin Nichols Distilling Company, Laurenceburg, Kentucky *(Fig. 64)*. The special decanter was etched with a wild turkey in flight encircled by a garland of leaves. The decanter was described as 'a priceless limited edition, one full litre of superb 101 proof Wild Turkey whiskey in a lustrous full-lead crystal, hand shaped and hand engraved by Wedgwood'. An instruction leaflet contained in the lined presentation box gave recommendations 'for maximum enjoyment of this fine product' and on the process to be used while opening the decanter for the first time. It also advised on the proper use of and care for the enclosed silver-plated ringed stopper 'designed for ease of corking and uncorking'. The fine product was eight year-old Wild Turkey Kentucky straight bourbon whiskey.
- A diamond cut decanter (made in Yugoslavia) containing 750 ml of 80 proof Drambui. The label round the neck of the decanter read 'Prince Charles Edward's Liquor. Produced and bottled by The Drambui Co. Ltd. Edinburgh, Scotland'. The gold label on the back of the decanter informed the purchaser the product was 'Imported by W. A. Taylor & Company, Miami, Florida. Sole distributors for the USA'. The decanter was stoppered with a red seal bearing a crown.
- A personally engraved suite of crystal for the Emirates.

Several 'hybrid' glass items have appeared in the secondary market. This has been the result of cameos becoming detached from the original pieces. The 'hybrids' have included several quite unusual combinations. One used the amethyst 1977 Silver Jubilee bell commissioned by John Sinclair. As was previously described, the original bore a portrait cameo medallion of the Queen and was etched with the royal cypher and had a lilac jasper clapper. The 'hybrid' bore a white on light blue jasper cameo medallion of Shakespeare. This is a totally wrong jasper colour combination, never mind the topic. Another example is a five-inch (12.75 cm) smoky blue goblet similar to that produced for the coronation Silver Jubilee. It bore a white on light blue jasper Olympic Torch Runner. The colour combination was right but that shape of goblet was not produced for the

Montreal event. Another is an amethyst tankard bearing a white on pink jasper cameo. It is worth noting that with the exception of the bell, the glass pieces for these items were seconds. They were not base-etched and none of these variations was a factory original.

9

GIFTWARE

For Special Occasions

From the set of different shaped blanks, customers could choose the one most suitable on which to have their own design created. For those who wanted to celebrate one of life's milestones, Wedgwood Glass had hand-made goblets, tankards, plaques, and bells already etched with special designs. The items came boxed and were accompanied by a gold embossed

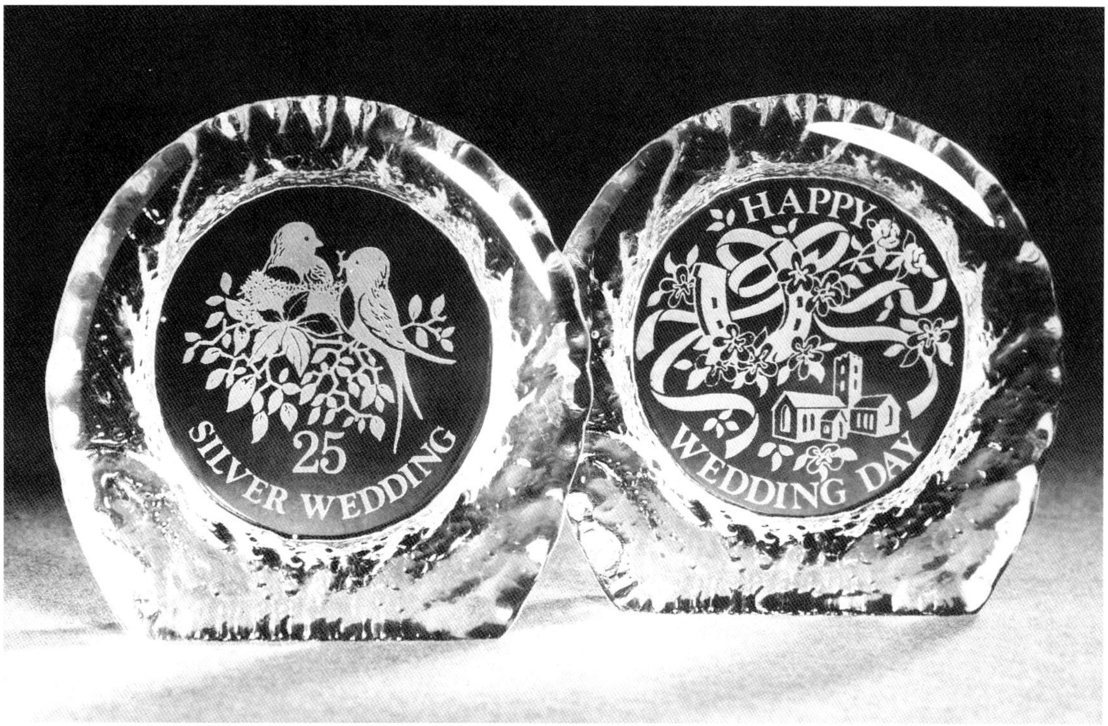

Plaques — Silver Wedding and the Wedding Day.

gift card on which to write the name of the presenter, recipient and the date.

The focus of the tankards was decidedly male. On them was etched a hot rod and 'Congratulations on your Eighteenth (or Twenty-first) birthday'. The grill of the car was replaced by the numerals '18' or '21' for the birthday boy. For the birthday girl there was a ring-stemmed goblet. The same two birthdays were celebrated with the etched age decorations with ribbons, flowers and leaves.

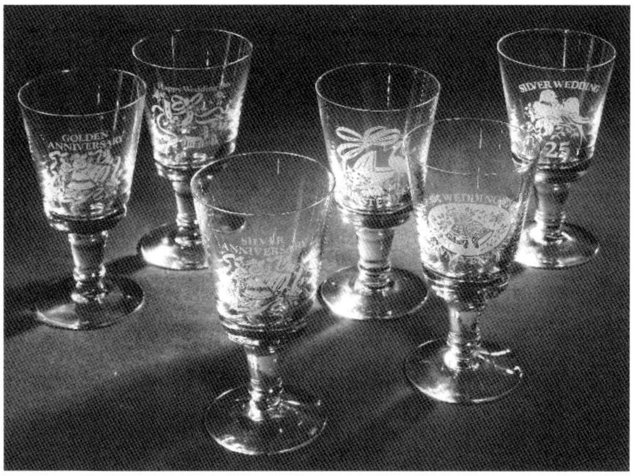

Etched crystal goblets — Golden Anniversary, Wedding Day, Silver Anniversary, Christening, Wedding Anniversary, and Silver Wedding.

One gift for a Christening was same goblet shape with an etching of a baptismal font also surrounded by ribbons within which was written 'CHRISTENING' over the font. Other decorations included an angel on each side of the font and flowers and leaves. A second Christening gift was a tea bell. The font was still the centre-piece. Above it were two doves, below a banner on which was inscribed 'CHRISTENING'. Flowers and leaves decorated the sides of the font.

There were also two choices for weddings, a goblet and a plaque. On both were 'Happy Wedding Day', a horseshoe, ribbons, stylised flowers and leaves above a church. A goblet and a tea bell were available for unspecified wedding anniversaries. Both bore an oval etching of two linked bells, but there were differences. On the goblet were 'WEDDING ANNIVERSARY' and a decoration of roses. On the bell were 'HAPPY WEDDING ANNIVERSARY', pairs of hearts, and daisy decorations. The clapper was amber glass.

For the silver wedding anniversary there was a choice of two goblets, a plaque and a bell. One goblet bore the linked bells, roses, ribbons, and 'SILVER ANNIVERSARY' above the design. The other goblet bore a pair of doves on leafy twigs below which were '25' and curved round it the words 'SILVER WEDDING'. The same pair of doves was on the plaque, but 'SILVER WEDDING' was curved over their heads and '25' was still below the twigs. The bell bore a slightly different design of doves, but this time they were surrounded by a wreath of leaves and separated by daisies. The anniversary details were in the same position.

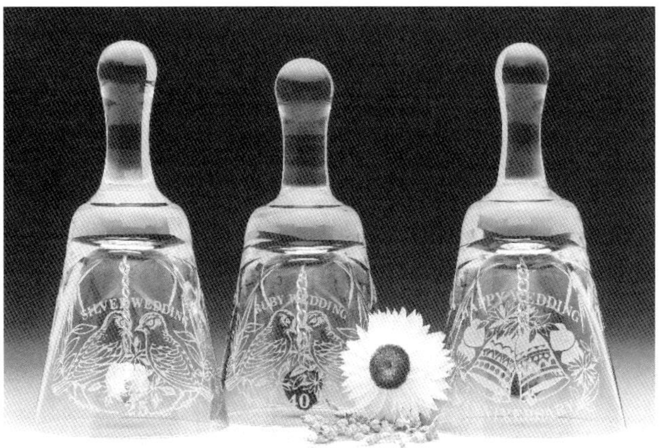

Etched crystal bells — Silver Wedding, Ruby Wedding and Wedding Anniversary.

Both the ruby and golden wedding anniversaries were celebrated. For the ruby anniversary there was a goblet and a bell. The design on the goblet was the same as that for the silver anniversary with the 'RUBY ANNIVERSARY' above the doves and '40' below. On the bell, the differences were the anniversary and the red glass clapper. The design for the golden wedding anniversary goblet was that of the silver wedding with the exception of the wording, 'GOLDEN ANNIVERSARY'. All goblets originally sold for six pounds and twenty-five pence.

For Any Occasion

The smoky blue tankards issued before Christmas 1971 were only the start of an extensive gift range produced at King's Lynn. The range of shapes produced by Wedgwood Glass for general giftware included all the shapes and colours so far described. Where tankards came in clear, smoky blue, amethyst, topaz, and less frequently in sapphire blue, amethyst was usually limited to royal events. There are exceptions to every rule and there was at least one edition of amethyst tankard onto which a bone china floral disc was attached as a seal. The floral decoration was in tones of pink and lilac to co-ordinate with the colour of the tankard *(Fig. 65)*.

Goblets were not frequently used for general giftware. They tended to be retained for use mainly for commemorating special events, most of which are mentioned earlier, although again there is at least one edition of smoky blue goblet on a clear glass stem and foot. A bone china floral disc was attached as a seal to the bowl. The seal was surrounded by hand-cut laurel leaves. To co-ordinate with the colour of the goblet, the floral decoration on the disc was in tones of blue. For other hand-cut, five-inch (12.75 cm) high goblets, the colours used were smoky blue and amethyst (and topaz for the special Silver Wedding commemorative). For the general gift range there is also an example of a topaz goblet similar in shape to the amethyst one produced for the Silver Jubilee of Queen Elizabeth II's coronation. There is a seal in which a small cameo could be set. This shape for the topaz goblet was used for the Egyptian theme depicting Tutankhamun and Ankhsenamun.

Coloured glass bells were produced in two forms. Cameo bells were in both smoky blue and topaz with amethyst being used for special events. Clappers of blue bells were light blue jasper, for topaz bells the clapper was black jasper, while for amethyst bells the clappers were lilac jasper to match the exterior cameos. Town Crier bells were in smoky blue, amethyst, topaz and green.

There were also cameo decanters from the 'Brancaster' suite. The standard 'Brancaster' decanter bore a white on light blue jasper portrait cameo medallion either of Churchill or Shakespeare. The Wedgwood Collectors' Society commissioned three 'Brancaster' ship's decanters. All bore white on light blue jasper portrait cameo medallions. One was of Horatio Nelson, the cameo being the same as that on the crystal paperweight. Another was of John Paul Jones *(Fig. 66)*, being a reproduction of a portrait medallion made c1906. The original was cast from a medal struck in 1779. The third was of James Cook, eighteenth century navigator and explorer, particularly of the Pacific Ocean during three voyages between August 1768 and his death in Hawaii in February 1779. The cameo was a reproduction of one designed by John Flaxman in 1784.

Prestige goblets/chalices *(Fig. 67)* bore a one-and-a-half inch (4 cm) tri-colour cameo of the Three Graces. The Graces were the daughters of Zeus and Eurynome and were the personification of the joy and well-being produced by fertile nature, beauty and love. They were always present at the celebration of human and divine marriages. Thalia (the Flowering), Euphrosyne (Joy) and Aglaia (the Radiant) also represented grace in giving and gratitude in receiving as well as true grace in behaviour. The first edition chalice in 1978 used a black, light blue and white jasper cameo. A later edition used lilac, light blue and white jasper. As with the royal commemoratives, the cameo was surrounded by hand-cut laurel leaves, while the reverse was cut with a garland. The smoky blue bowl was hand-formed, the rim sheared and finished in the traditional manner. The stem and foot were finished without the use of a mould. The stem was faceted and the foot star cut. All cutting was hand-polished. The editions were limited to one thousand and the first of these sold for forty-five pounds.

Other items for giftware were the drum and pumpkin shaped full lead faceted crystal paperweights each of which carried white on light blue jasper cameos, for example of Caesar's head, Cupid stringing his bow, Shakespeare, Dickens or one of the designs by Stubbs of horses. These crystal weights were in long-term production.

Packaging

During the years of glass production, the colours and designs for presentation boxes was quite varied. The most frequently used until 1982 were the foam lined lilac or mauve boxes for 'Wedgwood Glass'. Special editions and some gift lines were sold in satin lined crimson boxes on which was written in gold, firstly 'Wedgwood Glass' and later 'Wedgwood Crystal'. A label informed the buyer of the box's contents. Some labels also used the item's code.

Lilliput figurines were sold in cobalt blue boxes on which was depicted a leaping dolphin over the words 'Wedgwood Glass', brown and white boxes which described the contents as 'Lilliput's (sic) Handmade Crystal by Wedgwood Glass'. Silhouettes of an elephant, a duck, mushroom, dolphin and snail were the symbols. Boxes for special commemorative items, e.g. for the Silver Jubilee of accession of Queen Elizabeth II to the throne, the 1981 Royal Wedding and 1982 Papal visit to Britain bore a special descriptive label.

Most 'Wedgwood® Crystal' was sold in white boxes edged in black. The contents were described in word and illustration on the front of the box while on the bottom was the code, and on the back 'Handmade in England in 24% Lead Crystal. Designed by Frank Thrower'. Special boxes were used for the 1983–1986 Christmas bells. They were still black edged but the writing was red. Each described on the front which line of the first four of the 'Twelve Days of Christmas' was etched on the bell. The intention was to depict all twelve days as explained on the back of the box. 'The first in a series of twelve Limited Edition Crystal Bells to commemorate the twelve days of Christmas. Handmade in England in 24% Lead Crystal'. Also written was the code and description FJT33 Crystal Bell. Similar descriptions were on the back of the remaining three boxes of the series.

The 'Devon Collection' was presented in similar white boxes with black edging, black writing and the coat of arms of the county above and below which were 'Devon' and 'Collection' respectively. Like all other items of the period, 'Wedgwood® Crystal' was written on the front. In this case 'Handmade 24% Lead Crystal' was also there. The back of the box described its contents by code both for the North American market and for the British market, colour, height and the fact it was 'Designed by Frank Thrower'.

The boxes containing the commissions for the Danbury Mint were also white and edged in black. Their contents were described, 'Bird Crystal' and 'Wedgwood ® Crystal' on the front. On the back was a list of all the birds in the series. The particular item contained within the box was marked by a dot beside its name. For the 'Stag Crystal' the front also described the contents. This was a single item so there was no list on the back.

10

SPECIAL DAYS

Christmas

It is thought that Wedgwood was the first British hand-made glass producing company to make special items for Christmas. This was a five-and-a-half inch (14 cm) high clear glass, upright, circular plaque specially drawn by Ronald Stennett-Willson. Etched on it were '*CHRISTMAS* 1973' *(Fig. 68)* and the Madonna and Child, the surface of the design being matt. This edition was five thousand and produced only during 1973.

Between 1975 and 1979, Wedgwood produced a series of etched, clear glass, dome-shaped, Christmas paperweights *(Fig. 69)*. As with the 1973 paperweight, the central theme was matt. Each depicted scene was inspired by a Gospel text. The first of the series was 'The Christmas Angel' exemplifying the text 'the angel Gabriel was sent by God to a town in Galilee called Nazareth' (Gospel of St Luke, ch. 1 v.29).

In 1976, it the focus was 'The Annunciation'—'and the angel said to her, "Do not be afraid, Mary, for you have found favour with God. And behold, you will conceive a son and you shall call his name, Jesus"' (Gospel of St Luke, ch. 1 v. 3).

In 1977, the scene depicted was 'The Nativity',—'and she brought forth her first-born son and wrapped him in swaddling clothes, and laid him in a manger because there was no room for them in the inn' (Gospel of St Luke, ch 2 v.7).

On the 1978 paperweight, 'The Adoration of the Magi' was depicted—'they saw the young child with Mary, his mother, and fell down and worshipped him; and they presented him with gifts of gold, frankincense and myrrh' (Gospel of St Matthew, ch. 2 v 11).

The final weight of the series in 1979 was 'The Flight into Egypt'—'the angel of the Lord appeared to Joseph in a dream, saying, "Arise and take the child and his mother and flee into Egypt, and be thou there until I bring thee word"' (Gospel of St Matthew, ch. v. 20).

From 1980 to 1984 *(Fig. 70)*, the same five scenes were depicted and in the same order, but there were two major differences. The shape of the second series was that of the pointed Gothic arch. Each scene was presented in colour within the grooved outline shaped to resemble a traditional English church stained glass window.

From 1977 to 1979 a hand-blown, heavily etched, ring-stemmed, crystal goblet was produced each year *(Fig. 71)*. The shape of the goblets was specially commissioned with the bowl being supported on a tall stem which carried a six-ring annulated knop. All goblets were approximately seven inches (18 cm) high. Production of each goblet ended at the end of the year which it celebrated and the first originally sold for seventeen pounds and ninety-five pence.

On the front of the first goblet was the façade of St Paul's Cathedral above which was etched the Christmas Star. Below was inscribed 'ST. PAUL'S' and within a banner 'CHRISTMAS 1977'. Angels frame the cathedral, while the remainder of the surface is covered with foliage, feathers, and snowflakes. St Paul's, Cathedral of the City of London, is England's only cathedral built in the classical style, and was erected after the Great Fire destroyed the previous church in 1666. It is the masterpiece of Christopher Wren, being constructed between 1675 and 1710.

The centre-piece for the 1978 goblet was the western façade and the northern side of Canterbury Cathedral from the perspective of the north west corner. The cathedral in the metropolitan city of the Anglican community was erected between the eleventh and fifteenth centuries. Despite desecration of the building during and after the Reformation and bombing during World War II, it retains some of its mediaeval stained glass. The goblet bears the inscription 'CANTERBURY CATHEDRAL' and 'CHRISTMAS 1978'. The remaining decoration is similar to that of the previous goblet.

The final goblet in 1979 depicted the façade of Salisbury Cathedral. The foundations of the present Salisbury Cathedral were laid in 1220 and the structure, in early English Gothic style, was completed about 1280. England's tallest spire was added in 1334. Salisbury Cathedral is unique in that is it the only mediaeval cathedral built from start to finish by one master designer. The goblet's decoration was similar to that on the previous two goblets, with the wording 'SALISBURY CATHEDRAL' and 'CHRISTMAS 1979'.

A further addition to the celebration of Christmas was the full lead crystal tea bell, shape CG312. One was produced each year from 1978 to 1982. Each was four inches (10.25 cm) high. The Star of Bethlehem was hand-cut three times on the back of each edition of the bells, none of which had any etching to indicate the bells were made by Wedgwood, but all bore a production label. The clapper of each bell was clear, faceted crystal attached within the dome by a stainless steel chain. Each year the bell was presented boxed with a descriptive commemorative leaflet, on the front of which was a photograph of the item. In 1978, the price for the bell was three pounds and thirty-three pence, while the next year the price had risen to three pounds and sixty-seven pence.

The first bell was etched with a reproduction taken from a mediaeval woodcut of the Christmas angel. In 1979, the robed Bethlehem Shepherd holding his crook and a lamb was the etched picture. Two numerals of the year were etched on each side of the figure while 'CHRISTMAS' was inscribed within a banner below the figure *(Figs 72–73)*.

In 1980, the Magi carrying their gifts of gold, frankincense and myrrh, the etched star of Bethlehem, and a commemorative inscription, 'CHRISTMAS 1980' within a banner, were depicted.

On the 1981 bell was etched the Flight into Egypt, a depiction of Joseph, Mary and the Child Jesus surrounded by palm fronds, above the inscription, 'CHRISTMAS 1981', in a banner.

The Holy Family of Jesus, Mary and Joseph was etched on the 1982 bell. Again the banner was used to state the event, 'CHRISTMAS 1982'. (Examples of each year's bell were also produced without the commemorative date).

Departing from the Biblical tradition, in 1982, the etching was of holly leaves and the year. In 1983 another bell was produced. Etched on it was a 'Partridge in a Pear Tree'. From 1984 to 1986 the theme continued with 'Two Turtle Doves', 'Three French Hens', and finally 'Four Calling Birds' in successive years. The Star of Bethlehem was still hand-cut onto the bells, but it was cut only twice — on each side of the central design, and was much smaller. These five bells were four-and-a-half inches (11 cm) high in shape FJT33. It was intended that the theme of these bells be continued for all Twelve Days of Christmas. This is evident from the boxes in which the first four bells of the series were packed. Written on the back of all boxes were the twelve days, with the specific theme bearing a tick beside its name.

Though made in 1980, an undated two-piece Christmas tree was produced for use on the festive dinner table. It was sold, at the time, with candles, for eleven pounds and ninety pence. When the two pieces were separated, the base could be used as a candleholder.

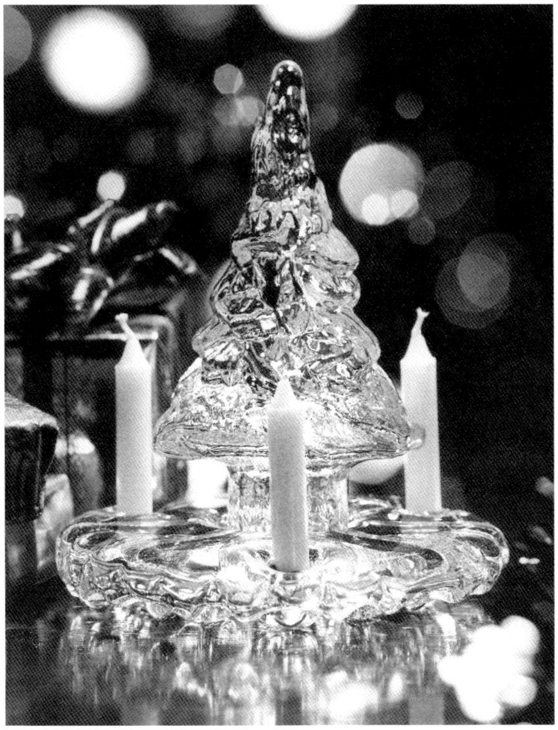

Two-piece Christmas tree. The base can be used as a candleholder.

Mother's Day

From 1980 to 1982 crystal bells in shape CG312 were etched for Mother's Day. Swans, a swimming pen and cygnet, above which was 'MOTHER 1980', were depicted on the first. In 1981, rabbits in long grass below which was 'MOTHER 1981' were the symbol. The third bell in the series depicted a doe with two fawns all seated in a ferny glade *(Fig. 74)*. Below them was 'MOTHER 1982'. The first bell originally cost three pounds and sixty-seven pence.

II

GALWAY CRYSTAL

According to a report *The Sunday Press*, February 23, 1975, on p. 5 'It was only an idea for making extra money when a group of seven invested in a small shop in Eyre Square, Galway in 1967.' By 1975, the 'intervention of Wedgwood and their own skills' (ibid) enabled an idea to mushroom into a factory employing one hundred and fifty people and a turn-over of almost one million pounds. Less than twelve months previously it looked as though Galway Crystal would close down because of insufficient capital, even though its quality cut glass was well accepted in the market place.

The assets of the Irish Crystal Glass Company (Galway) Limited were acquired by Josiah Wedgwood & Sons Limited on the 1st October, 1974. The new company, Galway Crystal Limited, took over the assets of the Irish Crystal Glass Company and re-engaged the employees. Wedgwood held eighty percent and Foir Teoranta twenty percent of the company shares on terms that permitted Wedgwood to acquire the balance at Wedgwood's option over a seven-year period. Roger Marsden was appointed managing director. He had previously been divisional sales manager at Barlaston.

A new purpose-built factory at the port city of Galway on the west coast of Ireland was constructed and equipped partly with grants from the Irish Industrial Development Authority. John Lyons, on behalf of the Authority, welcomed the arrival of Wedgwood in Galway. The *Wedgwood Review* in December 1974, on p.16 reported that he 'was confident the labour force of The Irish Crystal Glass Company—manufacturers of high quality lead crystal tableware and an extensive range of ornamental wares—would join him in welcoming Wedgwood to Galway'. At the time of sale there were one hundred and seventy-five employees, both glassmakers and craftsmen, and John Lyons further expressed the belief that the co-operation between the new management and employees would 'make and important contribution to the economy of the district and to the employees of Galway Crystal' (ibid).

Reports of production during these years state that a team of five men could blow one hundred and eighty 'Old Galway' liqueur glasses in one day, while the same time a team of four could blow thirty decanters of that pattern. When it came to cutting this pattern, work was much slower. It took a craftsman an hour to cut the liqueur glass, but five hours to cut the decanter.

As with the factory at King's Lynn, there was also construction of a new extension at Galway. Simon Kelly & Partners were employed as architects and John Sisk & Son the main contractors to extend the factory. The building on Dublin Road incorporated eight furnaces and all production was moved from the older building. Finished by mid-1975, it provided space for additional employees, expanding the workforce to almost two hundred and almost doubling output. To Ray Duly's responsibilities as technical director at King's Lynn were added those in a similar capacity at Galway. Donal Morrissy was works manager.

Glassmakers used fast-fire furnaces to produce hand-made full lead crystal tableware and a range of decorative items with the finest raw materials that came from around the world, e.g. sand from Belgium and lead from Mexico. The furnace master was responsible for every melting of raw materials to guarantee perfect homogeneity of the liquid before it was offered to the glassblowers. Any corded glass was rejected. (Flier advertising Wedgwood Irish Crystal from Galway).

Every Wedgwood Irish Crystal Item had attached a special emblem. The company commissioned the emblem from the Kilkenny Design Workshops. It interpreted the attributes of hand-cut lead crystal—shadow, symmetry, reflection, clarity, repeat of pattern and integrity of design. The base of all first quality pieces were etched 'Wedgwood' 'Galway'. On hand-cut bases this was often only visible when the piece was held obliquely to light (Advertising Flier).

Michael Garvey was master craftsman. There were twenty-two apprentices who would take seven years to achieve mastery. Patterns from Galway Crystal included 'Old Galway', 'Clifden', 'Killarney', 'O'Donnell', 'Galway Oyster' and 'Royal Irish'. The products were available in over fifty countries and sold through outlets such as Tiffany's, Bloomingdales, Nieman Marcus and Jensen. Cutting of designs onto the glassware was entirely freehand, but each item underwent extensive examination—twice before being cut and three times after.

In October 1975, Brian Berrington, at various times since 1964 area manager, divisional sales manager, new product development manager at Barlaston, and marketing director of Wedgwood Glass, relinquished the post of new product development manager to Richard Midwinter, group design co-ordinator. Brian Berrington was appointed marketing director for the glass division, succeeding David Marten who moved to be sales director of Coalport. In his new position, Brian Berrington was responsible for the sales administration and product development teams for both Wedgwood Glass and Galway Crystal. In London, Roy Wadland became director of the marketing division for Wedgwood Glass.

A statement from Sir Arthur Bryan, Chairman of the Wedgwood Group, reported in 1977, the growing strength of the Galway factory. 'Following a major expansion and re-organisation programme completed in September, 1975—resulting in substantially improved output and productivity—Galway Crystal is now able to introduce its designs into the British market.

'Since Wedgwood bought the factory and formed the new Galway Crystal Company in October 1974, production has trebled and, furthermore, the high quality of this hand-cut lead crystal has been consistently improved. Such progress has largely been achieved through the building of a new factory, completed just over a year ago, the subsequent re-organisation of production processes and the introduction of a well-structured training programme, which have combined to greatly improve the proficiency and efficiency of the skilled craftsmen and women among the 180-strong labour force at Galway.

'The demand for Galway Crystal from the USA continues to increase and nearly 80 per cent of

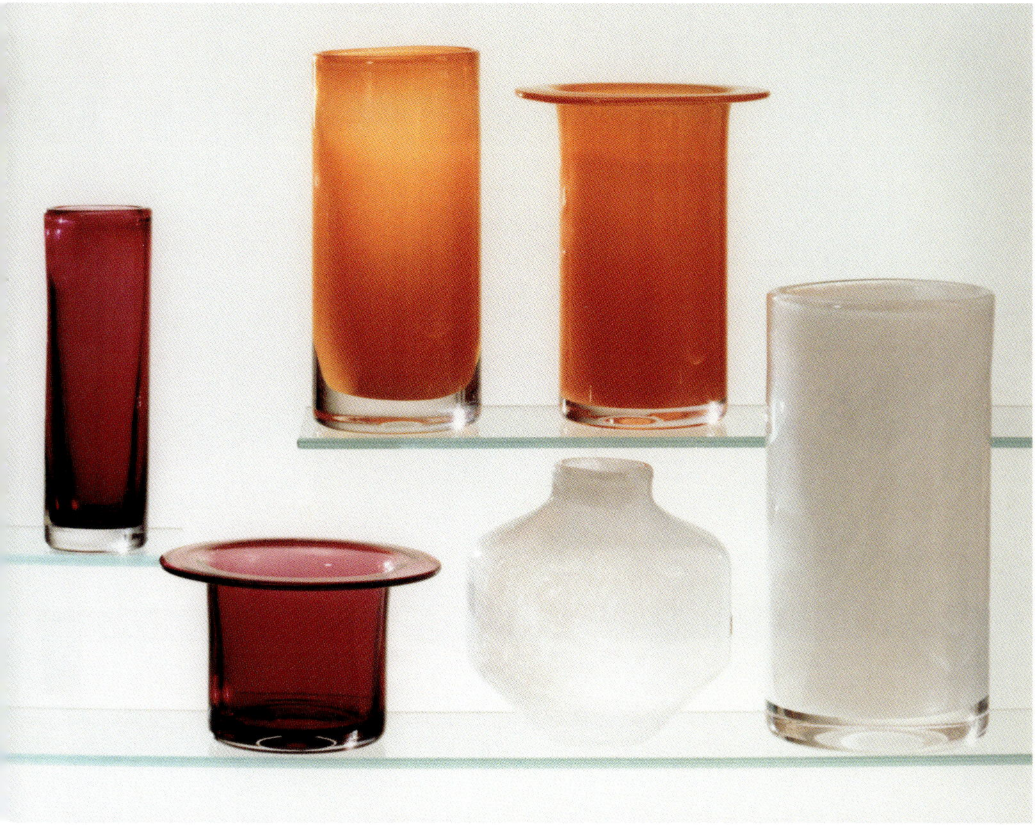

ʹig. 1: Single colour vases — top row: orange — RSW20/2, RSW21/2; niddle row: cranberry — RSW20/1; ʹottom row: cranberry — RSW21/1, white opal — RSW10, RSW20/3.

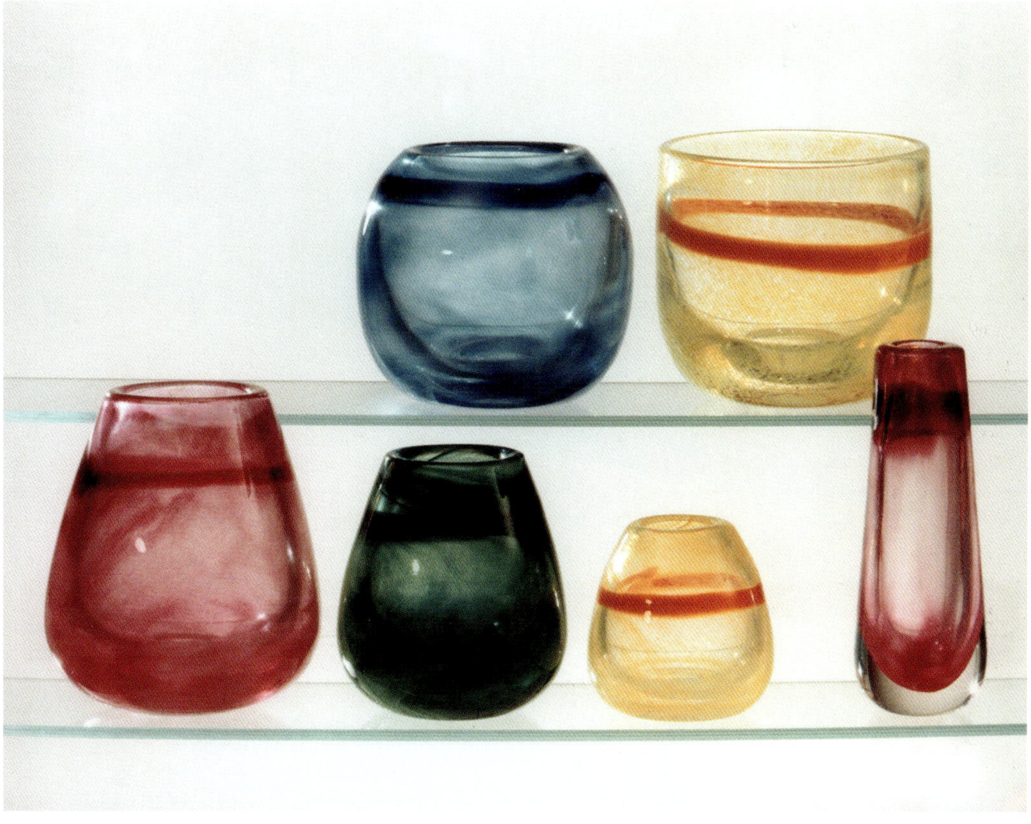

ʹig. 2: Colour combination vases — top row: lue/blue — RSW103/5, range/yellow — RSW103/6; ʹottom row: rose/rose — RSW103/3, reen/green — RSW103/2, range/yellow — RSW 103/1, ose/rose — RSW103/4

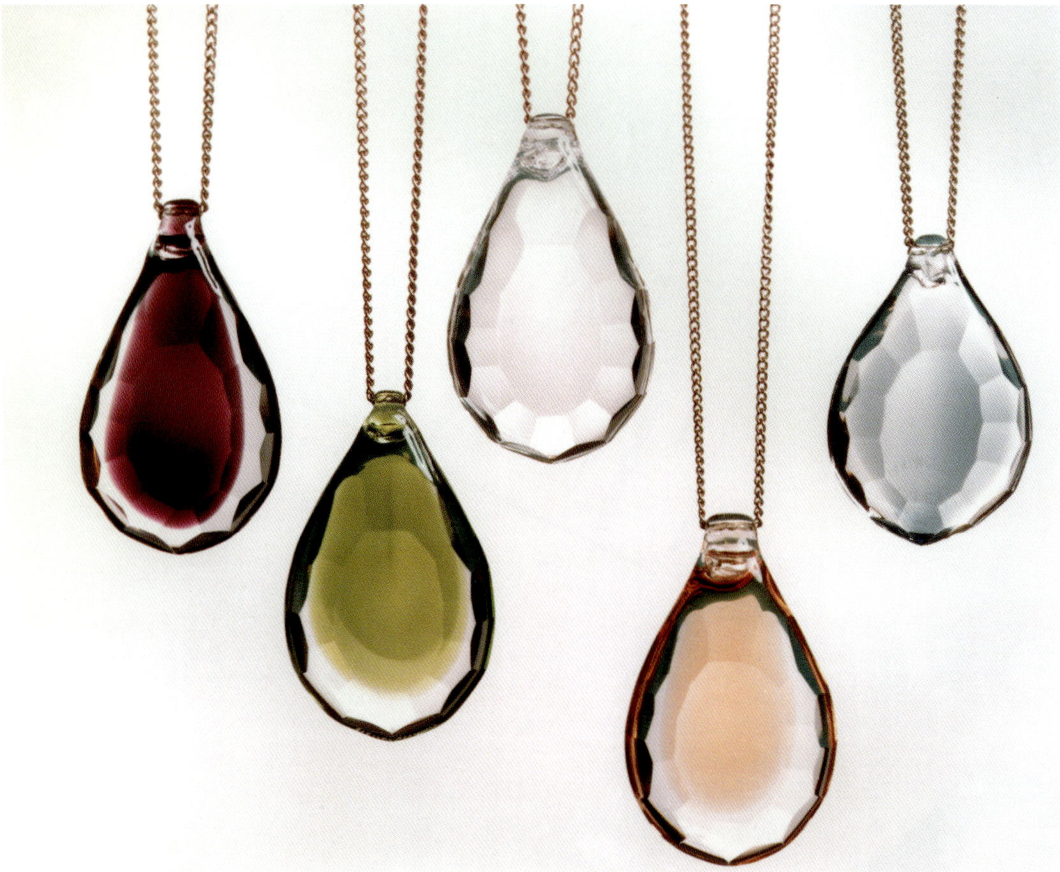

Fig. 3: Tear-drop crystal pendants.

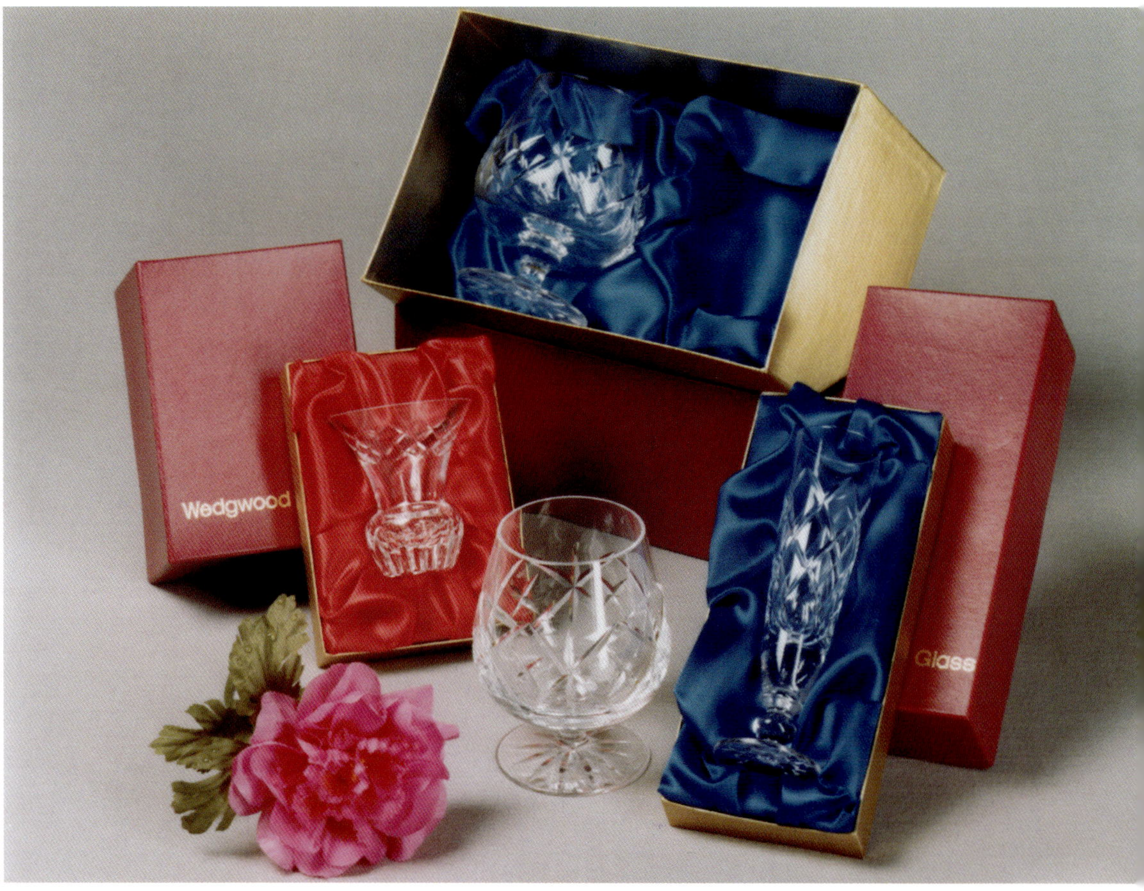

Fig. 4: Boxed crystal giftware.

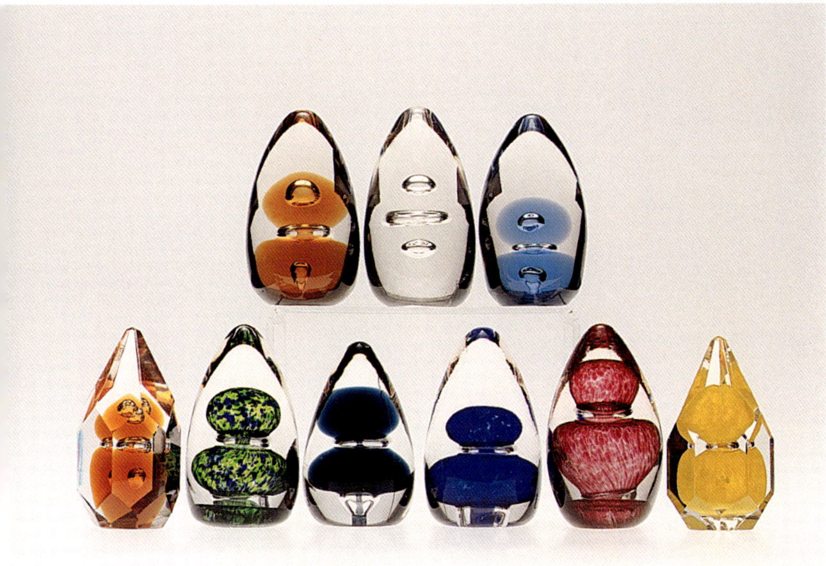

Fig. 5: Dome paperweights. Clear with air patterns only (centre top). All others with air patterns and clear and speckled colours. Faceted Galaxy *(extreme left and right bottom row).*

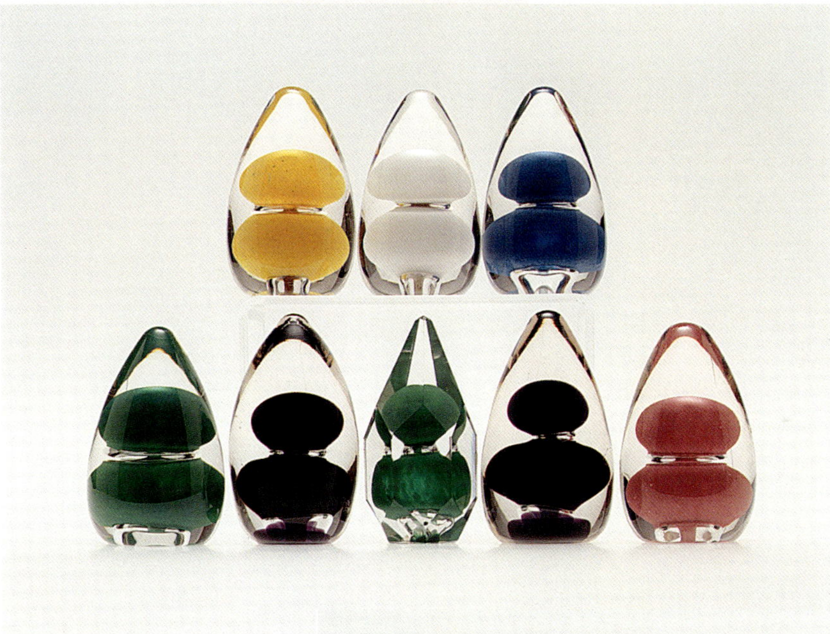

Fig. 6: Dome paperweights with opaque, powder colours and a faceted Galaxy *paperweight (centre bottom row).*

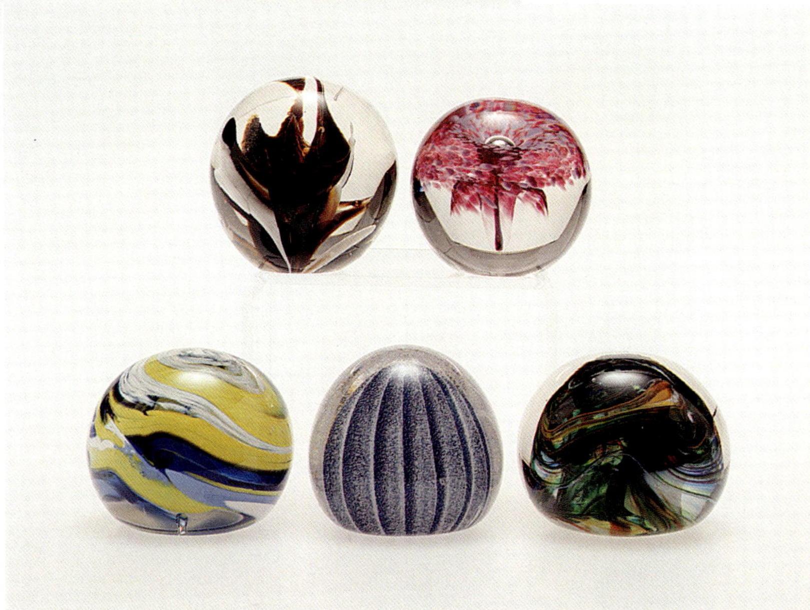

Fig. 7: Spherical paperweights — Top row: Seafern *and* Stardance*; bottom row: left and right* Spindrift, *centre* Galactic.

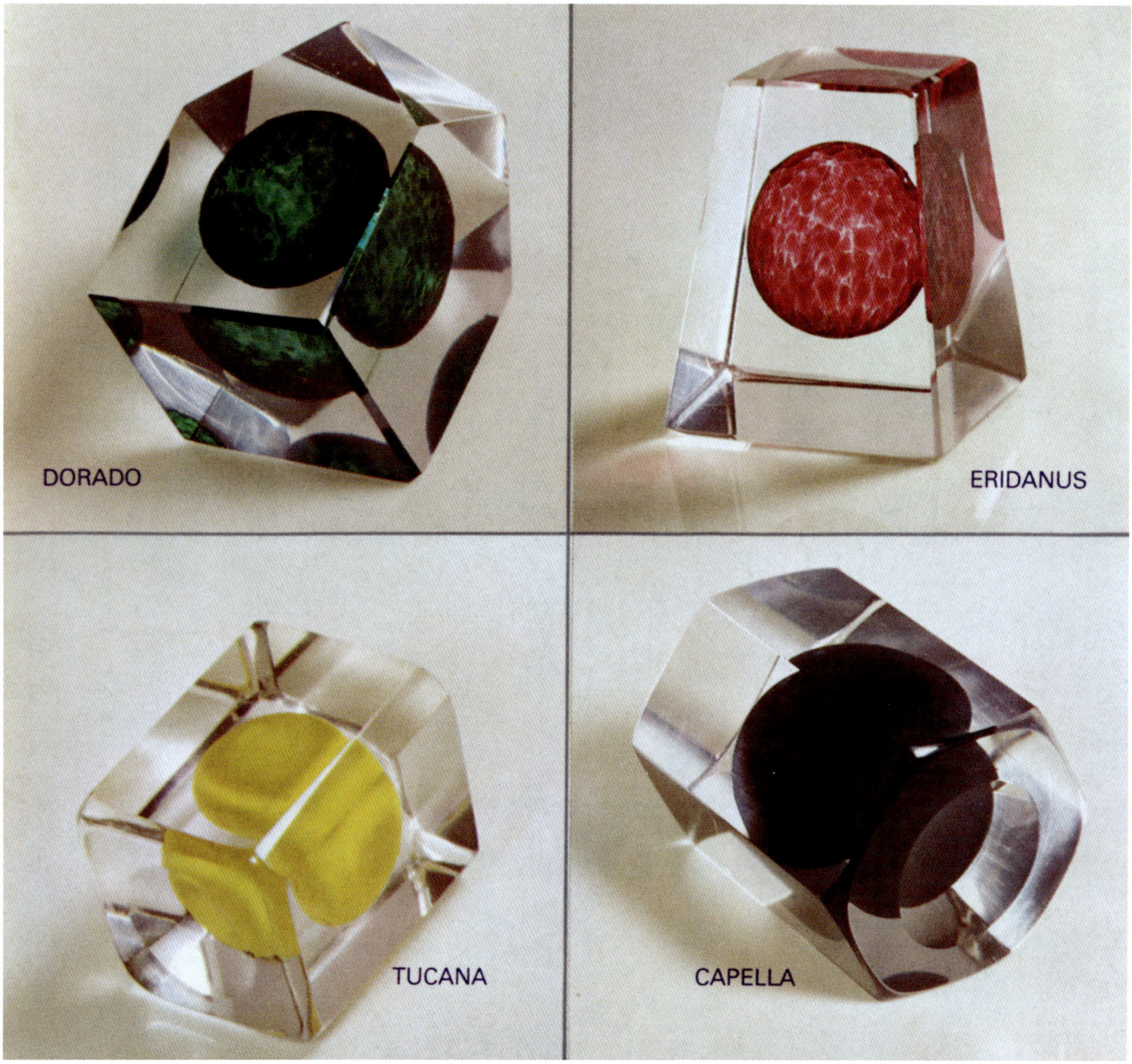

Fig. 8: Andromeda Collection.

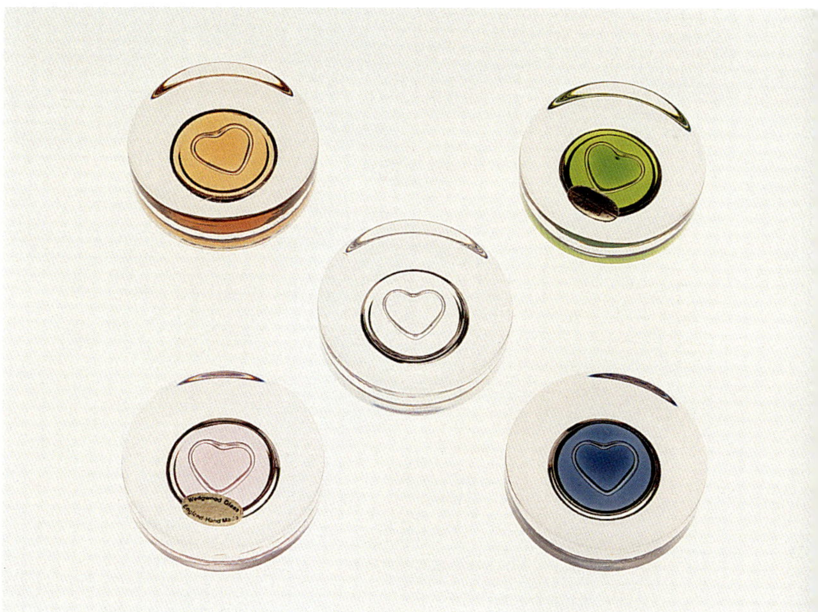

Fig. 9: Glass disc paperweights with central moulded heart shapes.

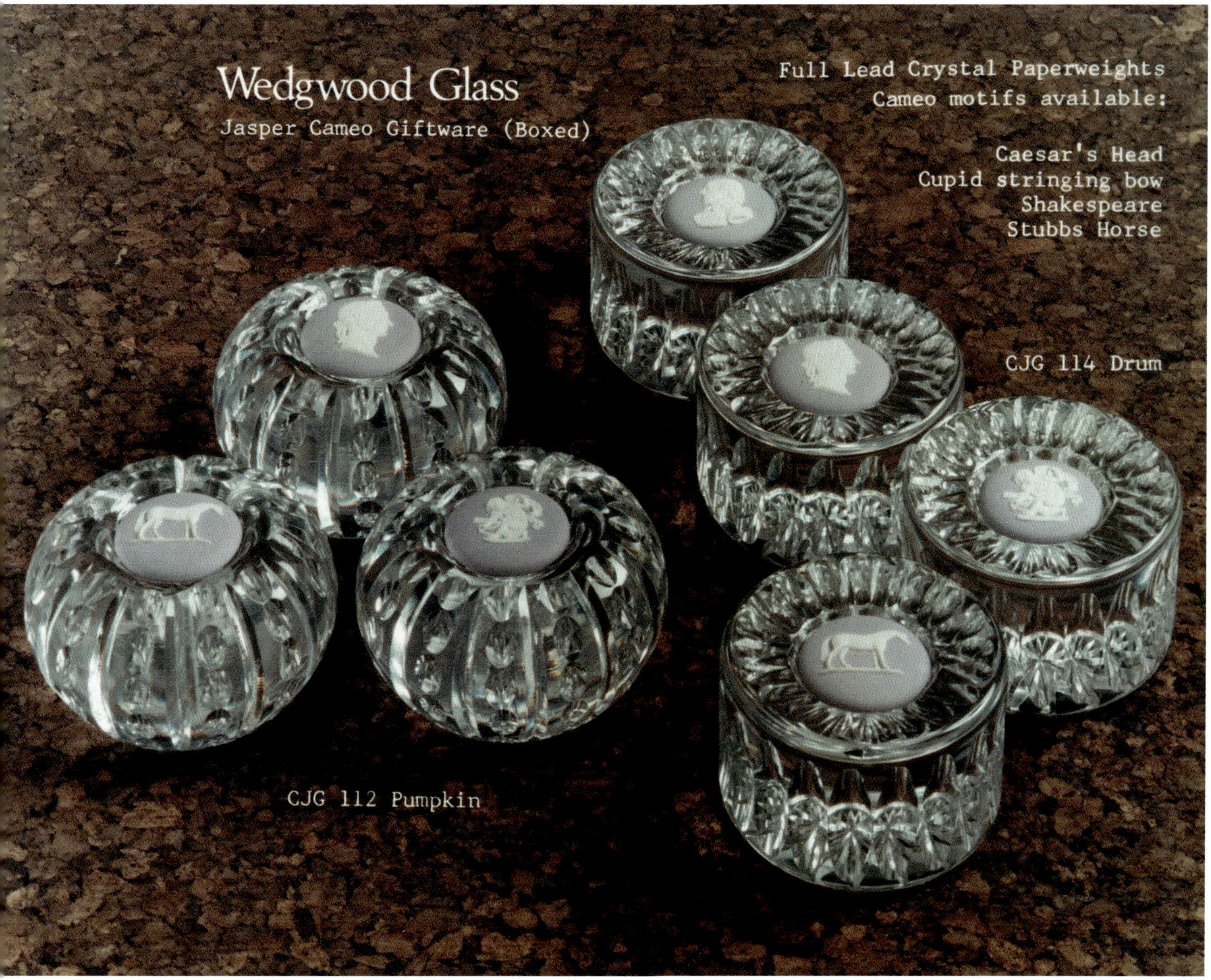

Fig. 10: Jasper cameo drum and pumpkin shaped crystal paperweights.

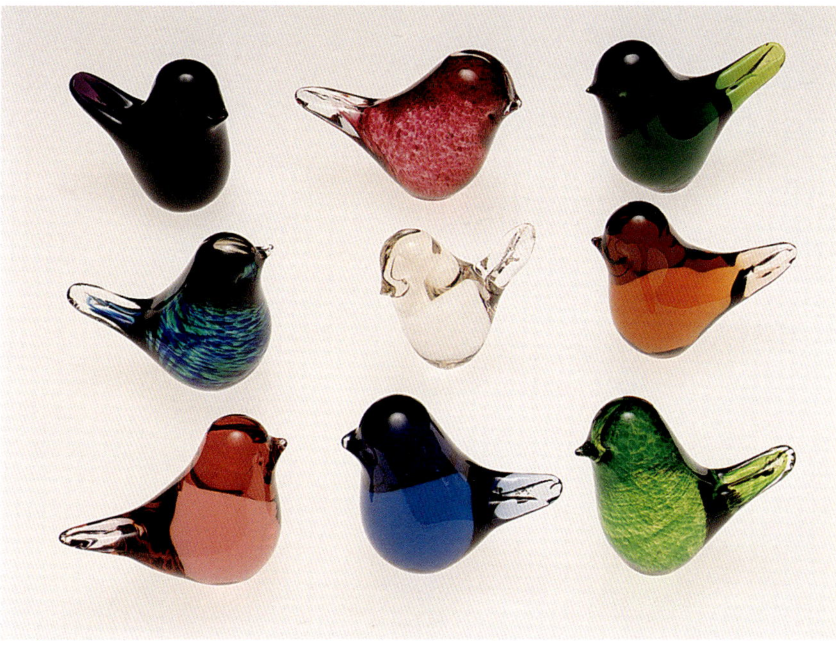

Fig. 11: Small birds — clear, plain and speckled colours.

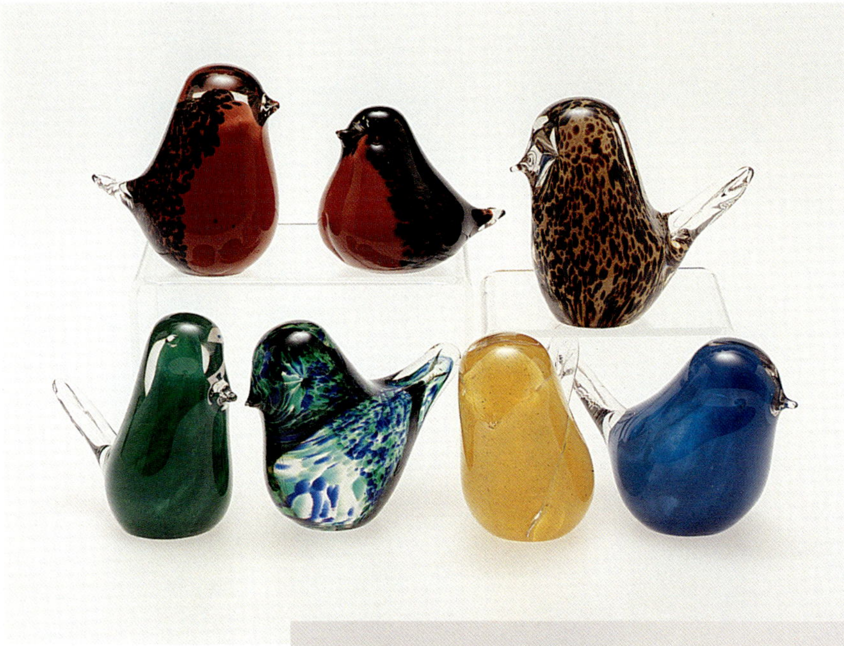

Fig. 12: Large birds — opaque powder colours and speckled colours. Top row: (right and centre) Robin and fledgling robin.

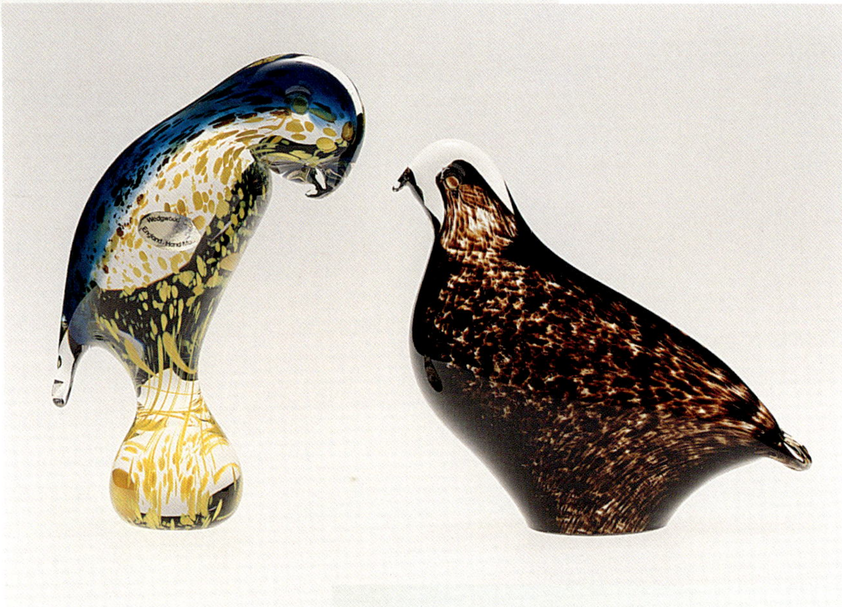

Fig. 13: Parrot and partridge.

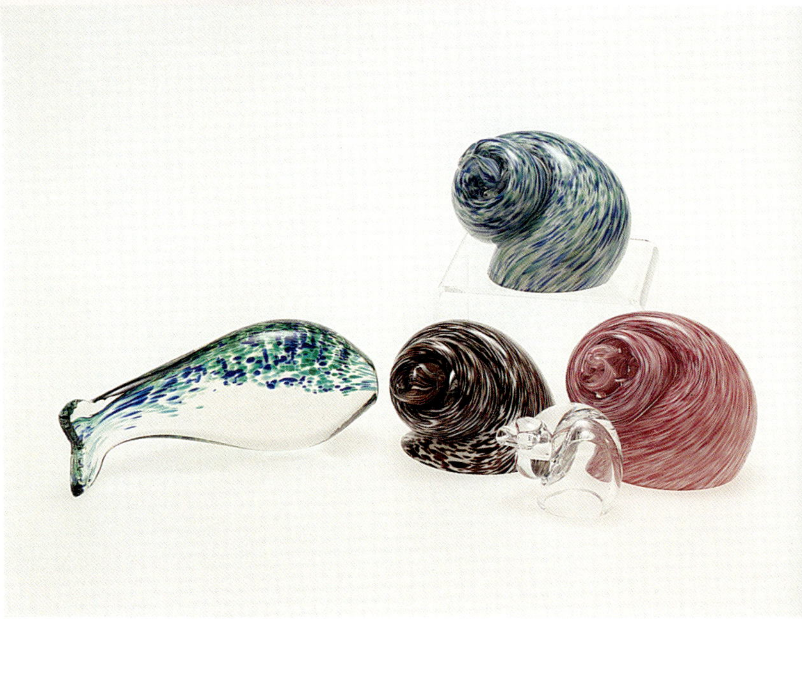

Fig. 14: Fish and large and Lilliput seashells.

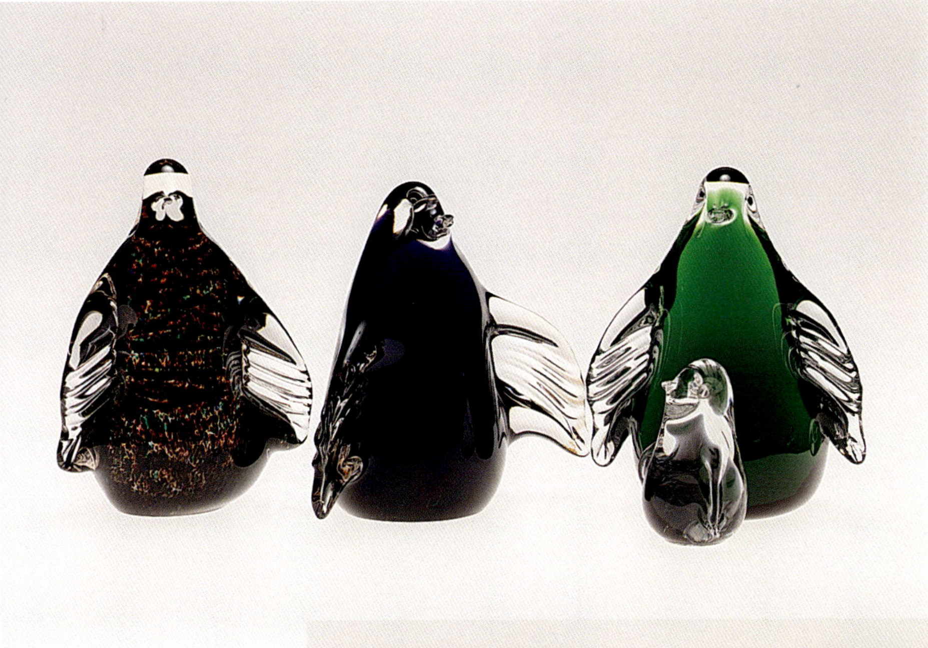

Fig. 15: Large and Lilliput penguins.

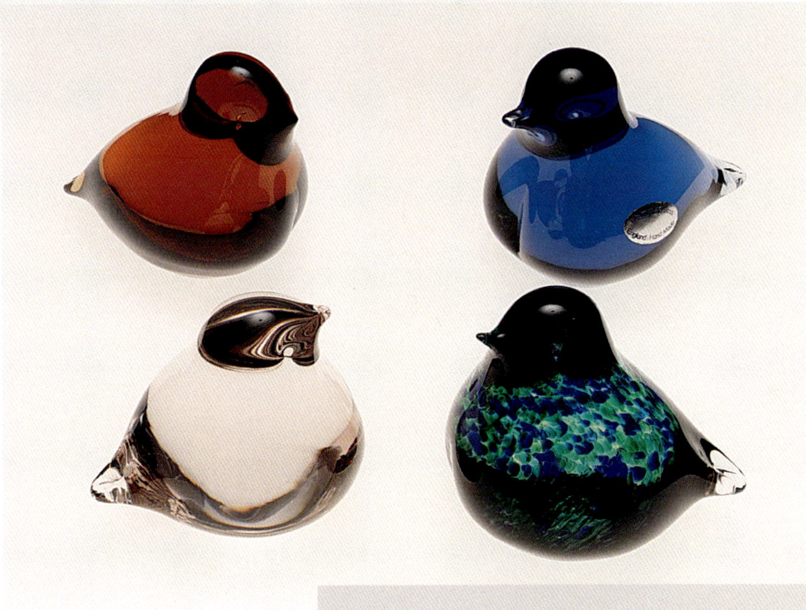

Fig. 16: Fledglings.

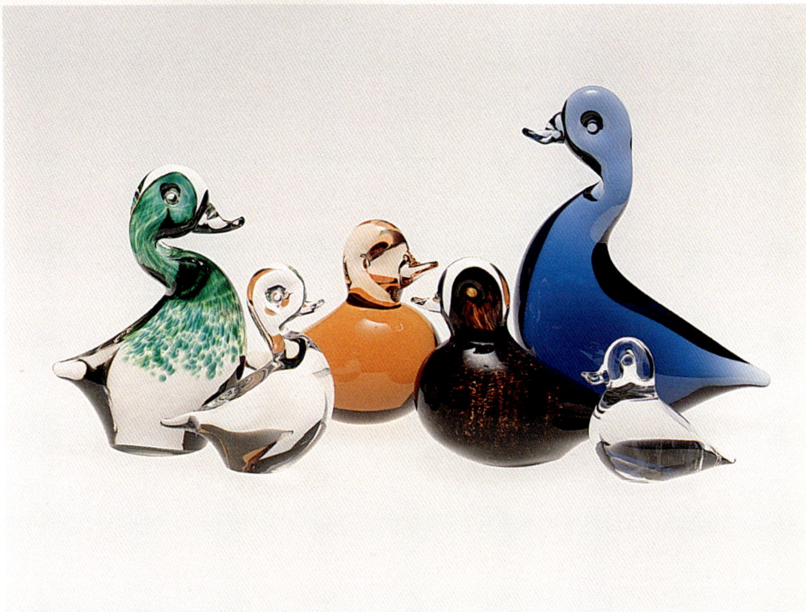

Fig. 17: Tall ducks and squat ducklings both large and Lilliput.

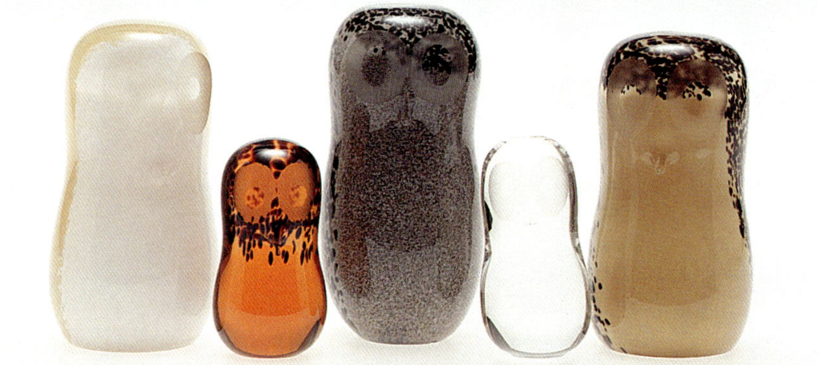

Fig. 18: Large and Lilliput owls.

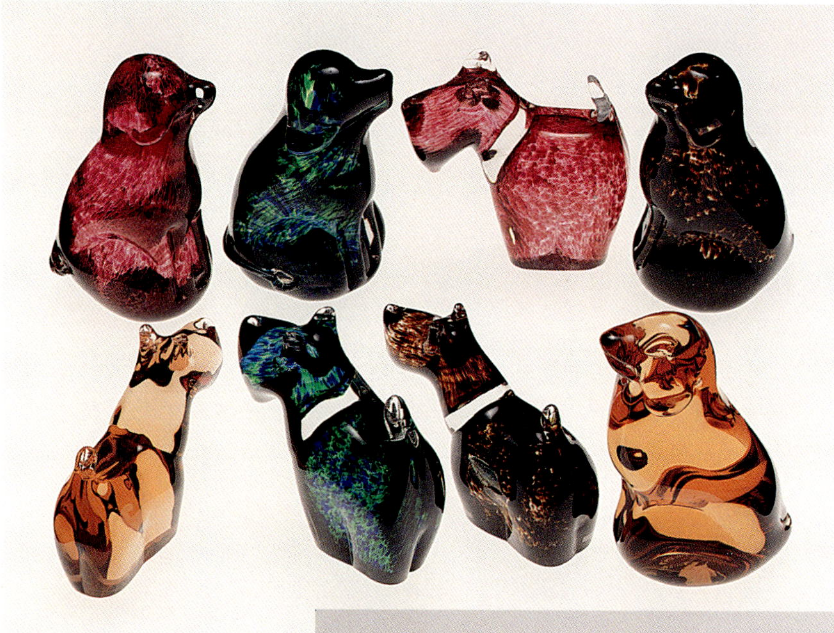

Fig. 19: Seated dog (puppy) and Scotty dog.

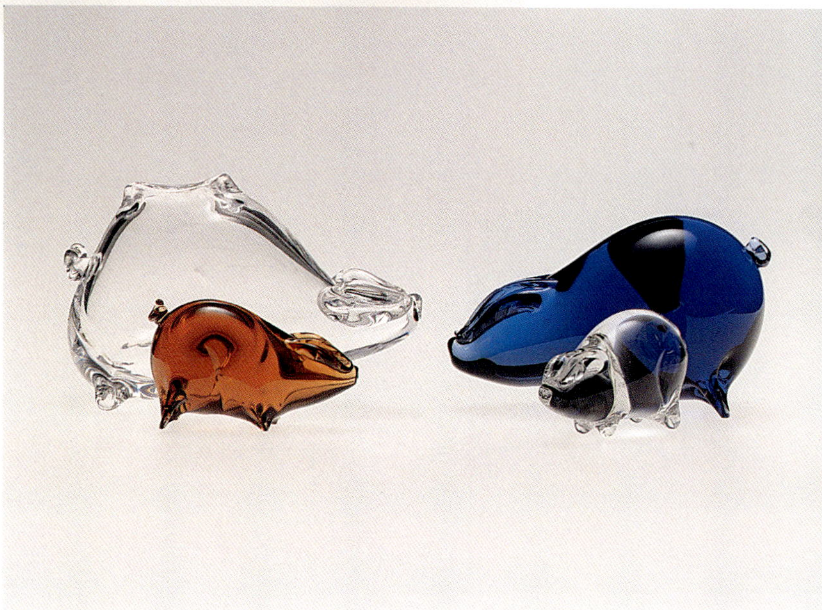

Fig. 20: Large and Lilliput pigs and a clear 'piggy bank'/money box.

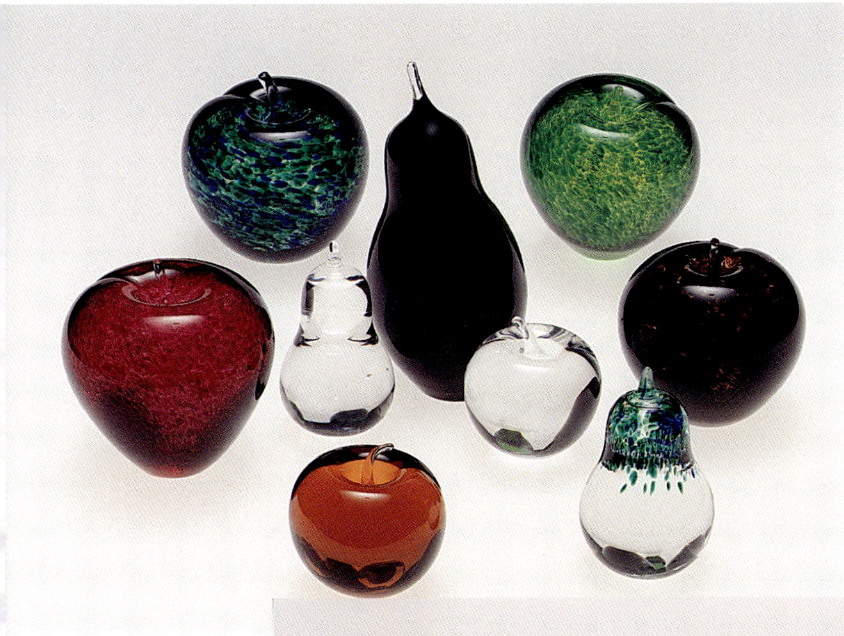

Fig. 21: Large and Lilliput apples and pears.

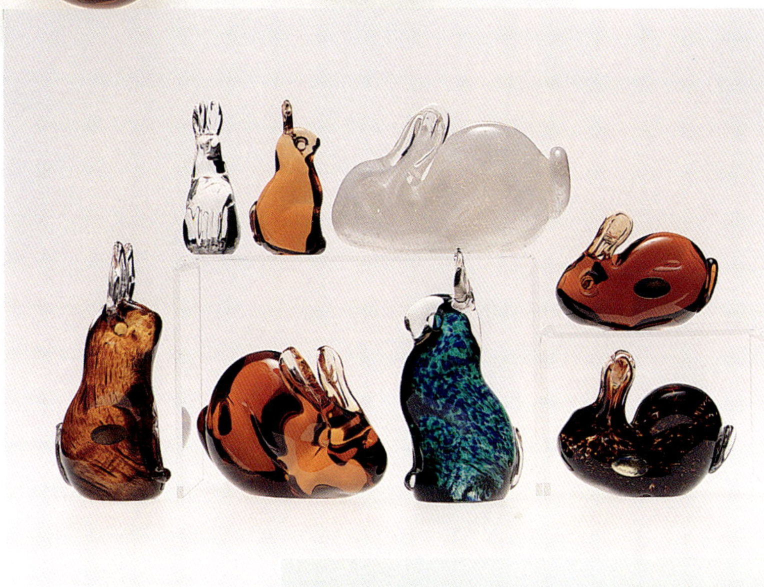

Fig. 22: From the field—small and large rabbits; upright large and Lilliput hares.

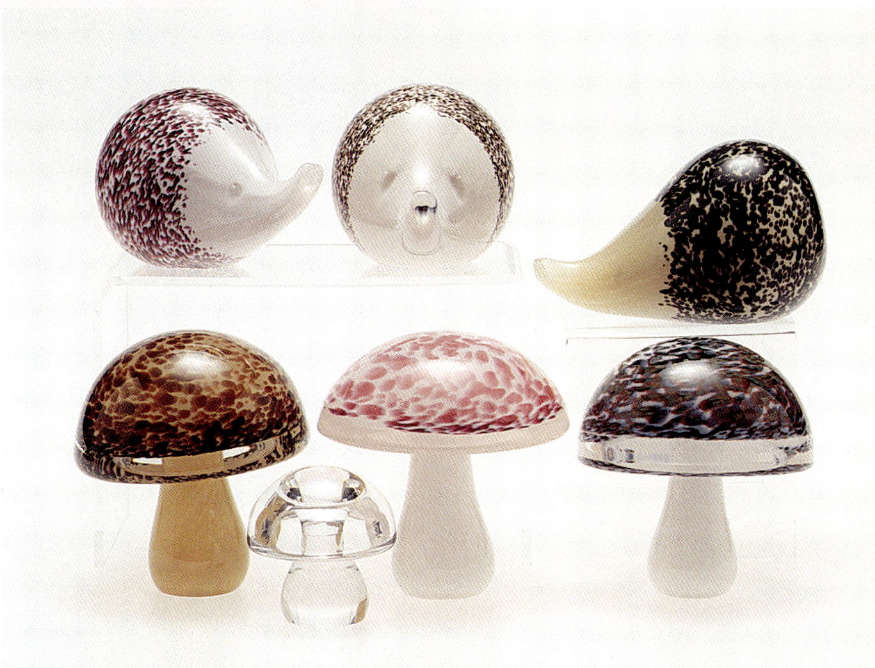

Fig. 23: From the field—hedgehogs and large and Lilliput mushrooms.

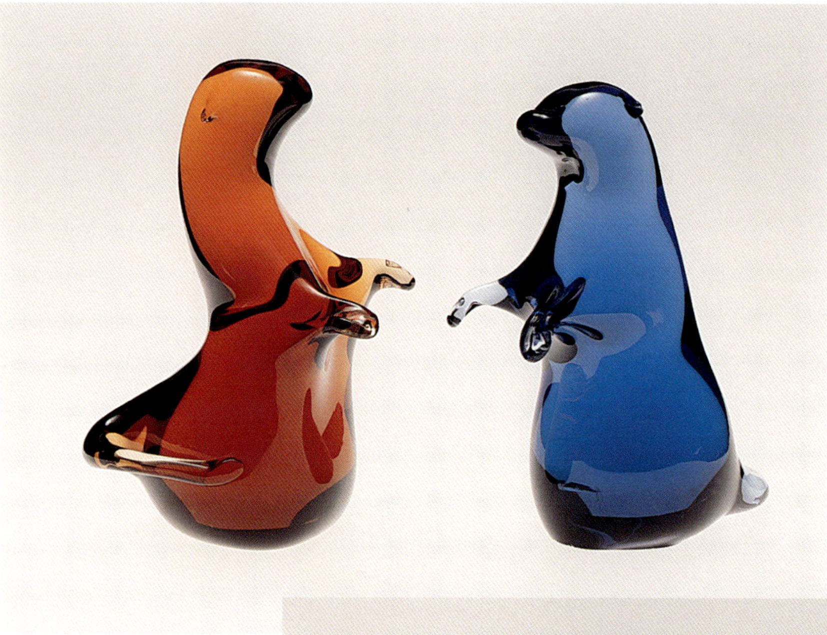

Fig. 24: By the creek and pond—otters.

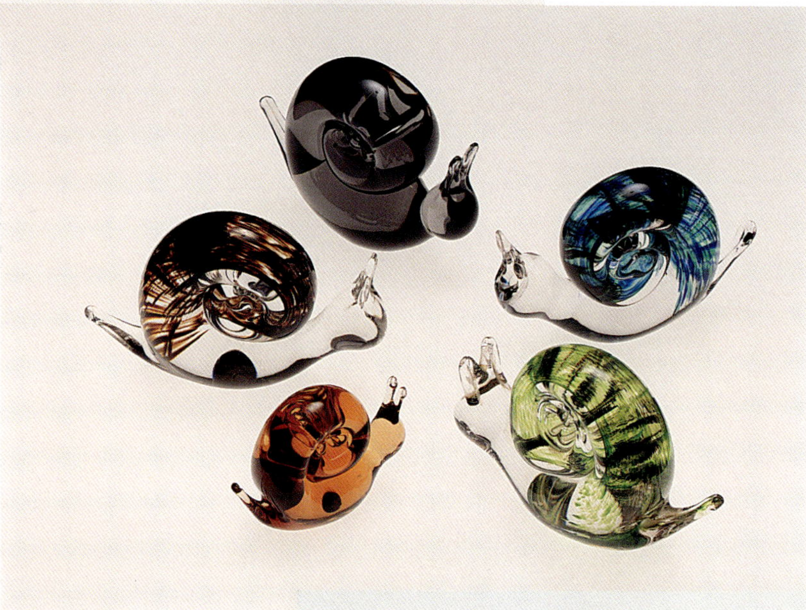

Fig. 25: By the creek and pond—snails.

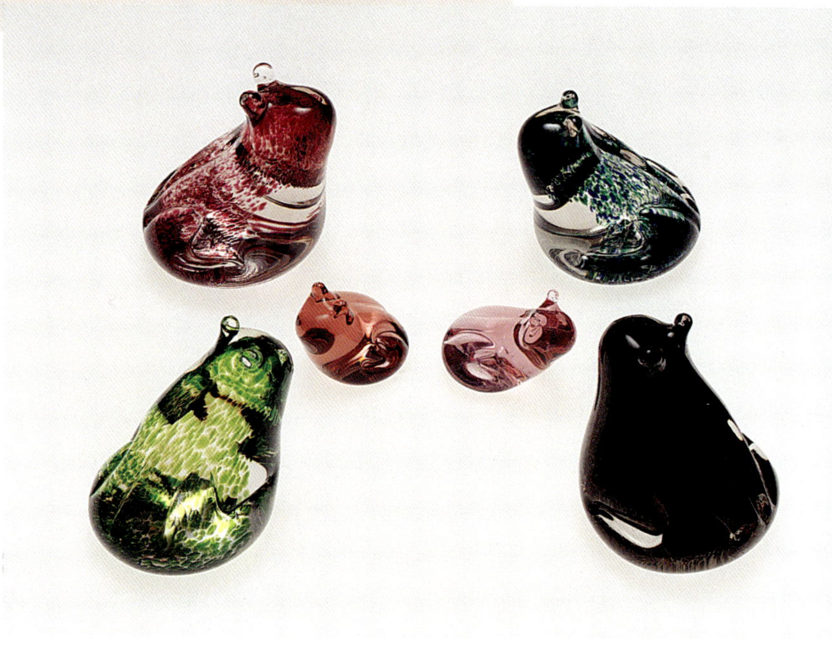

Fig. 26: By the creek and pond—large and Lilliput frogs.

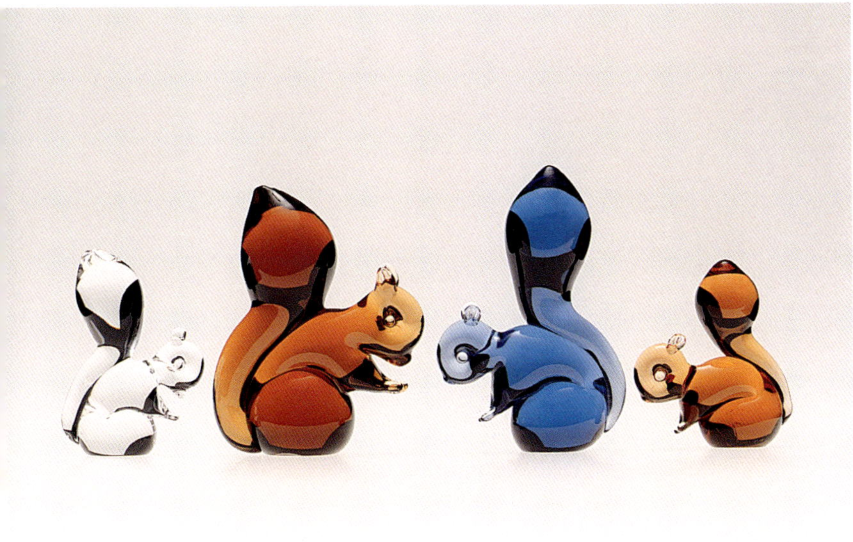

Fig. 27: In the forest — large and Lilliput squirrels.

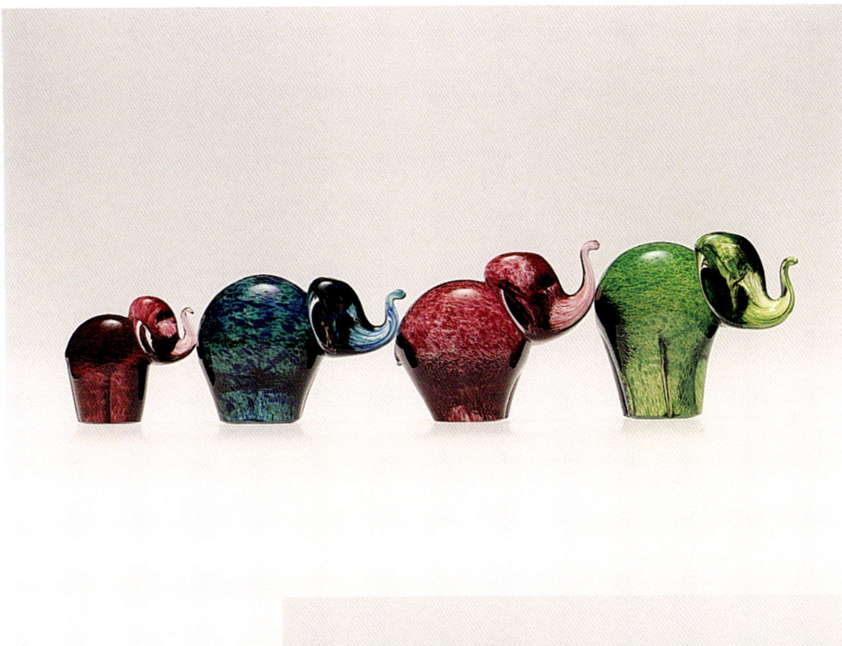

Fig. 28: From the wild — elephants with baby (extreme left).

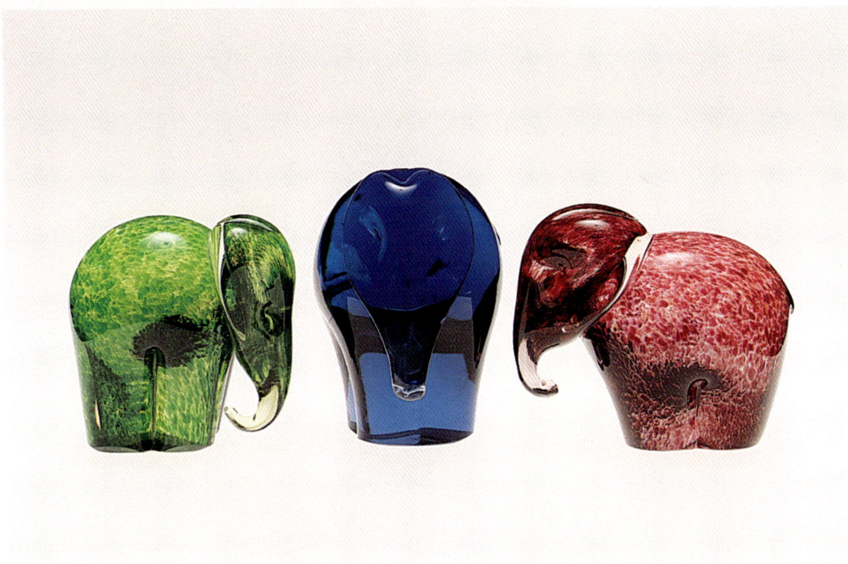

Fig. 29: From the wild — elephants.

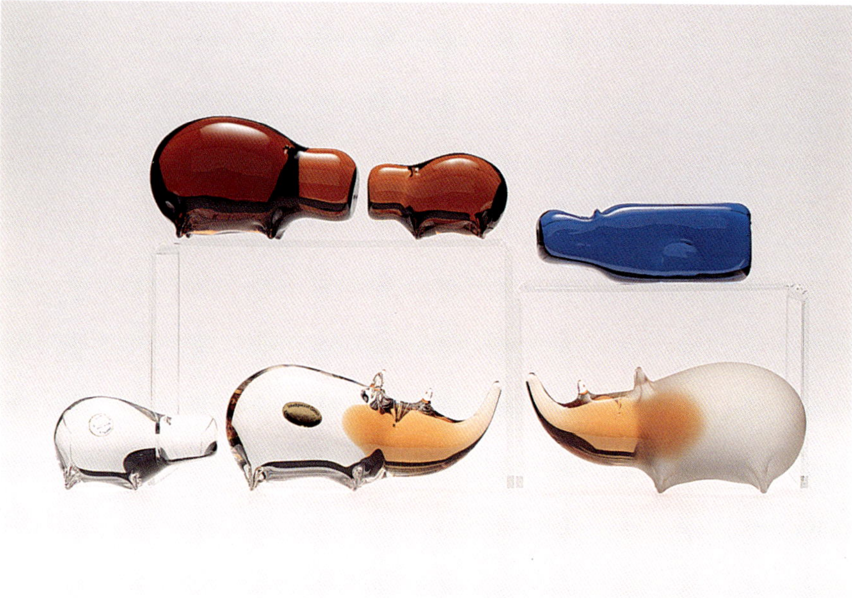

Fig. 30: From the wild—hippopotamuses large and Lilliput, and rhinos.

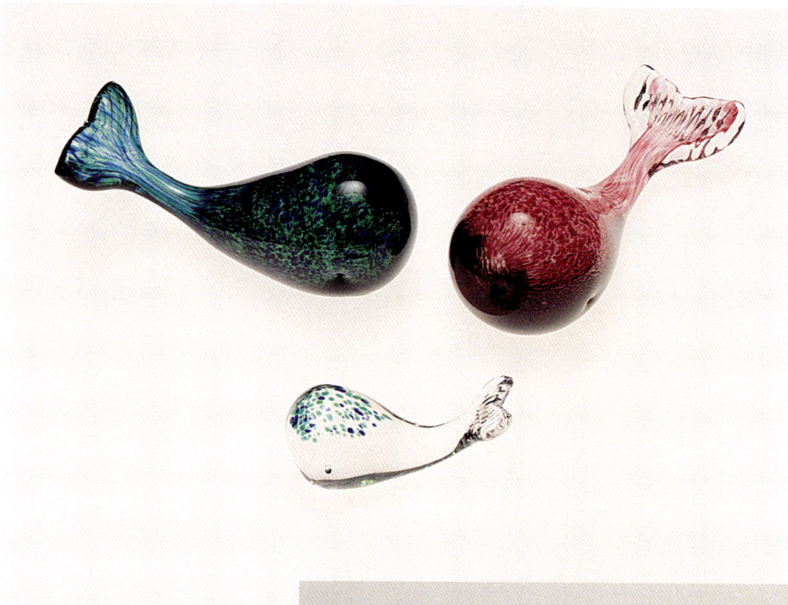

Fig. 31: Aquatic animals—large and Lilliput whales.

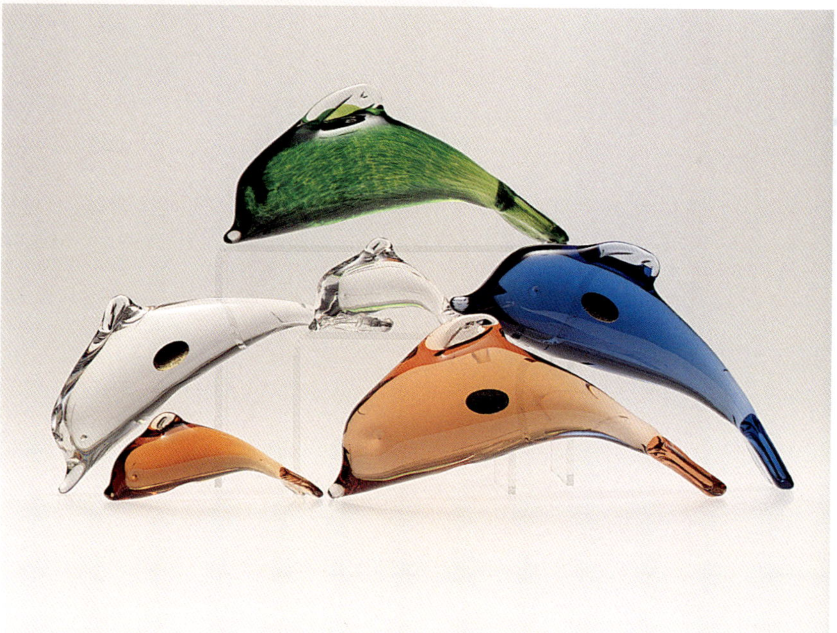

Fig. 32: Aquatic animals—large and Lilliput dolphins.

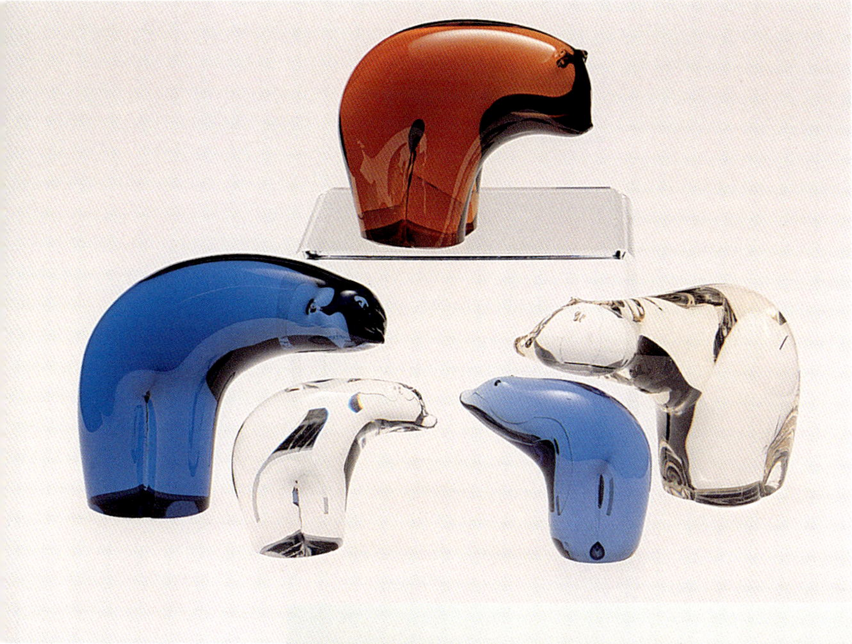

Fig. 33: From the frozen north—large and Lilliput polar bears.

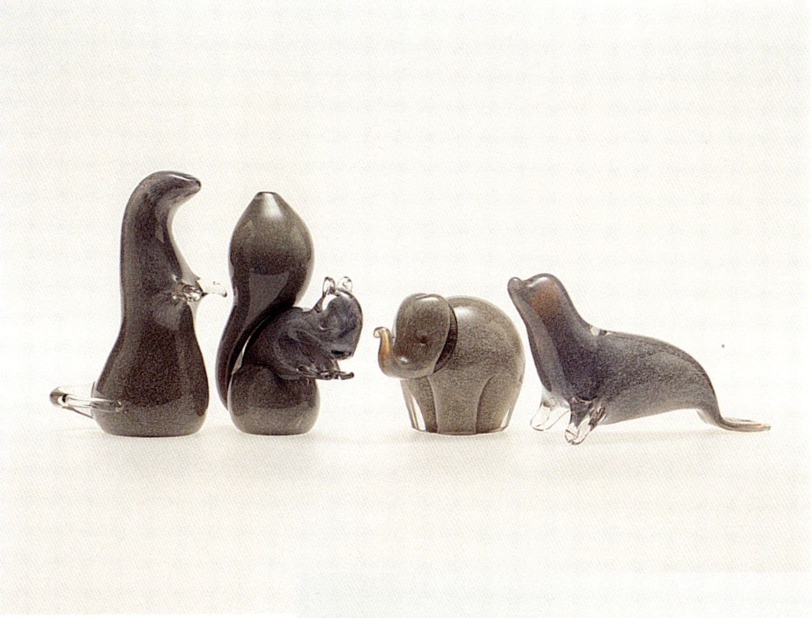

Fig. 34: Grey—otter, squirrel, elephant, seal.

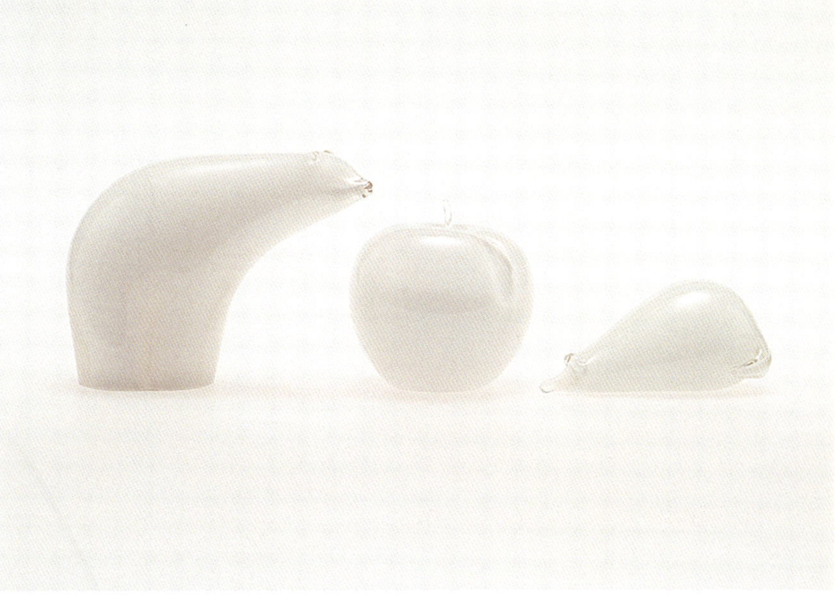

Fig. 35: White—polar bear, apple, mouse.

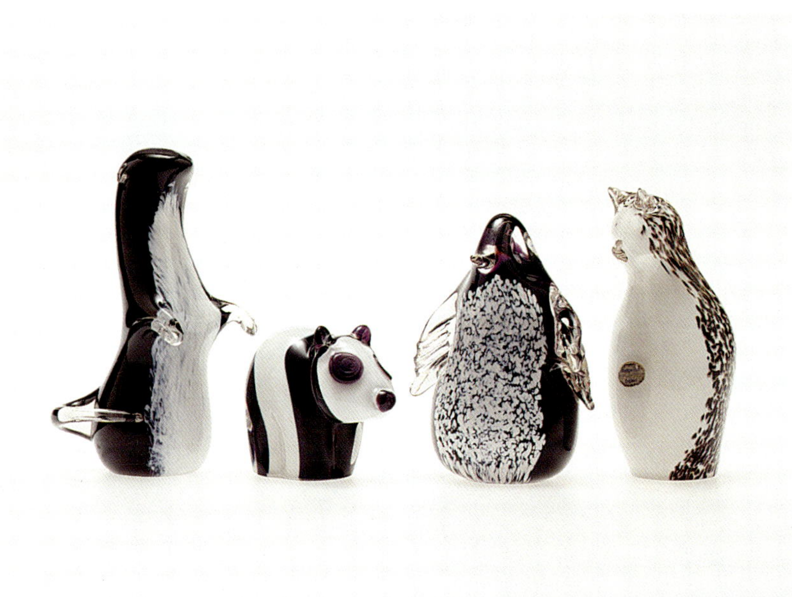

Fig. 36: Dark and white—otter, panda, penguin, cat.

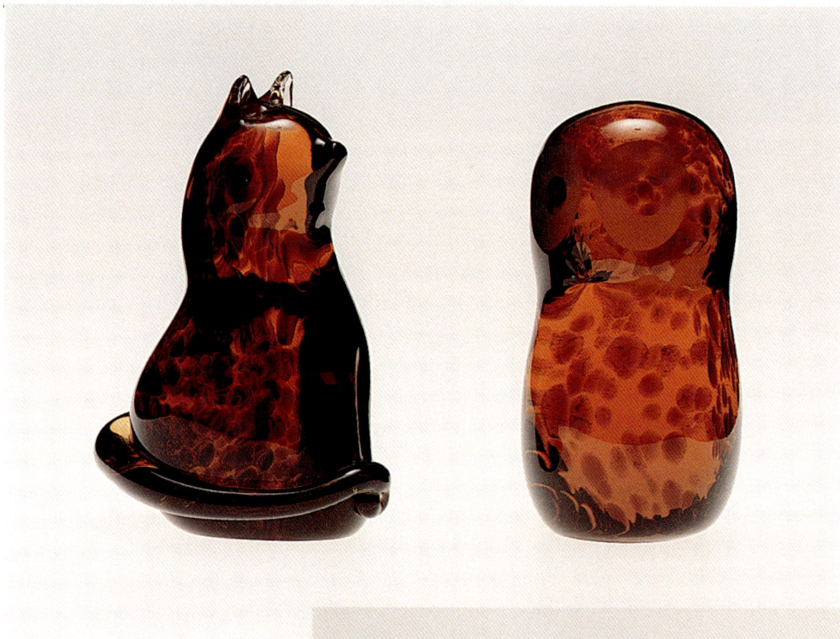

Fig. 37: Speckled topaz—'pussy cat' and owl.

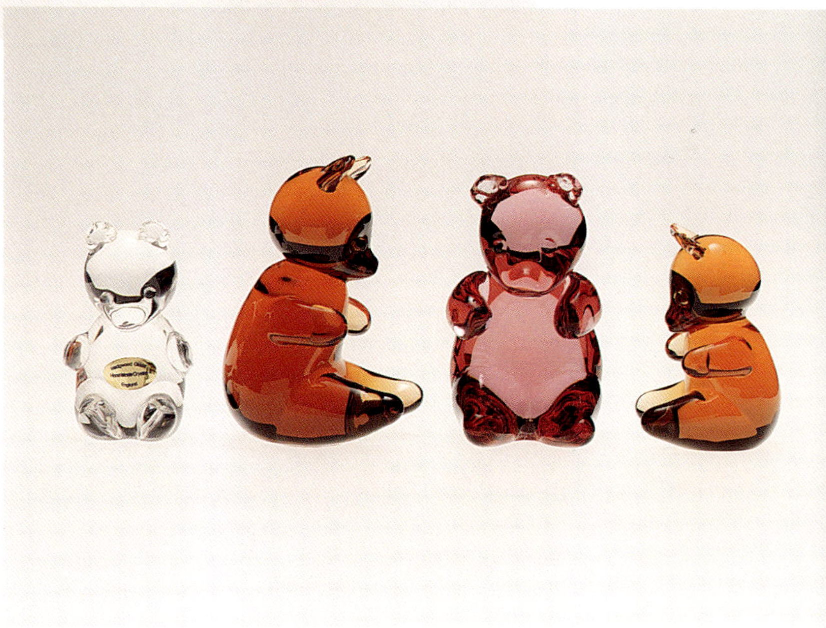

Fig. 38: Large and Lilliput teddy bears.

Fig. 39–41: Candlesticks and candleholders — top row: Sheringham, *middle row:* Sandringham *with a bulbous candlestick on the extreme right; bottom row:* Brancaster *with* Cromer *(second from left) and* Helix *(second from right).*

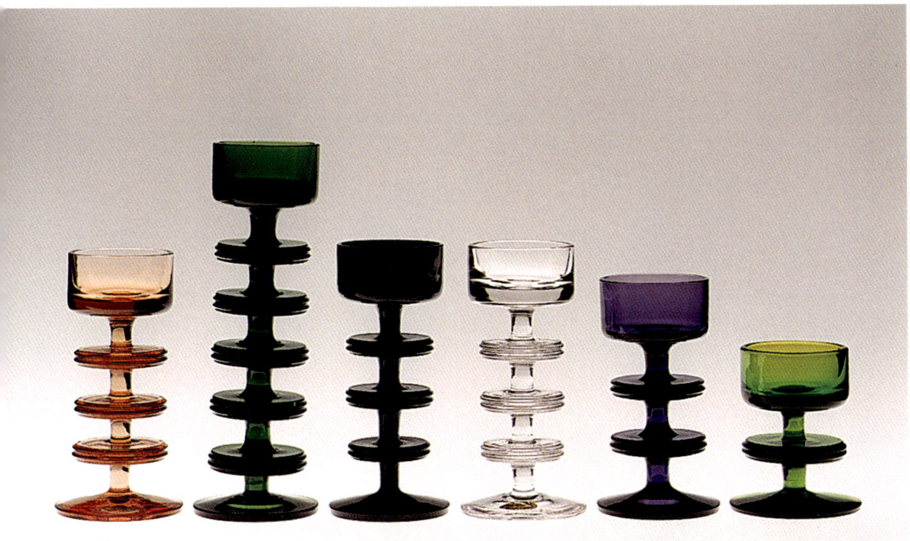

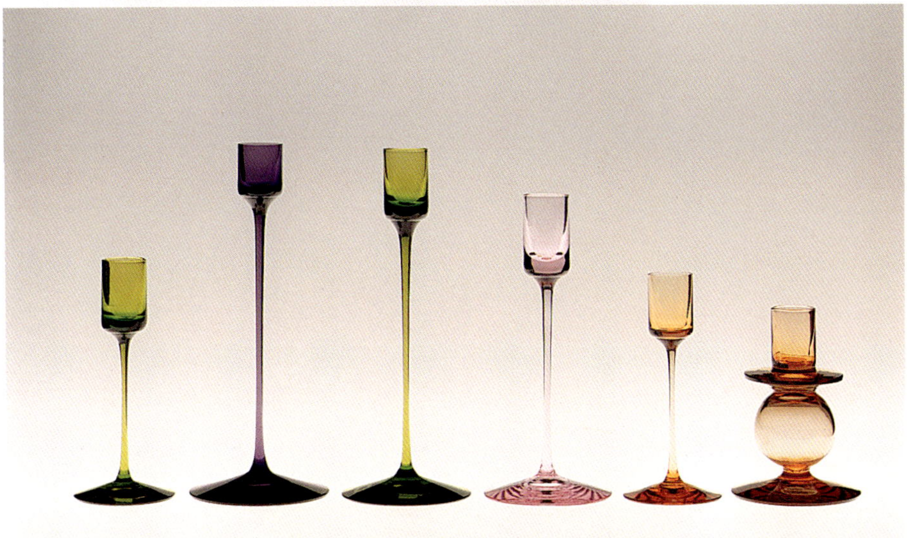

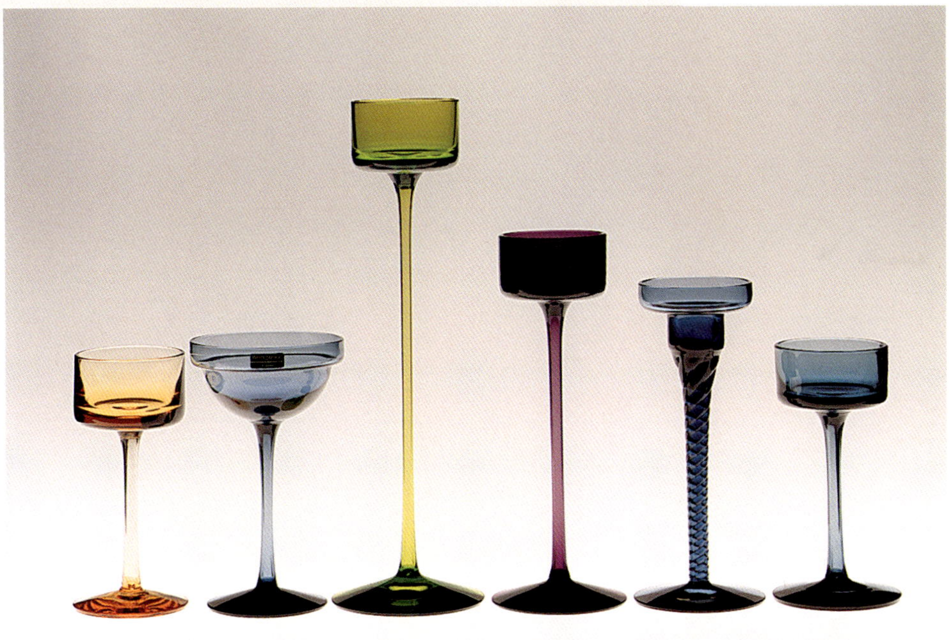

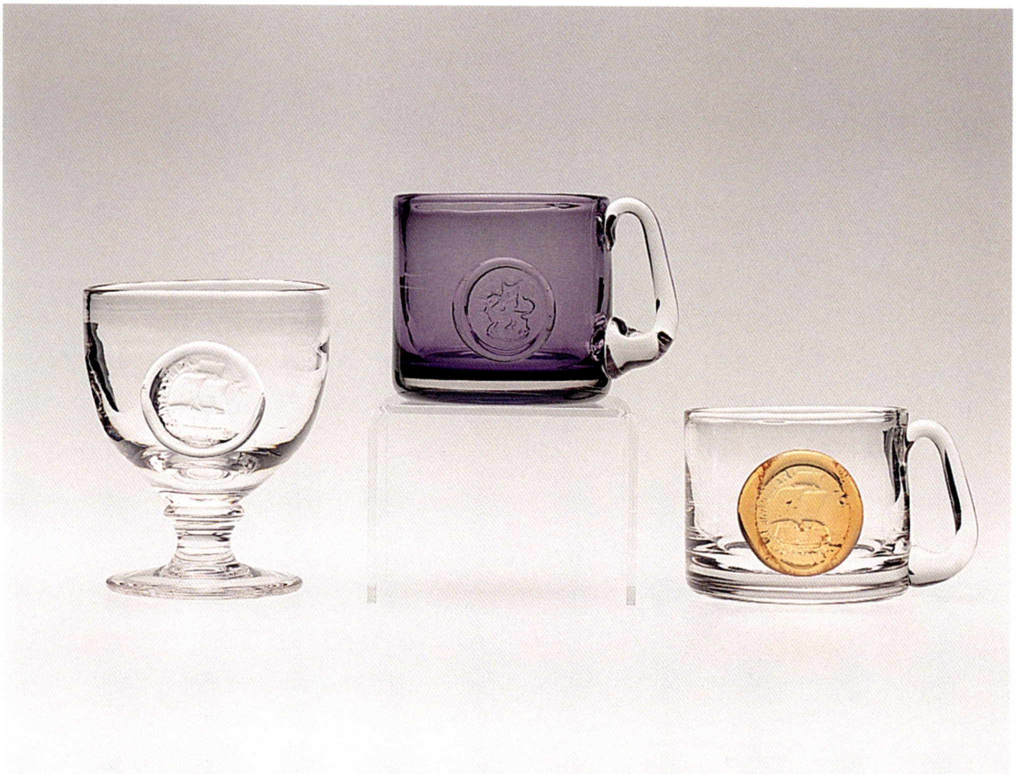

Fig. 42: (left) Top row: Amethyst goblet with the Welsh dragon pressed as a seal. It was produced for the Investiture of HRH Prince Charles as Prince of Wales (1969) Bottom row: Clear goblet with clear seal and clear tankard with topaz seal of the 'Mayflower' (1970).

Fig. 43: (left) Royal cameo goblets—smoky blue and topaz for the Silver Wedding Anniversary of Queen Elizabeth II and HRH Prince Philip the Duke of Edinburgh (1972); amethyst for the Silver Jubilee of Accession of the Queen to the throne (1977).

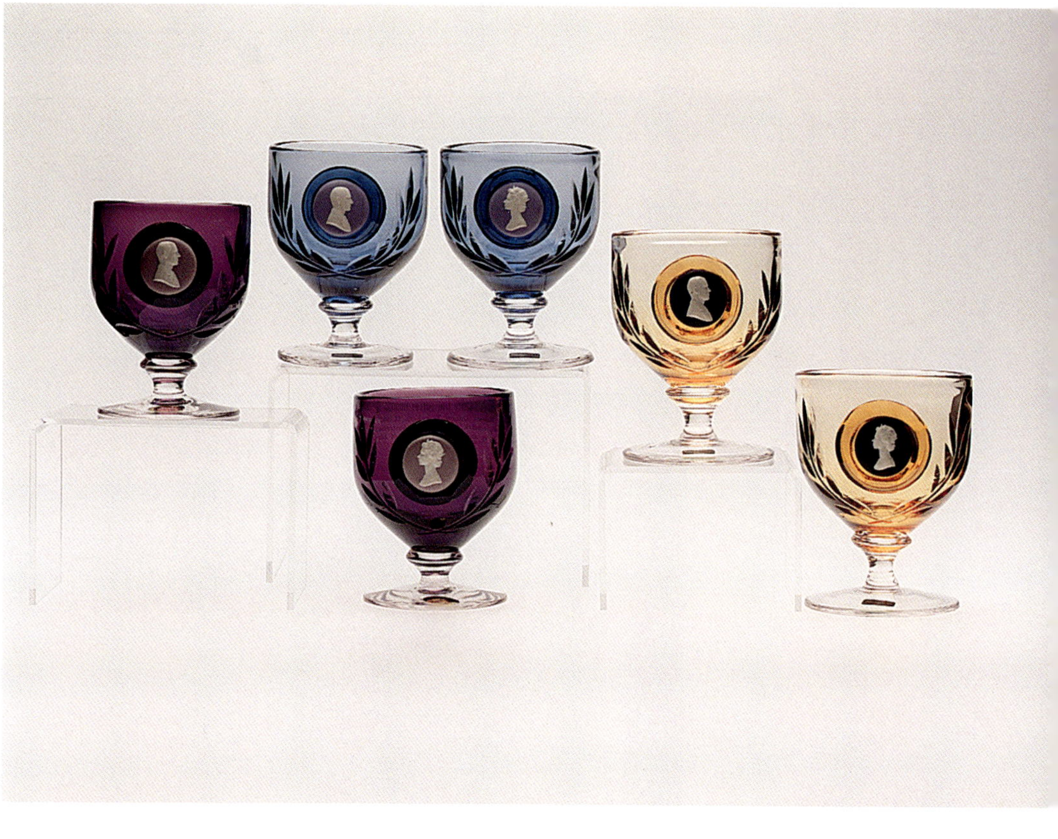

the total product is exported there, and, until now the remainder has largely been sold in Ireland. But with the recent improvements we can now enter the United Kingdom market—making a debut at the 1977 International Spring Fair at the National Exhibition Centre in Birmingham.

'Expansion in the United Kingdom will proceed from this February debut—with Wedgwood Glass sales representatives carrying the merchandise throughout England, Scotland and Wales, and supported by a new warehouse operation at our Wedgwood factory at King's Lynn, to supply the market with the best possible delivery service'. (*Counterpoint*, Spring 1977, p. 2).

Galway Crystal was previewed at a press reception held at the Gered shop in October, 1976. Retailers were informed through the *Wedgwood Review*, December, 1976 that Georgian or early Victorian shapes were available in long stemmed glasses for every occasion with matching decanters and carafes. Two shapes unique to Galway Crystal were 'Old Galway', a simple arched cut and 'Killarney' which used the same slender shape but in three cuts—simple vertical fluting between a fine diagonally-cut band above and a deeply faceted band below. 'O'Donnell' contrasted simple arching with deeply-cut diamond facets, 'Ashford' used cross-cutting interspersed with sunbursts, and 'Clifden' was a simple trellis pattern *(Fig. 75)*.

When Galway Crystal was available in the United Kingdom, sales literature was produced. It, too, made its debut at the 1977 International Spring Fair in Birmingham and included a two-colour broadsheet for the giftware, a two-colour catalogue for the stemware, *The Story of Galway Crystal* folder, and a *Wedgwood Glass* colour folder.

The same year, with existing patterns consolidated on the market, Galway introduced new items and new designs. Three covered chalices were elaborately cut to reproduce antique Irish designs. Two were twelve inches (30.75 cm) and one fourteen inches (35.75 cm) high. The *Wedgwood Review* of January 1979 reported that the winner of the Flying Childers Stakes at the St Ledger Day meeting at Doncaster in 1979 was presented with one of the twelve-inch (30.75 cm) chalices. 'Avoca' was much simpler in design. It was an eight-inch (20.5 cm) diameter, three-footed bowl with a fluted edge and its sides and base cut (*Counterpoint*, Spring, 1978).

From 1977 to 1979, Brian Berrington, based at Barlaston, was managing director of both Wedgwood Glass and Galway Crystal. A four man sales team was set up to cover the whole of the mainland United Kingdom: Peter Howell (Midlands and South West England), James Paul (Northern England and Scotland), Richard Midwinter (Central and Greater London), and Kevin Woolley (East Anglia, Lincolnshire, and South East England). Across the Irish Sea, John Crawford was responsible for Northern Ireland, while to the south, Kevin Barry was marketing manager and responsible for the Republic of Ireland.

During the late 1970s Galway Crystal produced four patterns. 'Claddagh', 'Clifden', and 'O'Donnell' were Shape 01; 'Burren', 'O'Brien' and 'O'Malley', Shape 10; 'Aran', 'Ashford', 'Castlerosse', and 'Galway Oyster', Shape 12; and 'Killarney', 'Old Galway', and 'Royal Irish', Shape 25. Each pattern was produced in different tableware items. Only Shape 01, with the exception of the 'O'Brien' suite, included all sixteen items. These were stemware—liqueur, port/sherry, white and red wine, goblet, saucer and tall champagne, tall hock and brandy balloon—a whiskey glass, two tumblers, a highball glass, a nut-bowl and a 32 ounce (1.2 litre) carafe. To complement the drinkware were a decanter and a water pitcher/jug in each pattern. The shape and long cut of the stems of Galway's wine glasses, e.g. 'Killarney', 'Old Galway', and 'Royal Irish' were unique. There were also a shot glass, 'Barna', 'Erin' liqueur glasses, and a coaster 'Leitrim'.

A 1977 catalogue for the North American market included explanations of the names chosen for the drinkware suites. The design depicted on 'Aran', and which was inspired by the rugged beauty of the isles, was of small tufts of grass which islanders raise in patches of sand and seaweed. 'Ashford' reflected the dignity and grace of the ancient Augustinian Royal Abbey, founded in the twelfth century by Turlough More O'Connor, King of Connaught. It is in the abbey that Rory O'Connor, the last High King of Ireland, is buried.

'Burren' is boldly cut and named for the treeless, rockbound district of County Clare. The unusual flora and fauna are of great interest to botanists and zoologists. The historian and archeologist are drawn to the area, too, because of the ancient stone remains. The 'Castlerosse' suite was intended to capture the stature of the remains of Ross Castle, County Killarney, and the natural beauty of the landscape.

The sails of the fishing boats on the sea out from the village of Claddagh are depicted by the vertical incisions on the pattern named for the village. The lower border is diamond cut to provide the sparkle of the sea, while the base is a sunburst. The scenic Atlantic coastal town of Clifden is a place of natural beauty and history, including twentieth century history. It remains a place of pilgrimage but it was here that Sir John Alcock and Sir Arthur Whitten Brown touched down after making the first transatlantic flight on 14th—15th June, 1919. The Clifden sea road has been called the brandy and soda road, so clear is the air. 'Clifden', then is an appropriate suite, the use of which can raise pleasant thoughts of such a place.

One of Galway's most famous products is its oyster, enjoyed locally and abroad. Although stout is the traditional drink with oysters, red or white wine would be equally enjoyable, especially from the elegantly simple suite, 'Galway Oyster'. The source of inspiration for the subtly strong 'O'Brien' suite was the ancient kings of Ireland from the O'Brien clan, the most famous of whom was Brian Boru who defeated the Vikings at the Battle of Clontarf in 1014.

Named for the O'Donnell clan who rebuilt their castle in 1610 at Donegal, the 'O'Donnell' suite is intricately cut in a diamond pattern to represent the shape of the town. Donegal was built around a spacious diamond adjacent to the castle. 'O'Malley' was cut to 'capture the brilliance and vitality of the legendary Irish heroine' Grace O'Malley. The custom of leaving the gates open at mealtime and having an extra place set at Howth Castle is traditionally linked to Grace O'Malley. She was a warrior, sailor and chieftain noted for bravery and courage in the sixteenth century. The legend is that on her seeking food at the castle, the gates were locked as the lord was at his meal. In retaliation O'Malley carried off his infant son. He was returned only when the family swore never again to lock the gates at mealtime. This custom of leaving the gate open, and that of having an extra place set for a visiting stranger, continues.

'Old Galway' sought to preserve the glories of the past for the city after which was named. Described in the sixteenth century as a compact town of handsome buildings, it was surrounded by fourteen bulwarks leading by gates to the fourteen principal streets, some of which can still be seen. The delicacy of line and form of the 'Royal Irish' suite seek to rekindle the spirit of the ancient heroic age enshrined in the Irish language and literature. The heroic era was the pre-Christian Ireland of folklore when the land was divided into almost two hundred kingdoms each ruled by a king and federated with its neighbours. The supreme ruler being the High King of Ireland residing at Tara in the County of Meath, the Royal Province.

Additional to tableware were different shaped decanters—'Sealord' was a ship's decanter, 'Dublin' an oblong spirit decanter, 'Ronayne' a spirit decanter, and a conical yachtsman's decanter.

There was also a Georgian Bottle. Claret jugs were produced in 'Galway Bay', 'Brandon' and 'Galway Sunset', and an ice bucket was produced in 'Ballina'.

There were further items for use at the dinner table. The pattern for a four-piece condiments set—salt, pepper, open mustard, and covered mustard—was 'Rosslare', while that for oil/vinegar was 'Ballinrobe'. There was also an open salt, 'Adare'. A sugar bowl and creamer set was 'Dingle' while a covered sugar bowl and footed creamer set was 'Kilronan'. 'Cara' and 'O'Malley' could be used either as a ginger jar or a honey pot. Marmalade pots were in 'Clifden', 'Kells' and 'Shannon'. A squat honey jar was in 'Blarney', a tankard in 'Dunloe', a butter dish in 'Achill', a sixteen ounce (57 cl) mug 'Sheebeen', and half-pint (28 cl) jug in 'Blarney'.

There were two compotes, 'Clifden' and 'Donegal'. A six-inch (15.5 cm) fruit/salad bowl was produced in 'Ballymagibbon' while an eight-inch (20.5 cm) bowl was in 'Blarney', and the largest bowl was 'Clifden', nine inches (23 cm). A footed-bowl was 'Avoca'. Sweets lovers could add a bonbonnier 'Old Cork', a candy box 'Bunratty' or a bob-bon dish 'Bantry'.

There was a wide range of vases of different shapes and patterns. These were 'Athlone', 'Ardagh', 'Bantry', 'Clare', 'Clonmel', 'Fermoy', 'Furbo', 'Gaelic', 'Kanturn' (or 'Kanturk'), 'Kilkenny', 'Kinrara', (or 'Kinvara'), 'Lahinch', 'Larne', 'Lynch', 'Mallow', 'Mayo', 'Moy', 'Old Cork', 'Ronayne', 'Shannon', 'Salthill', 'Sheelin', 'Sligo', 'Spiddal', 'Tralee', 'Westport', and 'Wicklow'. Sizes ranged from three-inch (7.75 cm) violet vases to heavy-based and/or footed eleven-inch (28 cm) vases. The exception to these relatively small vases was 'Antrim', a large presentation vase. (Separate catalogues spelled the names of 'Kinrara'/'Kinvara' and 'Kanturn'/'Kanturk' differently and there seems to be no data available to clarify which was the correct name given to each pattern).

There were fewer candlesticks. The patterns were 'Blarney', 'Connemara', 'Navan', 'Shannon' and 'Tuam'. Dinner bell patterns were 'Burren', 'Killary', 'Roscam', and 'Shandon', while tea bells were 'Burren' and 'Roscam'. Fruit baskets were in 'Dublin' and 'Galway Sunset'. 'Kilcogan' was the pattern for a large and small flower basket. Fourteen-inch (35.5 cm) lamp bases were 'Belfast' and 'Donegal'. Eighteen-inch (46 cm) lamp bases were 'Antrim' and 'Ballycastle'.

Crystal jewellery came in eight shapes. These were an oblong star 'Cliona', an oblong cross 'Fiona', a prism 'Grainne', a harp 'Mairin', a heart 'Orla', a pyramid 'Roisin', a prism 'Sinead' and a cone 'Siobhan'. A ring holder was 'Kerry'.

There were also accessories for the smoker—patterns with their relevant diameters for the ashtrays were 'Ballyroan', 4 inches (10.25 cm), 'Corrib', 'Delga', 'Donegal', 'O'Connell', and 'Shannon', five inches (12.5 cm), 'Mallone', five-and-a-half inches (14 cm) and 'Corrib', seven inches (18 cm). Cigarette urns were 'Claddagh' and 'Cleggan', while a cigarette box with a lid that could double as an ashtray was 'Ronayne'.

The last shape introduced at Galway was 'Kells' in 1980. The suite consisted of drinking glasses, a decanter and pitcher. There were three patterns. 'Iona' featured a star-burst and had a cut stem base. 'Durrow' was a simpler diamond cut version. 'Columba' was cut with a classical arch. The drinkware, described in *Counterpoint*, 1980, on p.11 retained the traditional settings of liqueur, sherry/port, wine, and water goblets as well as tall and saucer champagne glasses. In the bar ware there were highball, brandy and two sizes for old-fashioned glasses.

Galway Crystal had been introduced with great fanfare. It had been promoted in the Republic of Ireland, in the United Kingdom, and in the United States, but ultimately this experimentation with the production of crystal tableware was regarded by Wedgwood as a failure, even though the product was relatively popular in the United States. In 1980, the assets and business were sold, payments being made in installments over a period of three years. During this time Josiah Wedgwood & Sons Inc continued to market Galway Crystal in the United States and Galway Crystal continued under new ownership.

12

WEDGWOOD AND DARTINGTON— ENGLISH COUNTY CRYSTAL

Glass production, commenced in 1967, was only one of Dartington's educational, industrial and commercial enterprises begun in the 1925 by Leonard and Dorothy Elmhirst, following their purchase of the derelict Dartington Hall. Dorothy was an exceptionally wealthy member of the American Whitney family. She used her wealth to establish a charitable trust to provide employment in rural areas, to create viable communities in these areas, and eventually halt the movement of young people to the cities. In these communities, sometimes regarded as Utopian, but nevertheless successful in many aspects, people had the opportunity to strive for personal development as well as to earn a living. Funding was not intended for hare-brained schemes. Such would be a drain on the Trust and detrimental to the development of practical projects which could become self-supporting in a relatively short time.

In North Devon there was no history of glass making, although Bristol from the seventeenth century, and Bridgwater and Nailsea from the eighteenth and nineteenth centuries were centres for glass production. Evidence exists of some glass making near Exeter in South Devon, but it was at none of these sites that the proposed new glass factory would be established.

When the idea for glassworks was proposed, it was within the context of the Dartington Hall Trust's providing capital resources to fund industries to revitalise depressed rural areas in Devon. The road to realisation of this idea was long and convoluted. At a meeting in August 1962 between Euan Cooper-Willis of Portmeirion Potteries and adviser on several matters to the Dartington Hall Trust, and Peter Sutcliffe, a director of the Trust, the suggestion for glass manufacture was mooted. The idea was to base the glassworks on those of rural Swedish factories. The resultant products could be sold through the Portmeirion sales network.

In hindsight the procedures Peter Sutcliffe followed to bring about a Swedish style glassworks appear somewhat unusual. He had not done market research. He did not consult successful British glass manufacturers such as Chance Brothers, Pilkingtons, or Whitefriars, or companies in the Stourbridge area, although at some stage he made an attempt to find out about the new Caithness Glass Limited. There is little doubt people at these companies would have known about Swedish style glass and crystal and could have provided him with some assistance.

What Sutcliffe acquired was a folio of rejection letters from Scandinavian companies. These included Reijmyre, Kosta, Orrefors, and Riihimaen Lasi Oy. Why would a successful Scandinavian company want to go into some sort of partnership with an English organisation that had no idea of what the venture really entailed? Why would a successful manager from an established company give up a secure position to set up a company in competition and with no guarantee of success? How could a glass factory in Devon succeed? At Dartington there was no feasibility study, no plan of action, no factory, no skilled glassmakers, no raw materials nearby, but there was money.

That was the lure in January 1964 when advertisements were placed in Swedish, Finnish and West German newspapers informing all that 'an exciting opportunity exists for a really enterprising Glassworks Manager to assist in the development of a new venture in pleasant rural surroundings in South West England. Large organisation plans to set up one of the first factories in England to manufacture high quality hand blown stemware and other domestic glassware. There is a good market in Britain and the Commonwealth for good, modern glass which at present is imported, and as there will be ample financial backing, the right man could build up a very important concern'. Almost all responsibility for the success of the venture devolved on this man. 'He must be highly qualified and experienced, as well he will be expected to play a leading part in the technical planning and design of the works, furnaces, etc ... in the first instance find and engage a nucleus of skilled craftsmen from Europe to train local labour'. It was to be a two year contract, and almost as an afterthought the advertisement mentioned that 'a knowledge of English is desirable but not essential'.

Concern about the effect an English company making Swedish style glass prompted the managing director of Bjorkshult Glassworks to try to find out how the new enterprise would operate. To this end he had works manager, Eskil Vilhelmsson, who had not even seen the advertisement, apply for the position. What happened next was almost something out of a slapstick movie. Peter Sutcliffe, Frank Thrower and George Warburg went to Stockholm to interview Vilhelmsson. Unfortunately neither side knew for whom they or he was looking at the hotel at which the meeting had been arranged for June 9th, 1964. This major breakdown in communication led to both sides leaving with the feeling of being stood up and the English group's going home!

All was not lost as Sutcliffe contacted Vilhelmsson. A second meeting was organised for June 20th. This time only Thrower went. Communication was through an interpreter, even though Thrower spoke some Swedish, and the result was positive. In September, Vilhelmsson travelled to Devon where he was formally offered the job on October 20th, 1964.

Dartington had a managing director, from July 1965, and a designer. A capital and a business plan were developed. It was still short of a factory and labourforce. The comedy was not over. The original factory site at Winkleigh had several flaws. It was outside the Bideford Developmental area. That limited the grants it could attract. The Ministry of Aviation objected to the height of proposed chimneys. They would interfere with radar reception at the station it planned to build. There were also local authority funding problems. To avoid all of these it was easier to move the factory to Torrington, a flatter site than Winkleigh, but an easier problem to solve by redesigning certain elements of the factory. On March 5th, 1966 the public was informed.

Vilhelmsson began recruiting twenty skilled Scandinavian blowers. Eight local apprentices were to be taken on each year to undertake a four-year training programme. The aim was to have six teams composed of skilled blowers and apprentices.

Almost simultaneously a final 'glitch' occurred which was with government funding. Grants could not be made to Trusts. They could only be made to a company and that had not legally been formed. Solicitors drew up the appropriate papers. On May 2nd, they confirmed the name Dartington Glass Limited was available, and on 14th June, 1966, it was formally incorporated.

From May 1967 all was in readiness—company formed, factory built (by another Dartington company, Staverton Contractors), workforce recruited and raw materials on hand. On 12th June, 1967, the factory was officially opened, in the same month as King's Lynn Glass began on the other side of the country.

Of all its business ventures, glass production has been the most successful for Dartington. Glass manufacture fulfilled a major role of the Trust—the production of quality hand-made items which can be a showcase for the best of British crafts. Furthermore, some of the profits from the venture were re-invested into the business which generated them while the balance was redirected to other projects of the Trust.

In November 1982, the Directors of Josiah Wedgwood & Sons Limited and the Trustees of Dartington Hall Trust reached an agreement to merge their respective interests in glass tableware and giftware. It was mutually beneficial. It gave Wedgwood the manufacturing, design and marketing abilities of Dartington to create an attractive range of products. It gave Dartington Crystal access to Wedgwood's United Kingdom and international distributions organisations to sell its products. The new holding company acquired the business operations of Dartington at Torrington, Devon and of Wedgwood at King's Lynn, Norfolk. Where up to this point, Wedgwood had used the name 'Wedgwood Glass', from the merger 'Wedgwood Crystal' became the title. Shares in the new holding company were held equally by Wedgwood and Dartington. Eric Dancer became the Chairman of the holding company, 'English County Crystal Limited', Frank Thrower was Chief Designer and Marketing Director, and Gordon Kessler the Sales Manager. At the respective sites, Jan Mollmark became Managing Director of Dartington Glass Limited and Ray Duly Production Director of Wedgwood Crystal Limited. The combined workforce was just over three hundred.

The products from the two factories were complementary. It was reported in *Counterpoint,* Spring 1983, that 'their combined strengths—embracing advertising techniques, design and marketing—are anticipated to lead to stronger growth and to provide wider opportunities to managers, staff and operatives'. Distribution to existing markets—the home market, the United States, Australia, South Africa, Canada, and smaller markets continued. The varieties of products continued to expand, mainly through the designs of Frank Thrower. Both glassworks maintained their spin-off—tourism and the sale of products, often 'seconds' at the factory shops.

Tableware

In the early 1980s, the production at King's Lynn took a different direction. Ronald Stennett-Willson had retired. He had been the main designer of decorative wares, commemorative wares and a wide range of tableware. After his retirement, most commemorative items ceased to be produced and the focus continued on functional glassware—drinkware, decanters, jugs, vases, bowls, ice buckets, lanterns and candleholders and candlesticks. The colour range was gradually reduced to two, and many styles and patterns were much simpler.

Frank Thrower was the main designer during this period. *Counterpoint*, 1985, on p.10 referred to his 'talent for designing handmade lead crystal glass with a unique yet distinctive English air'. His designs used clear, uncluttered lines. Items were produced in one or both of the colour/shape choices—clear, clear optic, midnight, an 'elegant caviar grey tone' (ibid), sometimes referred to as 'smoky', and midnight optic. Optic items have vertical rippled surfaces. Some of Ronald Stennett-Willson's readily identifiable animal paperweights were produced in midnight, bore the new etched base-stamp and were marked with a clear label, while others bore a 'Wedgwood' only etched base-stamp. Another range of items was produced in hand-cut crystal. Among the exhibits at Wedgwood's 1985 Trade Exhibition were several of Frank Thrower's glasses.

The stemware patterns were 'Olivia', 'Portia', 'Theo', 'Philippe', 'Nicole', and 'Napoleon'. The first four suites included sherry, claret, goblet and tall champagne glasses produced in clear and midnight. In 'Philippe', there were also port and liqueur glasses. The 'Nicole' suite came in clear optic. 'Napoleon', appropriately named, was a clear brandy balloon. To complement the stemware, 'Philippe', there was a one litre clear port or sherry decanter in clear and midnight.

Other decanters, 'Gaston' and 'Marcel', were produced in both colours and in plain and optic. Each pattern had an air-filled stopper. 'Horatio' was an admiral's decanter produced in clear and midnight. 'Torquil' and 'Tarquin' were hand-cut, clear decanters. These two patterns had matching clear drink ware, the former pattern being a highball, an old-fashioned and a double old-fashioned tumbler, the latter being only a highball and an old-fashioned tumbler. The only other highball and old-fashioned tumblers were 'Rufus'. In a table setting these tumblers were a close match for 'Philippe'. The midnight hexagonal ice bucket, 'Eugene', did not exactly match the drinkware but it did complement it *(Fig. 77)*.

Jugs and pitchers came in several patterns and for various purposes. 'Alexander' in both colours and forms was referred to as a water jug/pitcher. 'Nautilus' in clear and clear optic was called simply a jug/pitcher, while 'Zelda' in clear optic and midnight optic was a cocktail mixer with a stirrer. Two other jugs came as a set each with a sugar basin. One was the midnight, 'Genevieve', the other in both clear optic and midnight optic was 'Devon'. Two other small, clear jugs were 'Roberta' and 'Clifford'.

Very similar in design to 'Genevieve', almost to the point of being a perfect match, was the Irish Coffee mug, 'Seamus'. For variety, there was also a Gaelic Coffee mug, 'Dougall'. For beer there was clear 'Brendan' and for ale, 'Falstaff' in clear and midnight.

Two comports, in clear and midnight, were 'Helene' and 'Harry'. The former stood on a tall drawn stem. The latter was squat. 'Cybill', a clear, footed bowl came in two sizes. Annular fruit or salad bowls, 'Marcus', came in two sizes—for individual use and for serving. Also annular in design, but with fewer rings, were pudding/sweets dishes, 'Charlotte'. There was a clear cheese bell 'Louise'. 'Brutus' tableware was an octagonal design. It included a serving bowl, fruit bowl and cocktail bowl in midnight. Avocado lovers had their own special dishes, 'Desmond'. In all patterns, bowls or dishes for personal use always came as boxed pairs.

Anita Harris was the inaurgural winner of the Dartington Glass Design Bursary at the Royal Society of Art (London). One of her designs, 'Wave', was produced in dishes in four sizes for fruit or salad. The largest three sizes were serving bowls. The smallest was for individual use. All three patterns were in midnight. The 'Wave' design was also used for four plates—a cheese platter, a large and a small plate and a butter platter. They were in clear as well as midnight.

Table accessories were available. The salt and pepper set in clear and midnight was 'Tessa'. The clear jam, jelly or honey pot, 'Georgia' came in two sizes and with a spoon.

Dick Terlier was employed in the United States to develop a wider spread of awareness of the Wedgwood Crystal brand and to win business previously held by Lennox Crystal. One of the

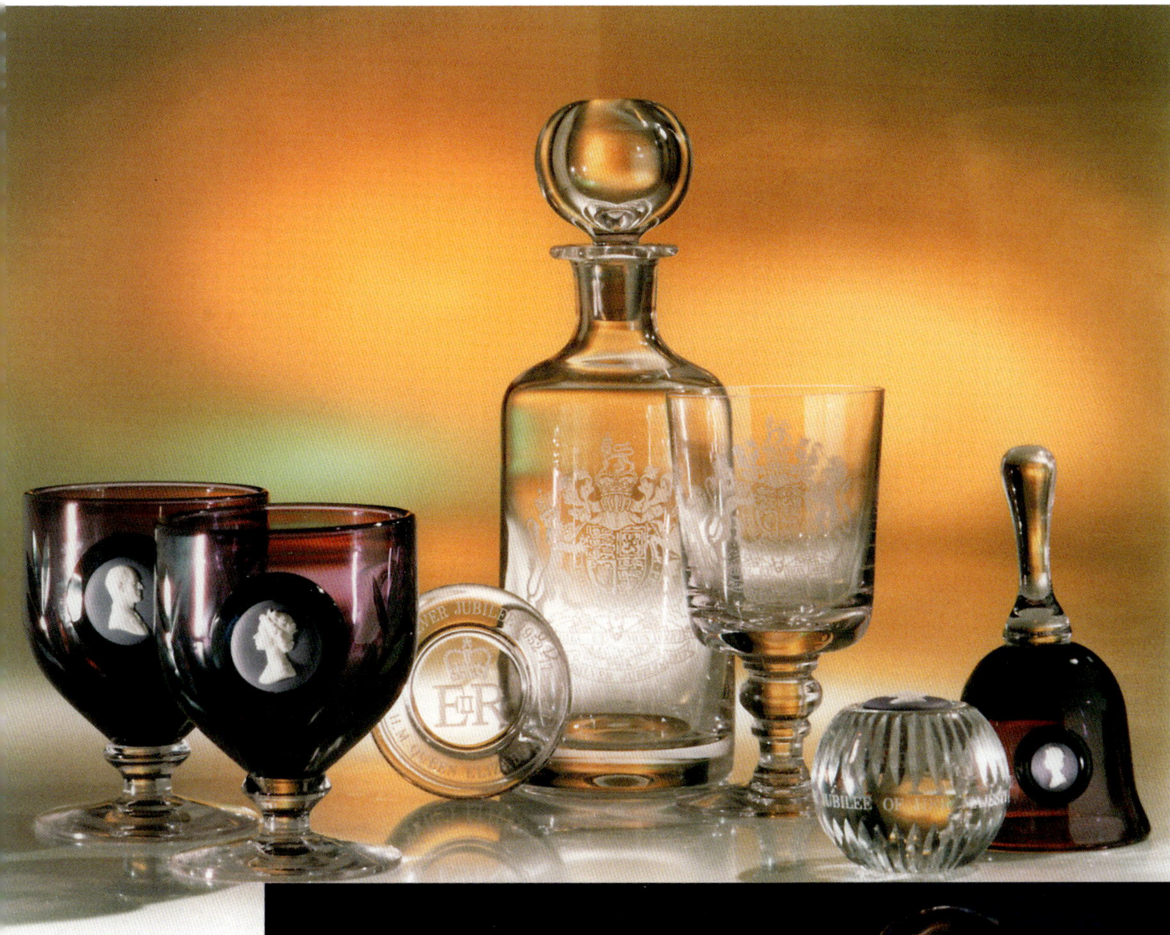

Fig. 44: Silver Jubilee of Queen Elizabeth's accession to the throne — amethyst cameo goblets, etched disc paperweight, etched spirit decanter, clear goblet, cameo crystal orb paperweight, amethyst cameo bell.

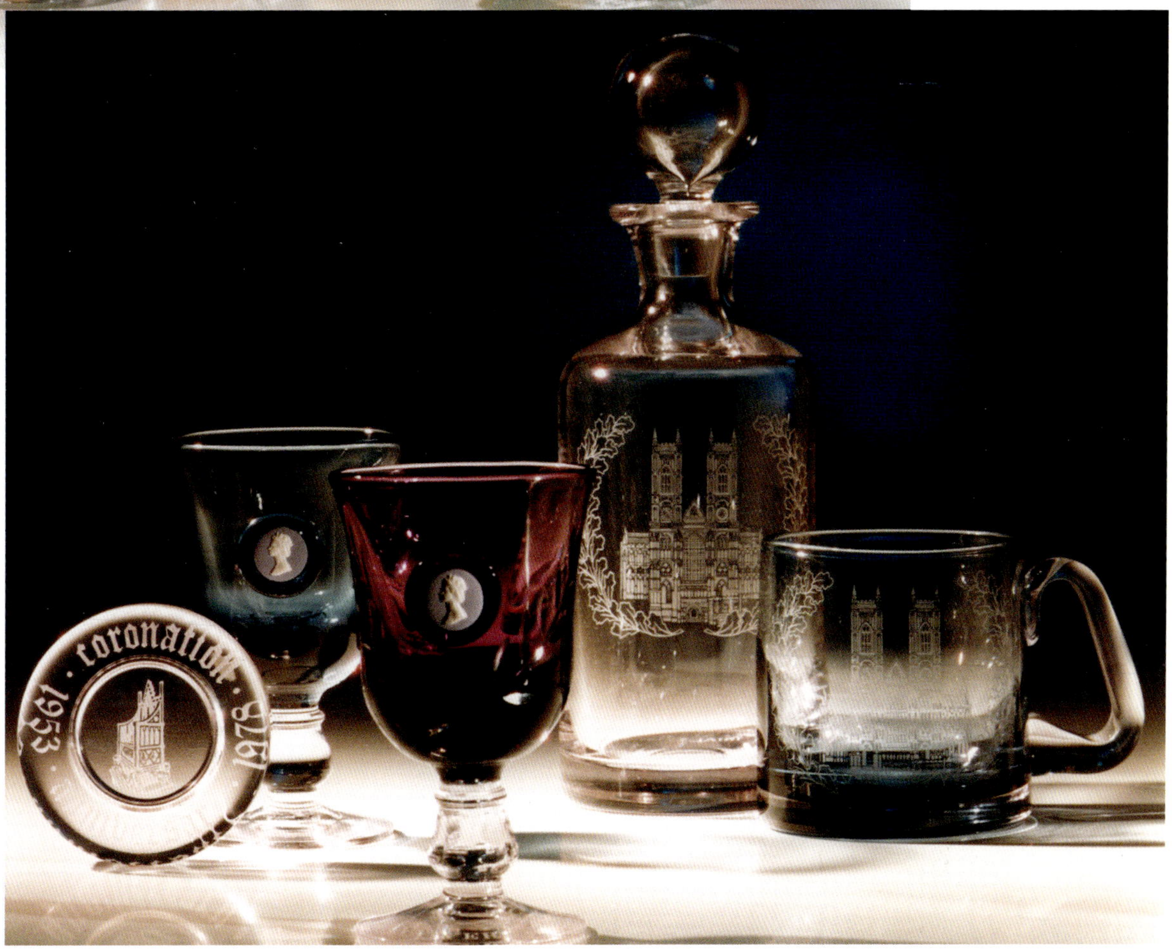

Fig. 45: Silver Jubilee of Queen Elizabeth's coronation — etched disc paperweight, smoky blue cameo goblet, amethyst cameo goblet, etched spirit decanter, smoky blue etched tankard.

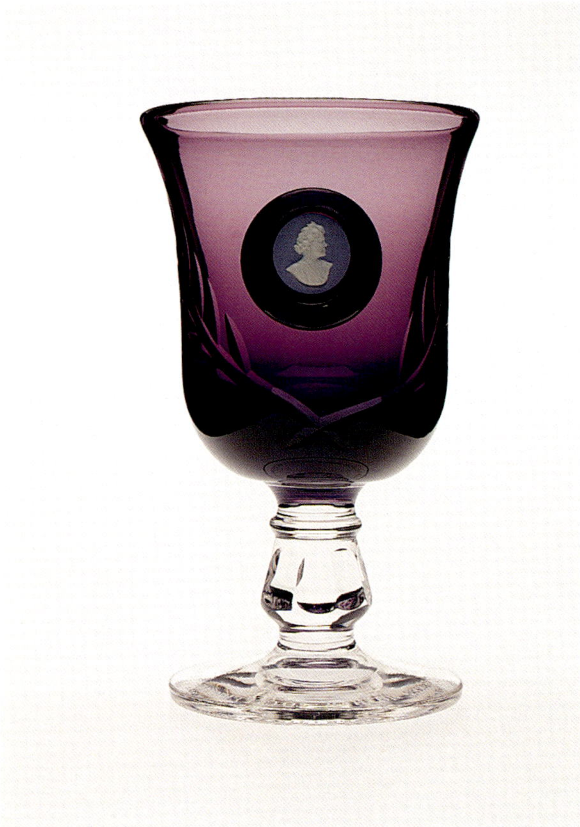

Fig. 46: Amethyst goblet to commemorate the 80th birthday of Queen Elizabeth the Queen Mother (1980).

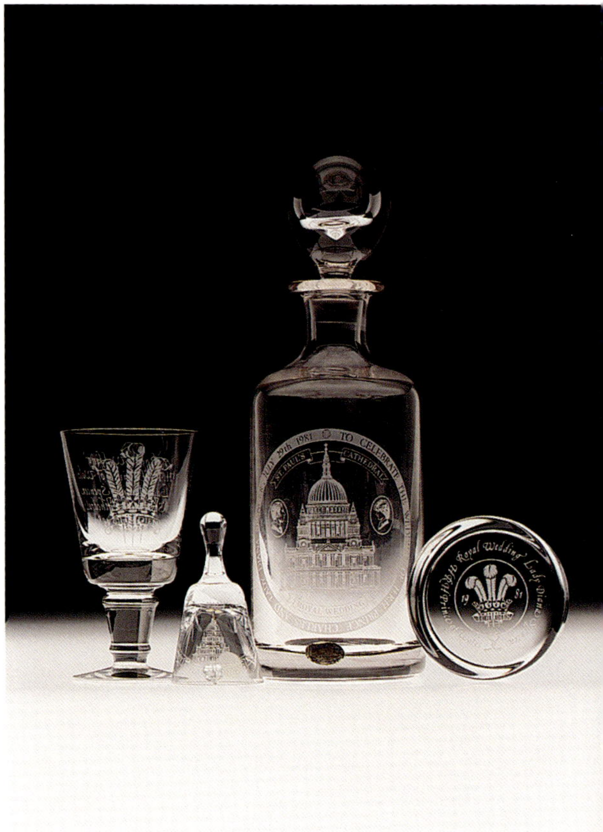

Fig. 47: Royal Wedding of the Prince of Wales and Lady Diana Spencer—etched crystal goblet, crystal tea bell, spirit decanter and disc paperweight (1981).

Fig. 48: Royal Wedding—etched crystal dinner bell, amethyst loving cup, cameo crystal paperweight (1981).

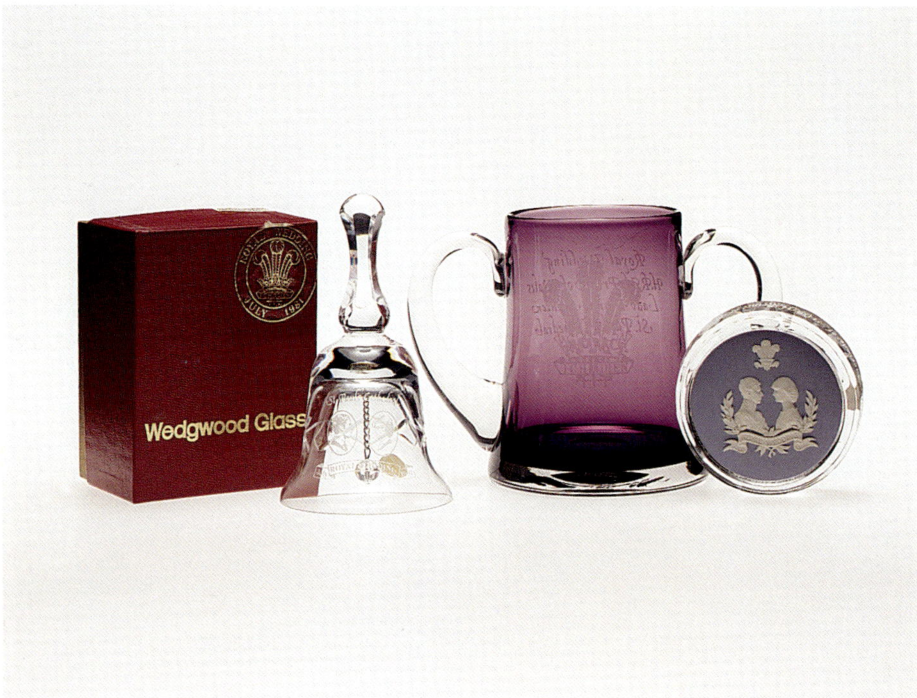

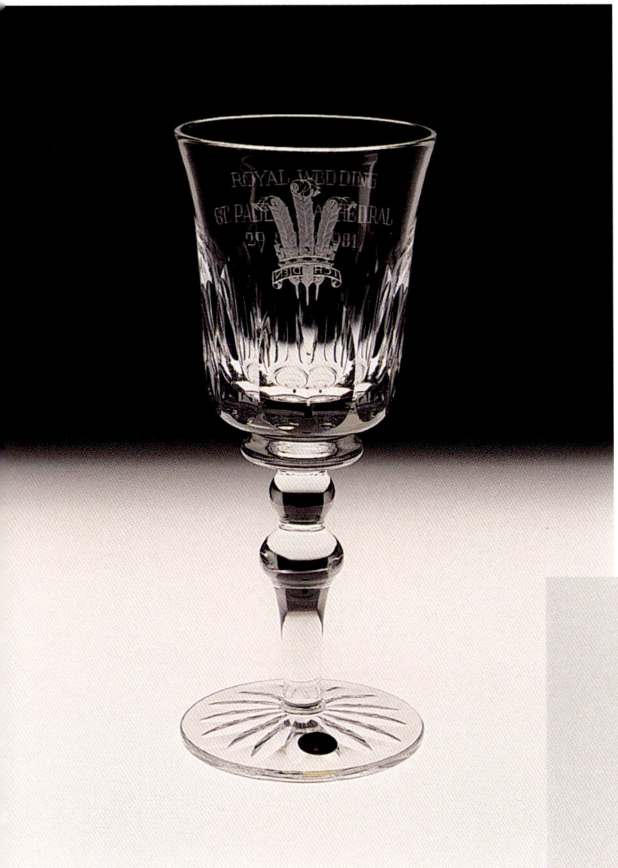

Fig. 49: Royal Wedding — etched, hand-cut crystal chalice (1981).

Fig. 50: Souvenirs of the Olympic Games in Montreal, 1976. Topaz cameo tankard, etched smoky blue tankard, smoky blue cameo bell and goblet.

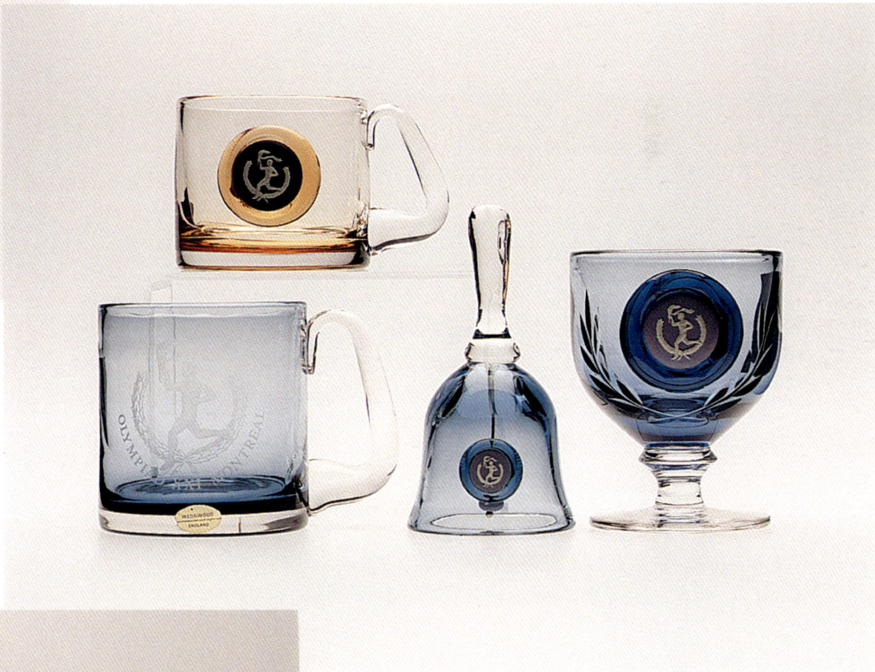

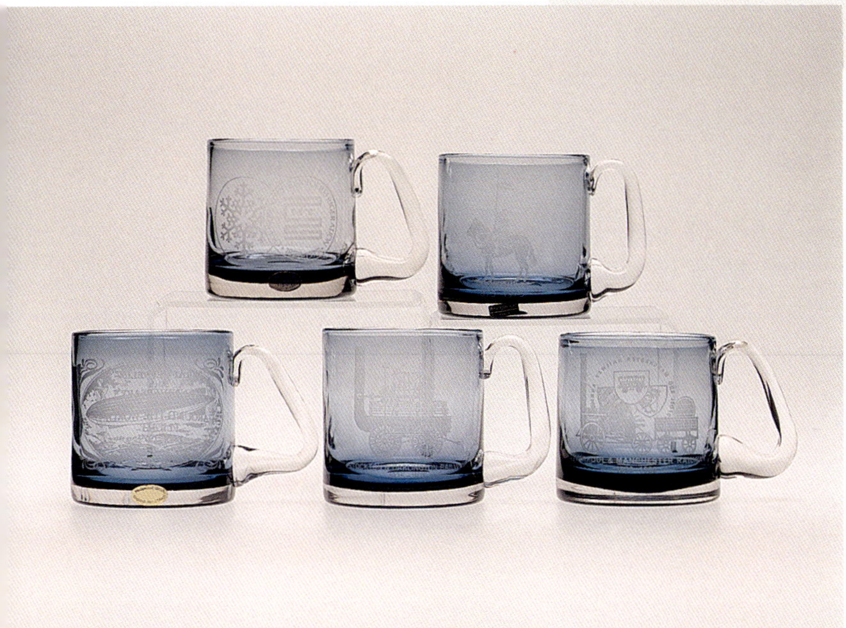

Fig. 51: Commemorative smoky blue tankards — Top row: Hall Thermotank's 100 Years of Refrigeration 1877–1977, Centenary of the Royal Canadian Mounted Police 1873–1973; Bottom row: Graf Zepplin — 50th Anniversary of the Around the World Flight 1929–1979, Stockton & Darlington Railway 1825–1975, Liverpool & Manchester Railway 1830–1980.

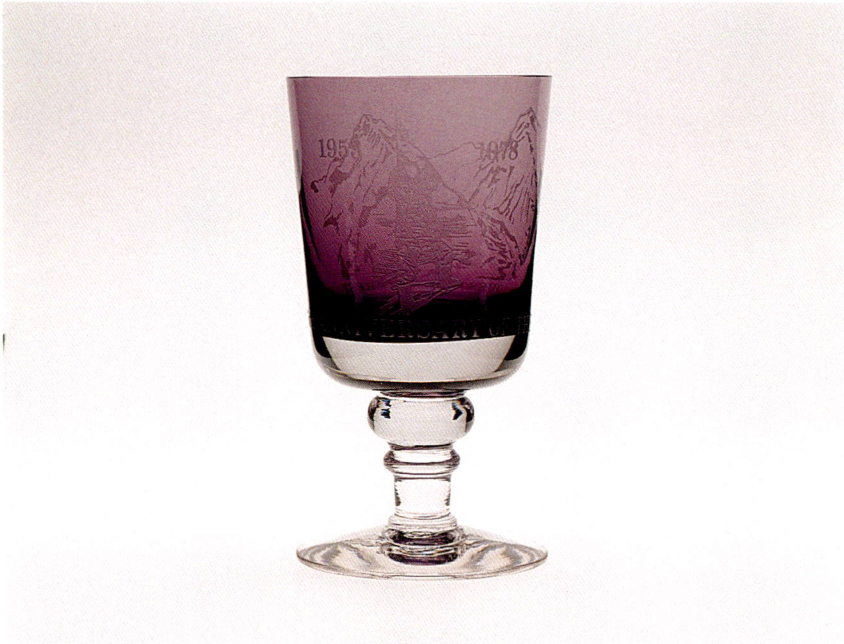

Fig. 52: Amethyst goblet to commemorate the 25th Anniversary of the Conquest of Everest.

Fig. 53: Novocentenary of the Tower of London — etched disc paperweight, smoky blue tankard.

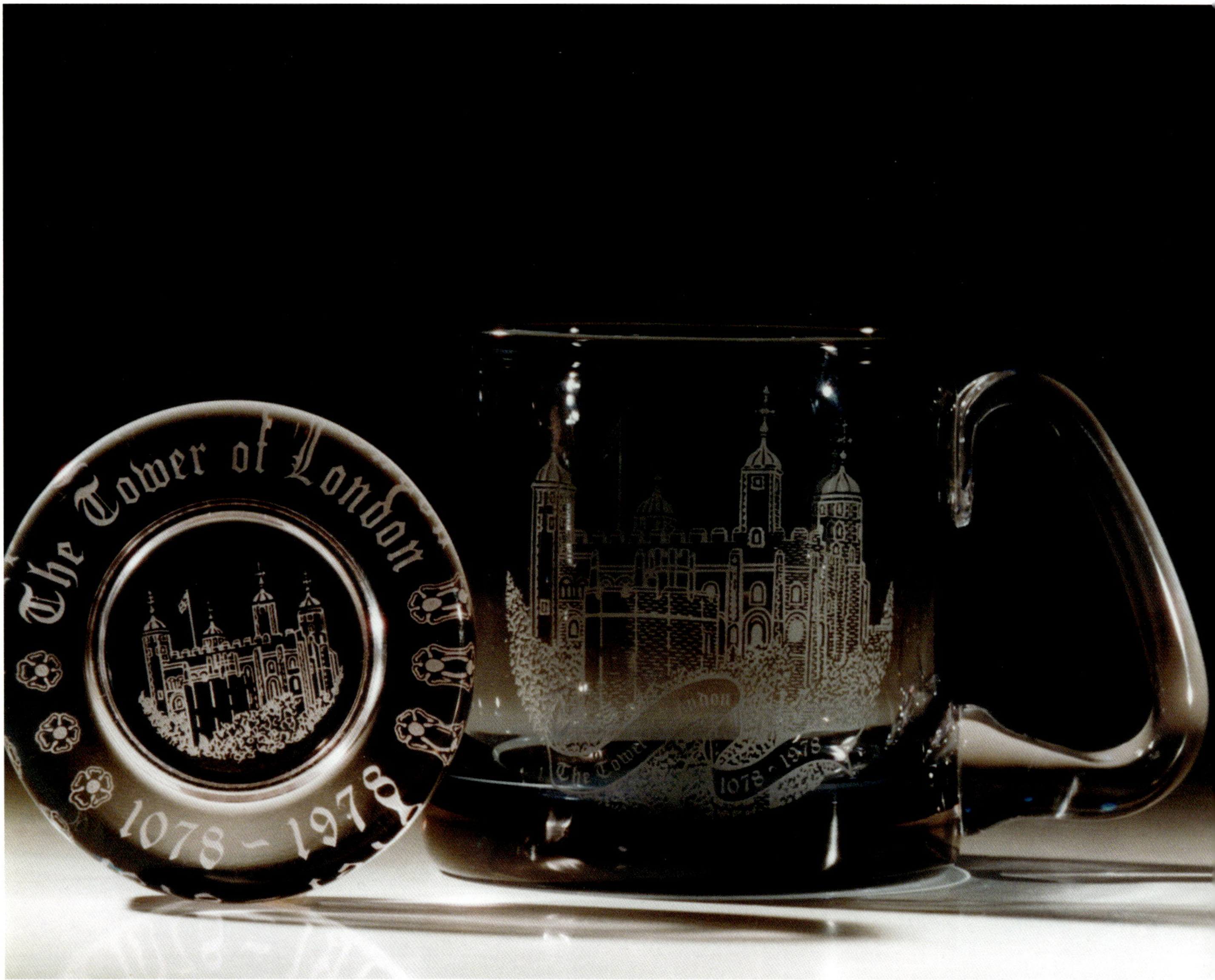

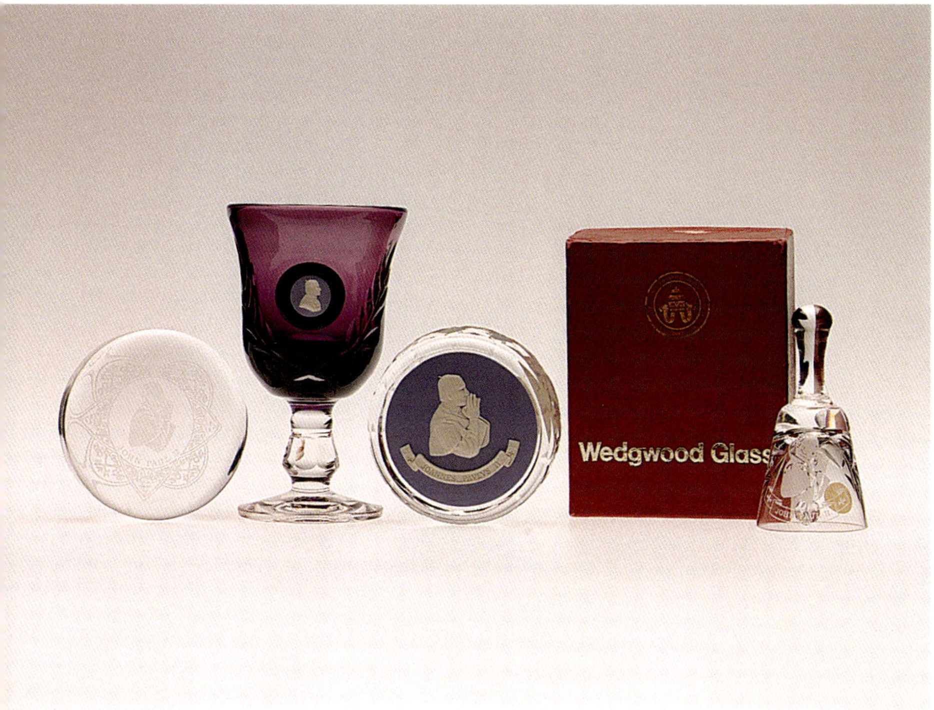

Fig. 54: Commemorative items for the Papal visit to Britain in 1982 — etched disc paperweight, amethyst cameo goblet, cameo crystal paperweight, etched crystal bell.

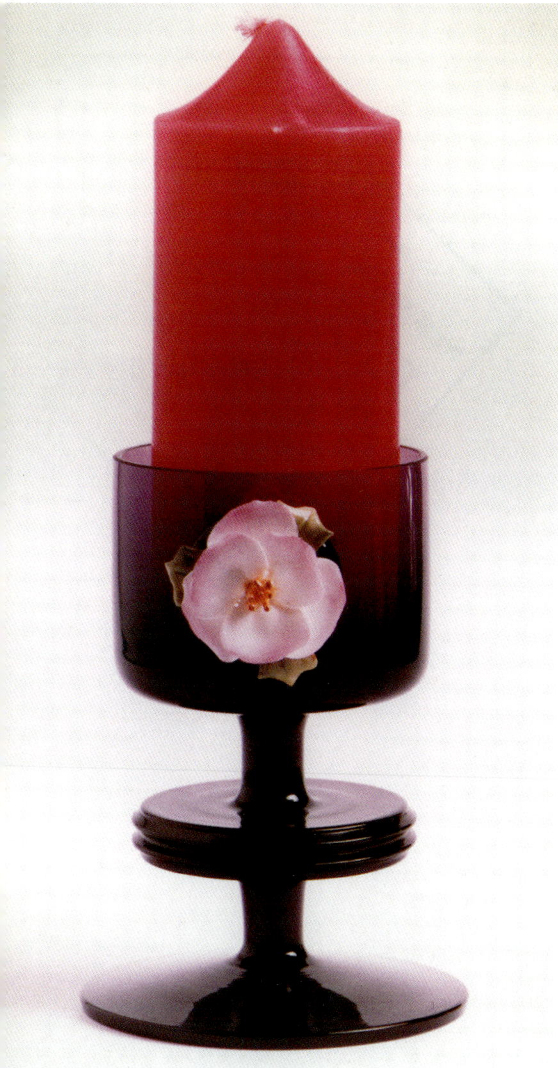

Fig. 55: (left) Coalport bone china flower on a Sheringham *candleholder*

Fig. 56: (below) Tankards commissioned by the British Defence Forces — Smoky blue for the RAOC (Royal Army Ordinance Corps), sapphire blue for the disbandment of the XIIIth (PR) Squadron (Royal Air Force), 1982, smoky blue for the XIIIth (PR) Squadron's return from overseas duty, 1978.

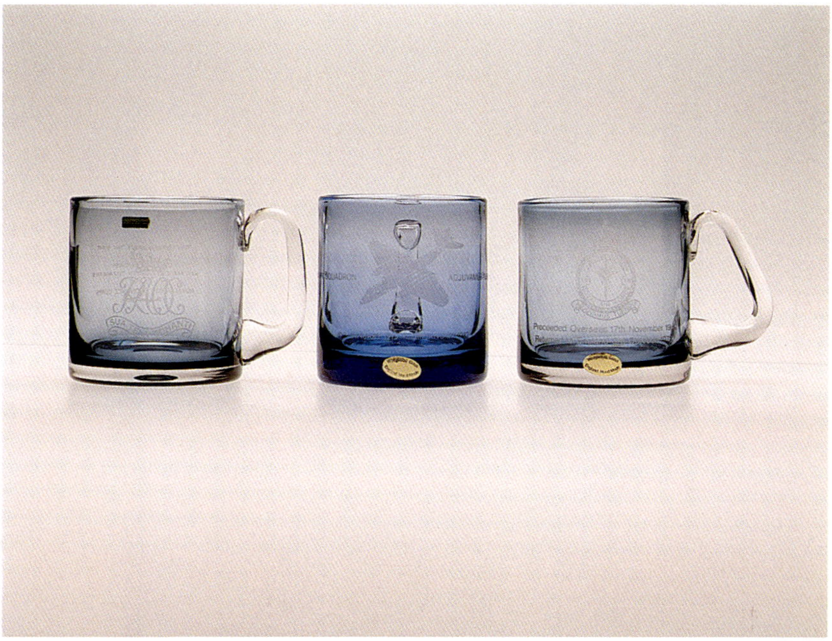

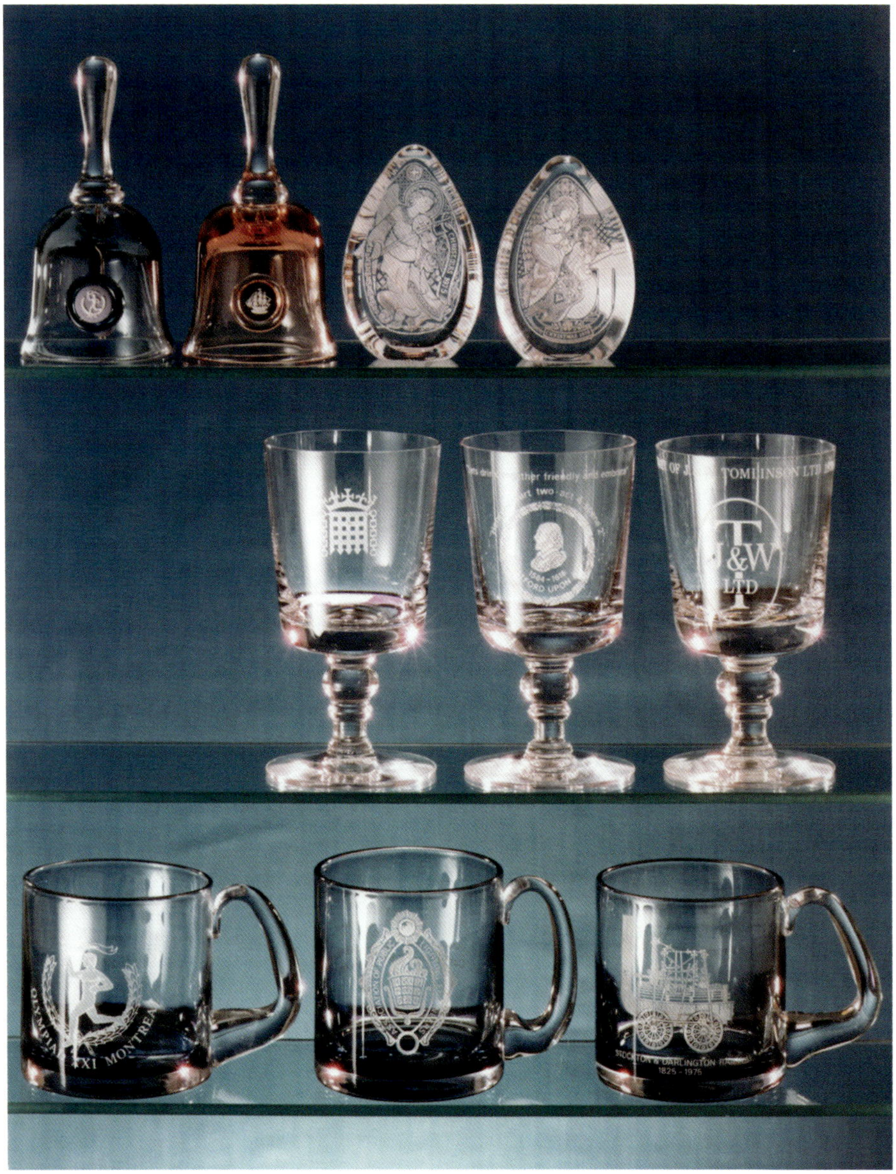

Fig. 57: Souvenirs, commemoratives and commissions — top row: Olympic cameo smoky blue bell, Golden Hind *cameo topaz bell, Christmas paperweights 1975 and 1976; middle row: goblets British Parliament, Shakespeare/ Stratford-upon-Avon, Centenary of J & W Tomlinson Ltd;*
bottom row: smoky blue tankards — Montreal Olympic Games, Association of Public Lighting Engineers, Stockton to Darlington Railway.

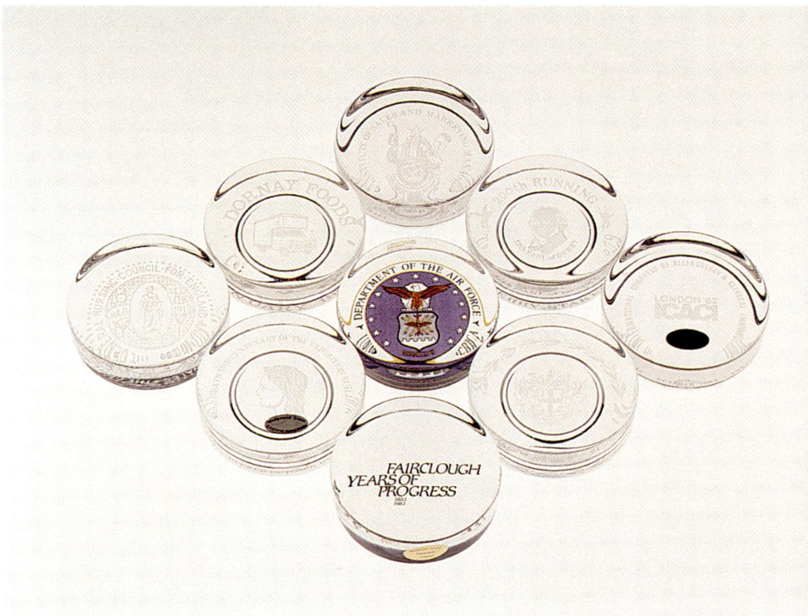

Fig. 58: (left) Clockwise from the top, commissioned disc paperweights: Institute of Sales and Marketing Management, 200th Running of the Derby Stakes, XI International Congress of Allergology and Clinical Immunology October 1982, Coat of Arms of the City of London, Fairclough 100 Years of Progress, To Celebrate the Centenary of the Exhibition Building Opened October 1st 1880 (Melbourne, Australia), The Central Nursing Council for England and Wales, Dornay Foods;
Centre: Seal of the Department of the Air Force of the United States of America.

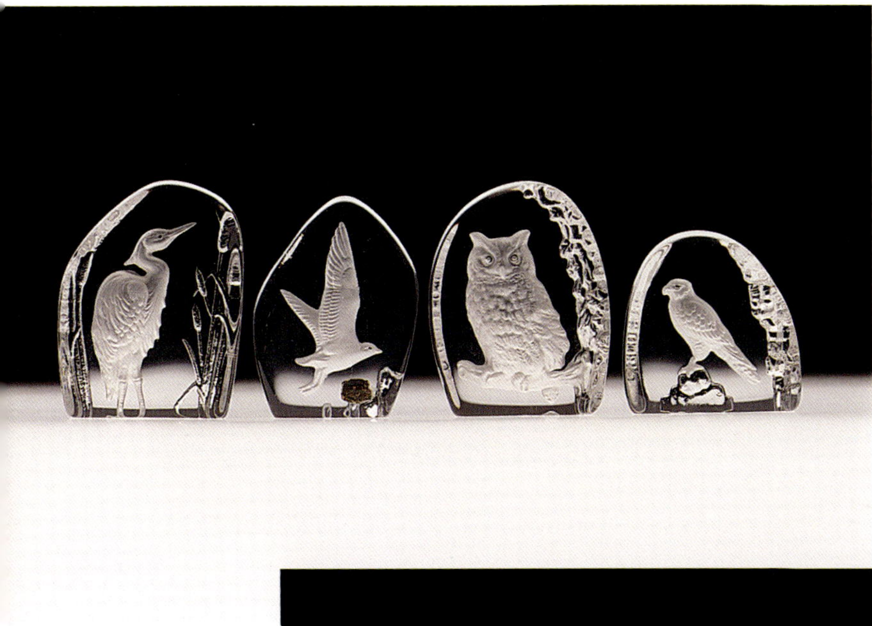

Fig. 59–61: Bird Crystals for the Danbury Mint — Top row: Heron, Seagull, Owl, Eagle;
Middle row: Kingfisher, Snipe, Pheasant, Falcon and Chick;
Bottom row: Duck, Woodpecker, Goose, Swan.

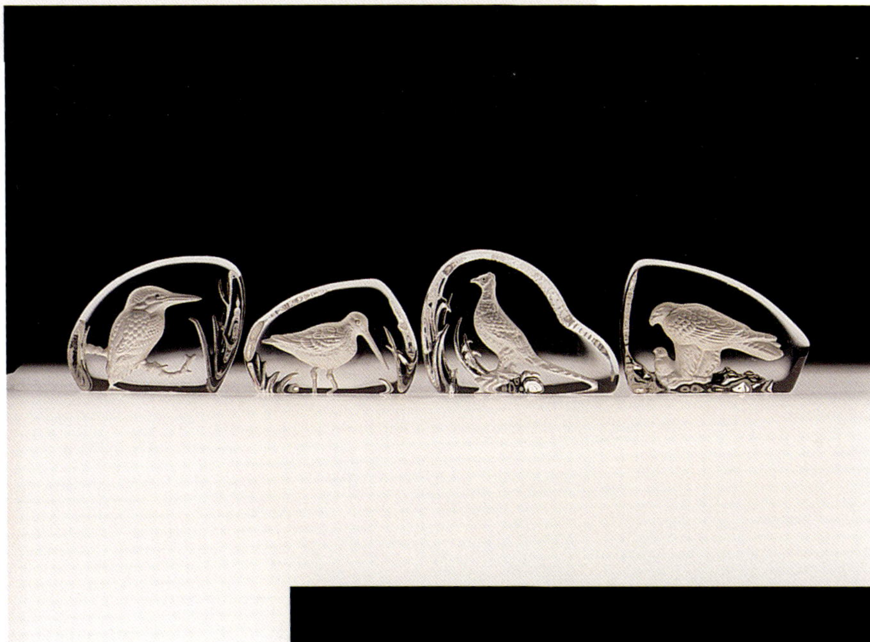

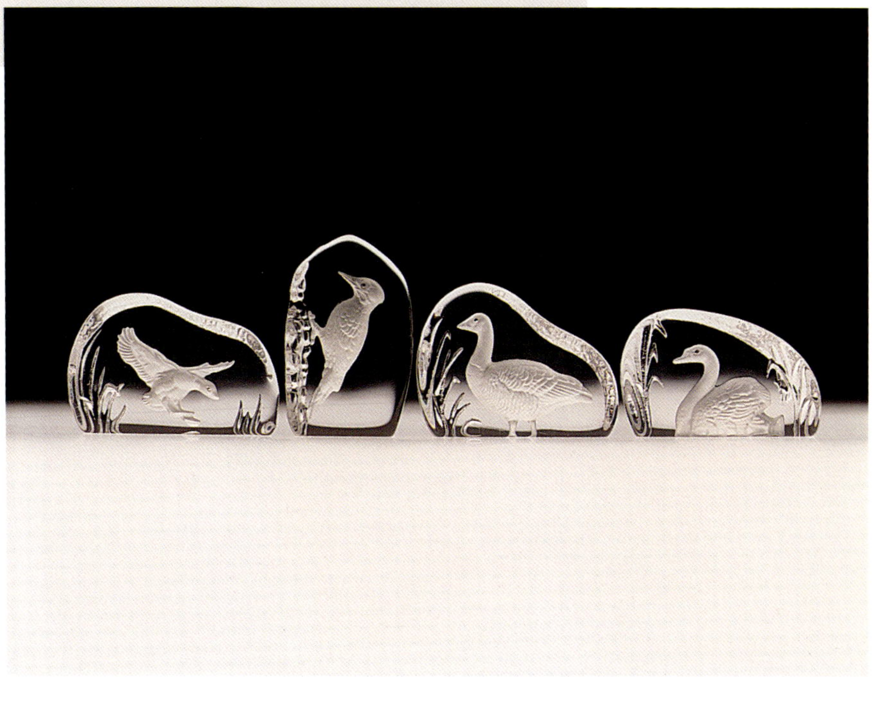

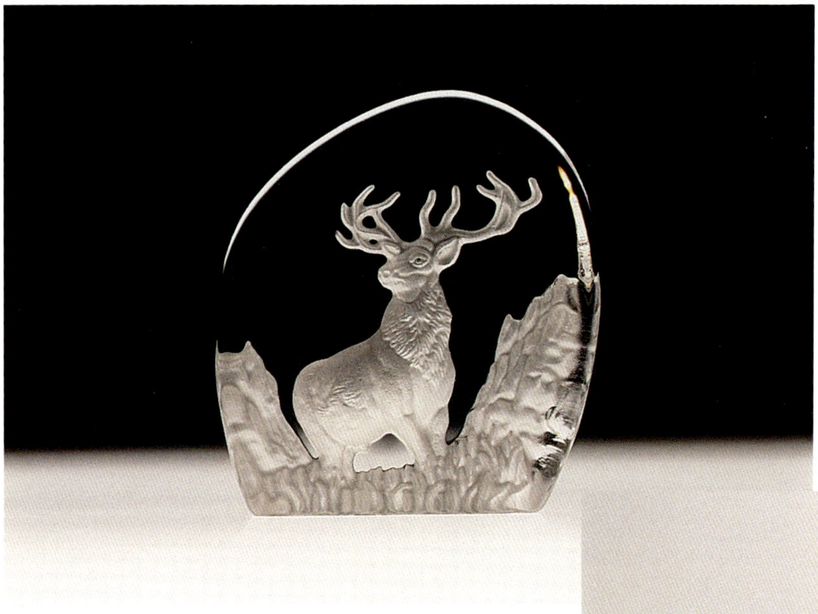

Fig. 62: Stag Crystal for Danbury Mint.

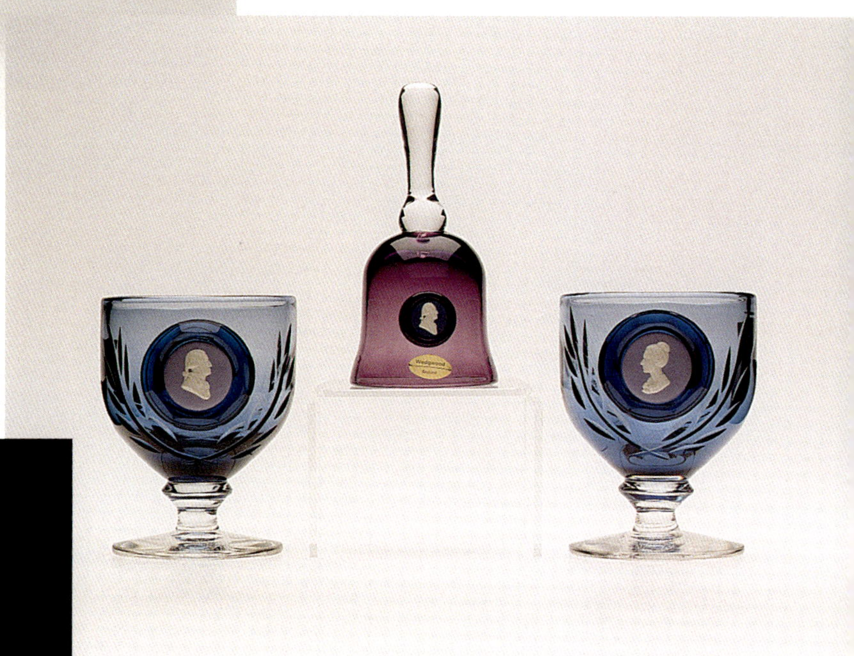

Fig. 63: A pair of smoky blue goblets bearing cameos of George and Martha Washington and a cameo of George Washington on an amethyst bell.

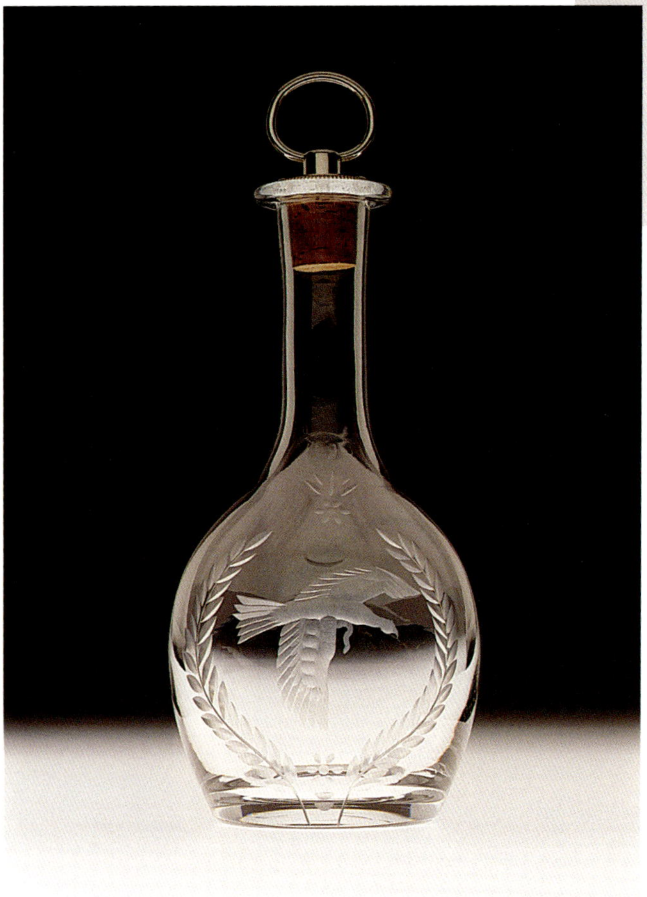

Fig. 64: Wild Turkey Crystal Decanter for the Austin Nichols Distilling Company.

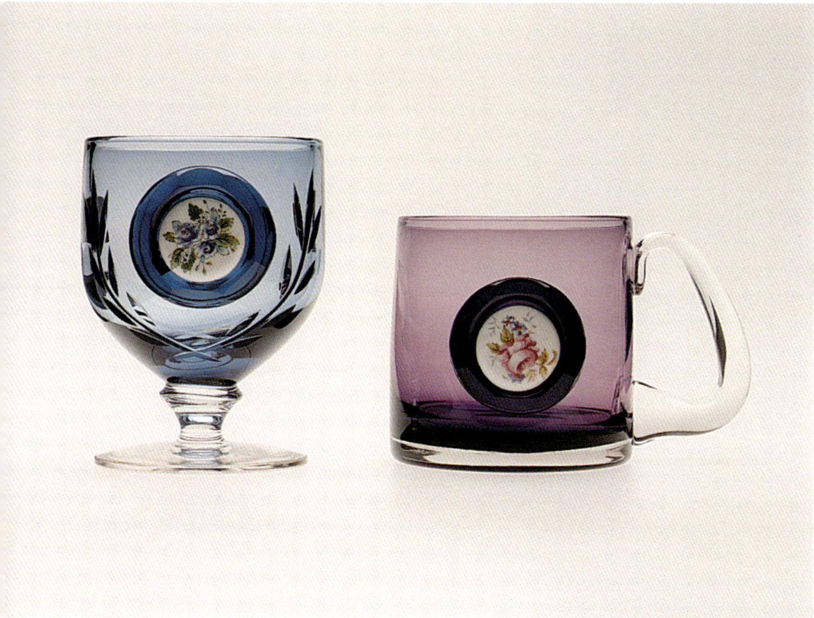

Fig. 65: Smoky blue goblet and an amethyst tankard each bearing a bone china disc.

Fig. 66: Brancaster *decanter bearing a cameo of John Paul Jones.*

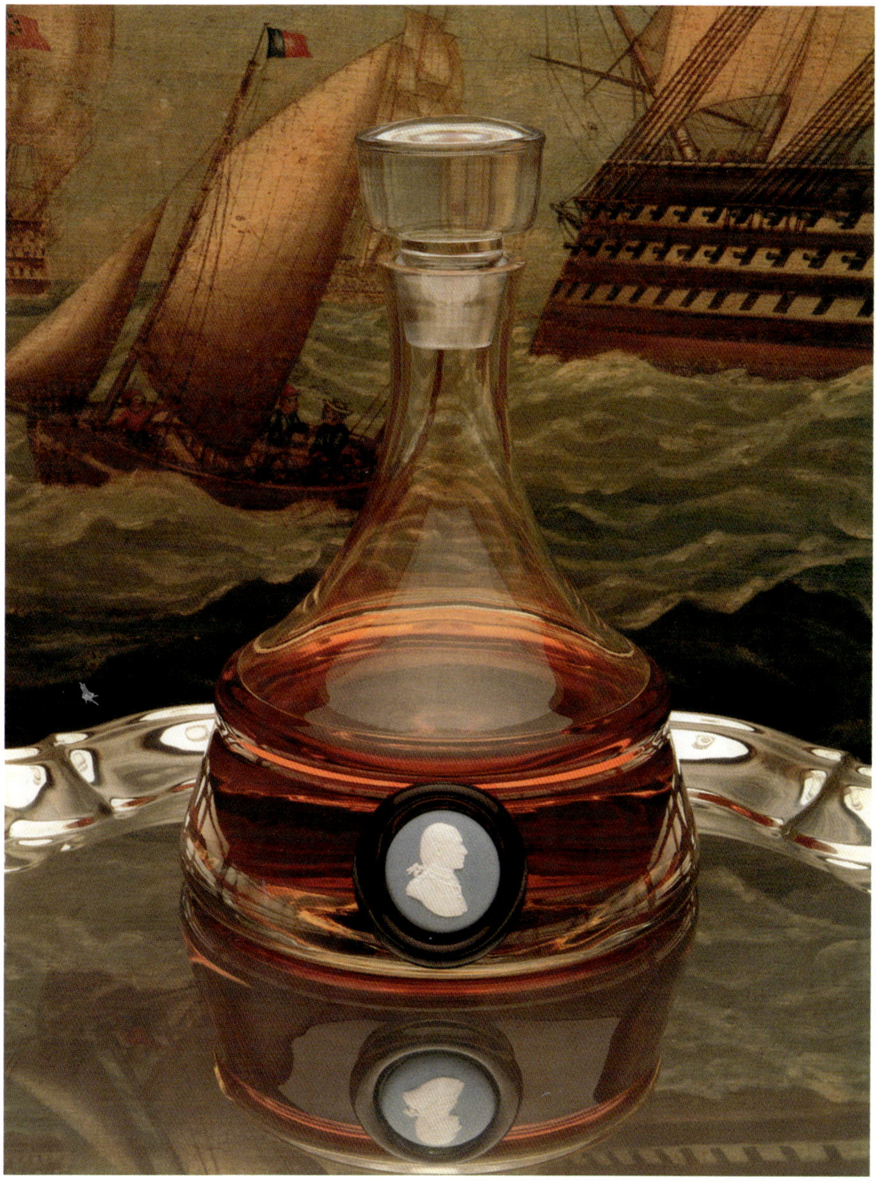

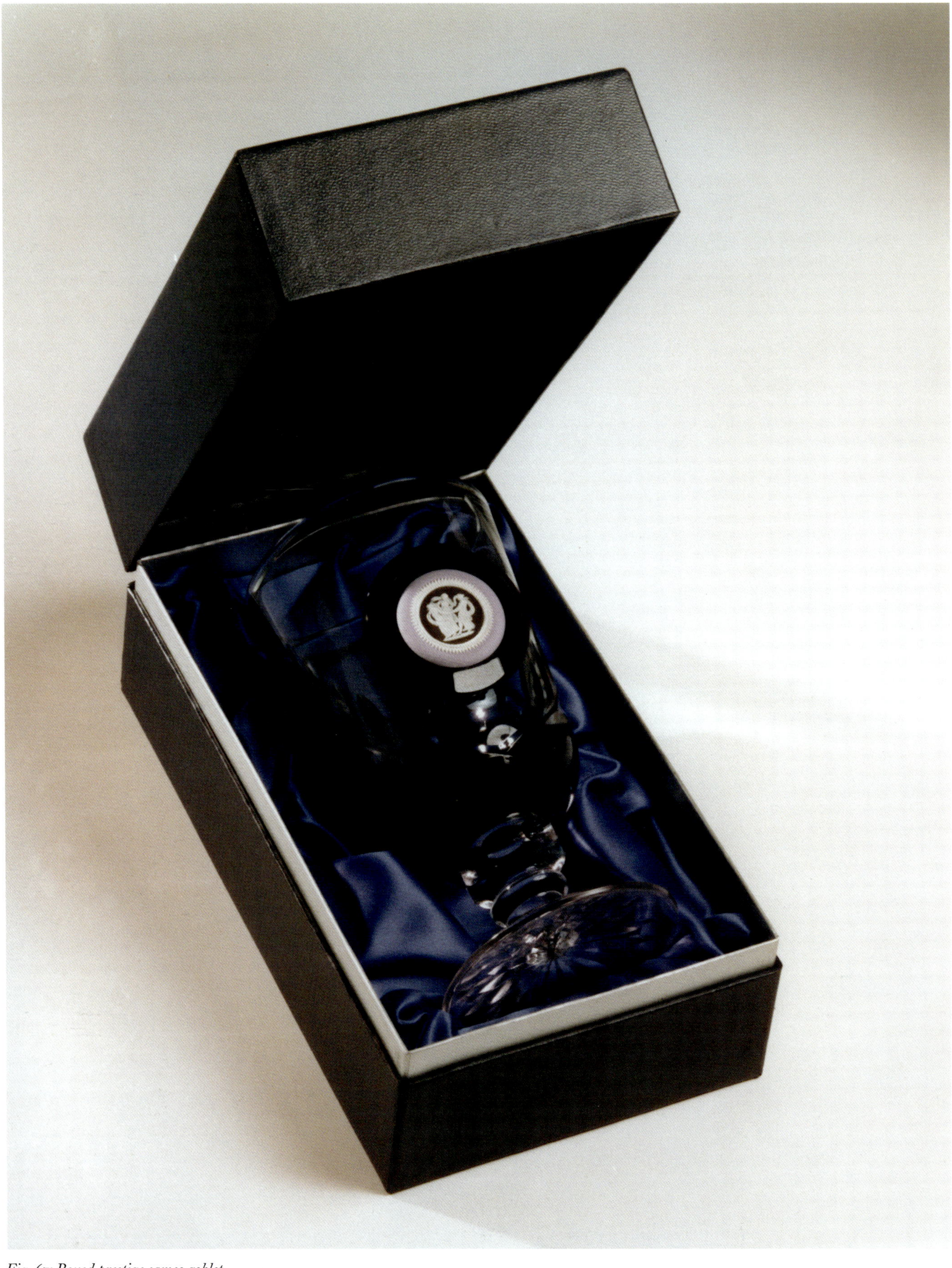

Fig. 67: Boxed prestige cameo goblet.

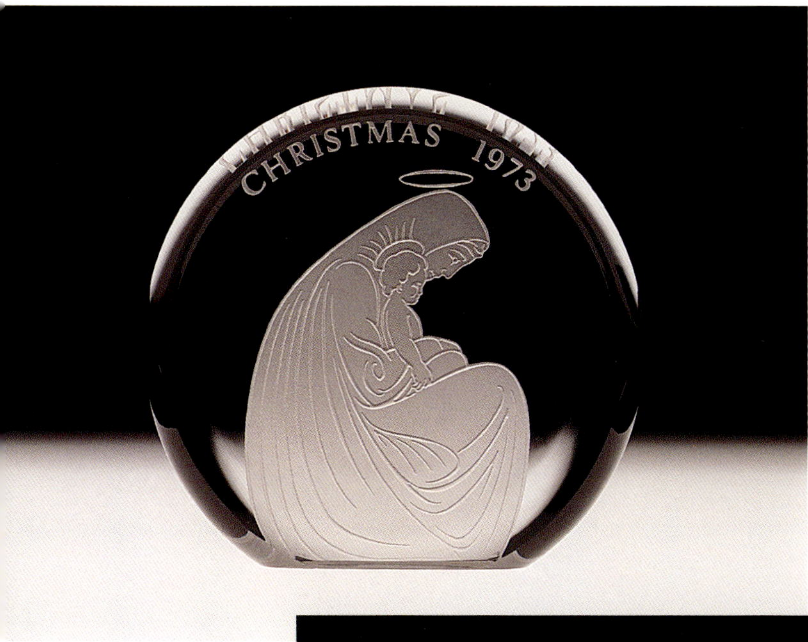

Fig. 68: Christmas 1973 plaque.

Fig. 69–70: Top row: Clear etched dome paperweights for Christmas 1975–1979;
Bottom row: Coloured Christmas scenes on a Gothic arch paperweights 1980–1984.

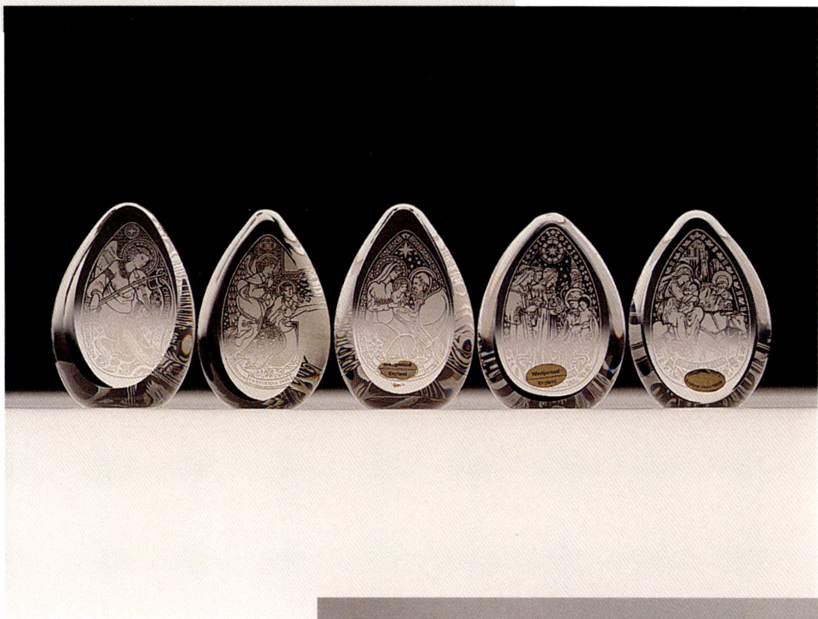

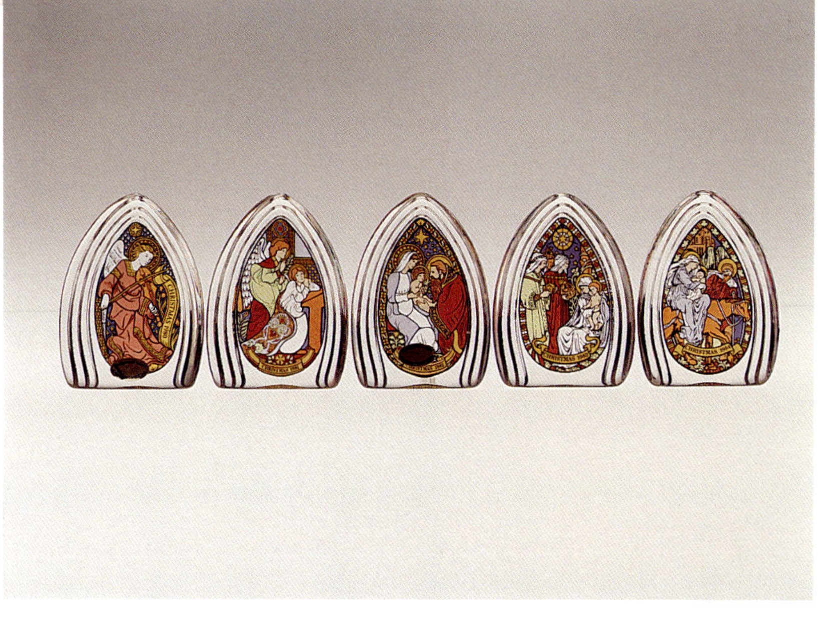

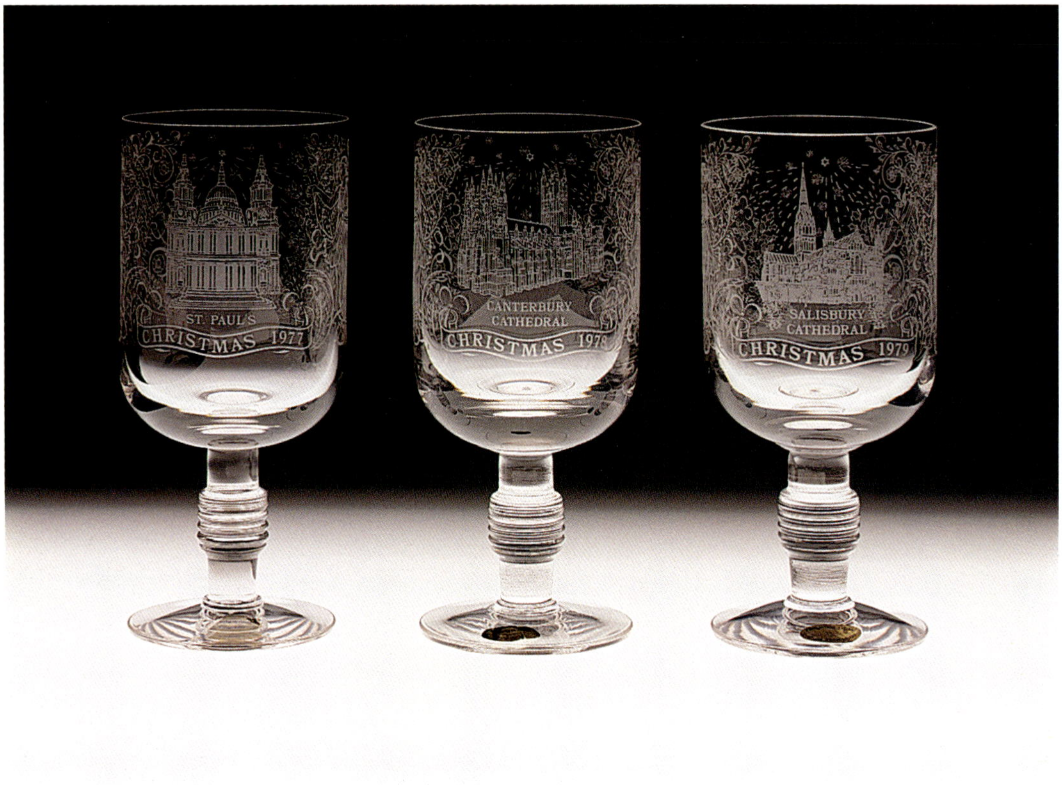

Fig. 71: Etched Christmas goblets — St Paul's (1977), Canterbury (1978) and Salisbury (1979) Cathedrals.

Fig. 72: Etched crystal Christmas bells — Bethlehem Shepherd (1979), Magi (1980), Flight into Egypt (1981), Holy Family (1982)

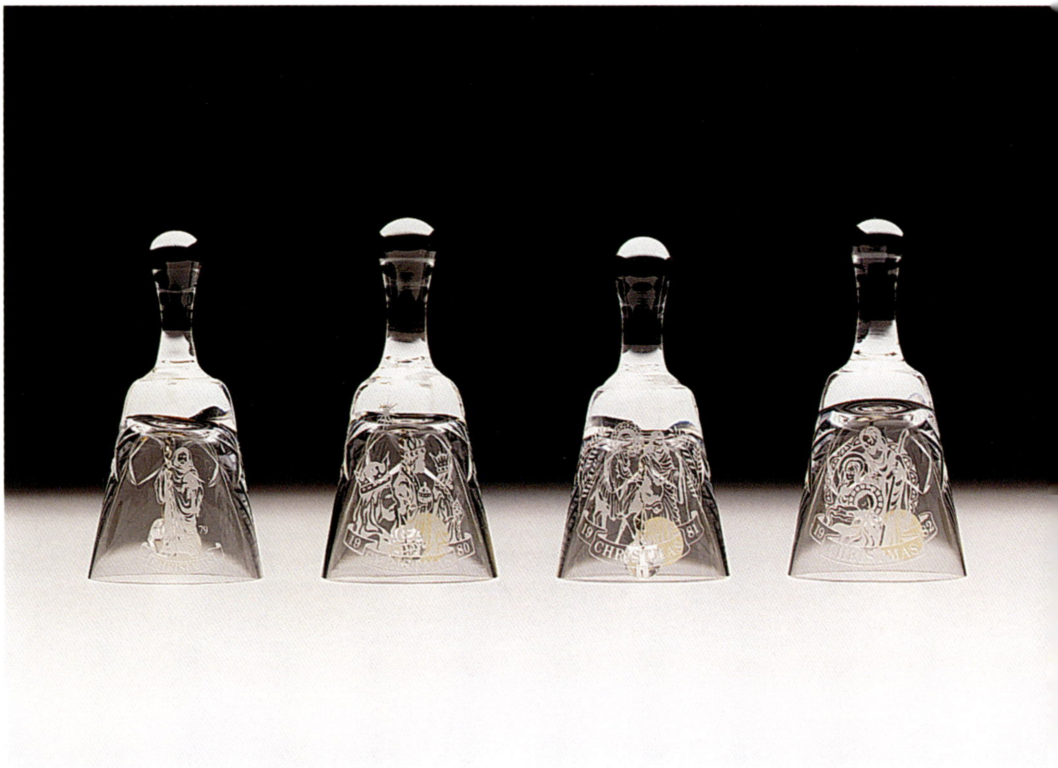

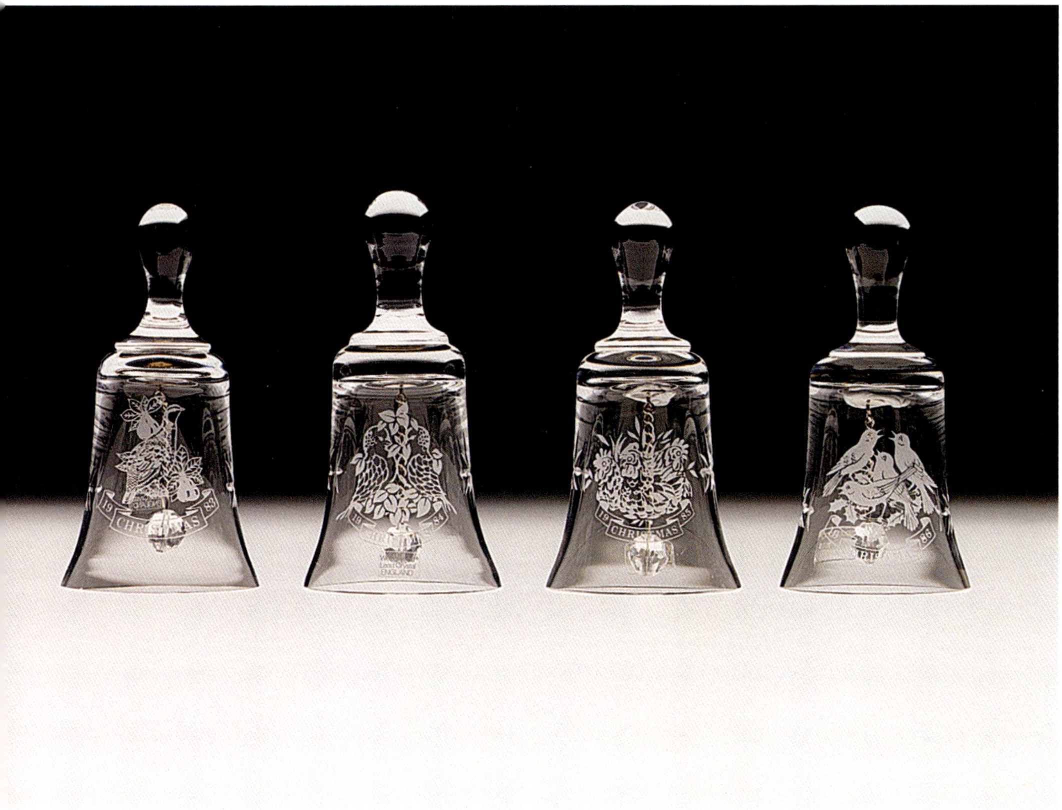

Fig. 73: Etched crystal Christmas bells — A Partridge in a Pear Tree (1983), Two Turtle Doves (1984), Three French Hens (1985), Four Calling Birds (1986).

Fig. 74: Etched crystal Mother bells — Swan and cygnet (1980), Rabbits (1981), Doe and fawn (1982).

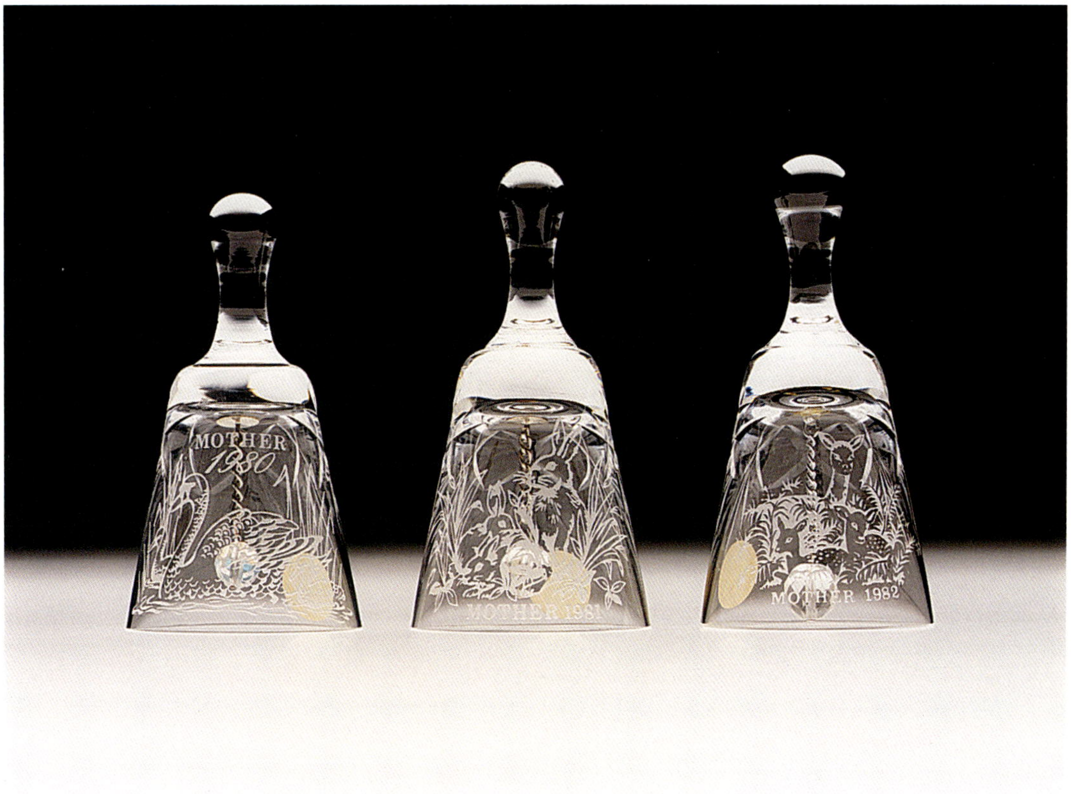

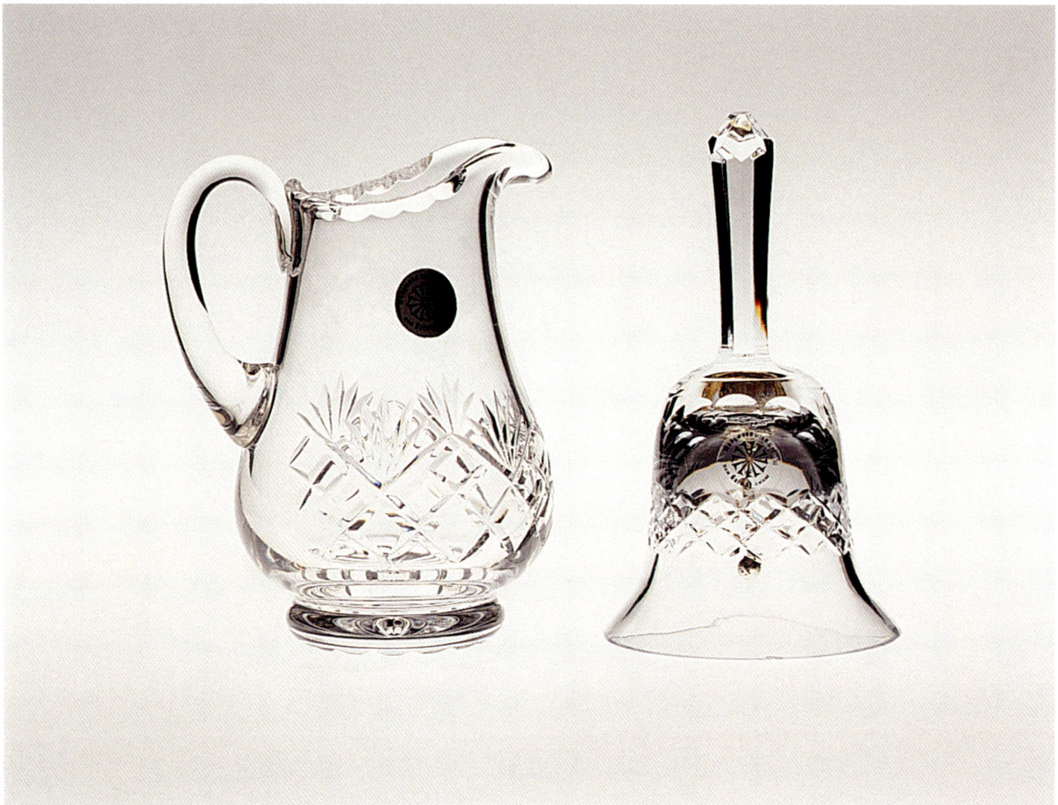

Fig. 75: Galway Crystal—Footed cream jug, Killary *dinner bell.*

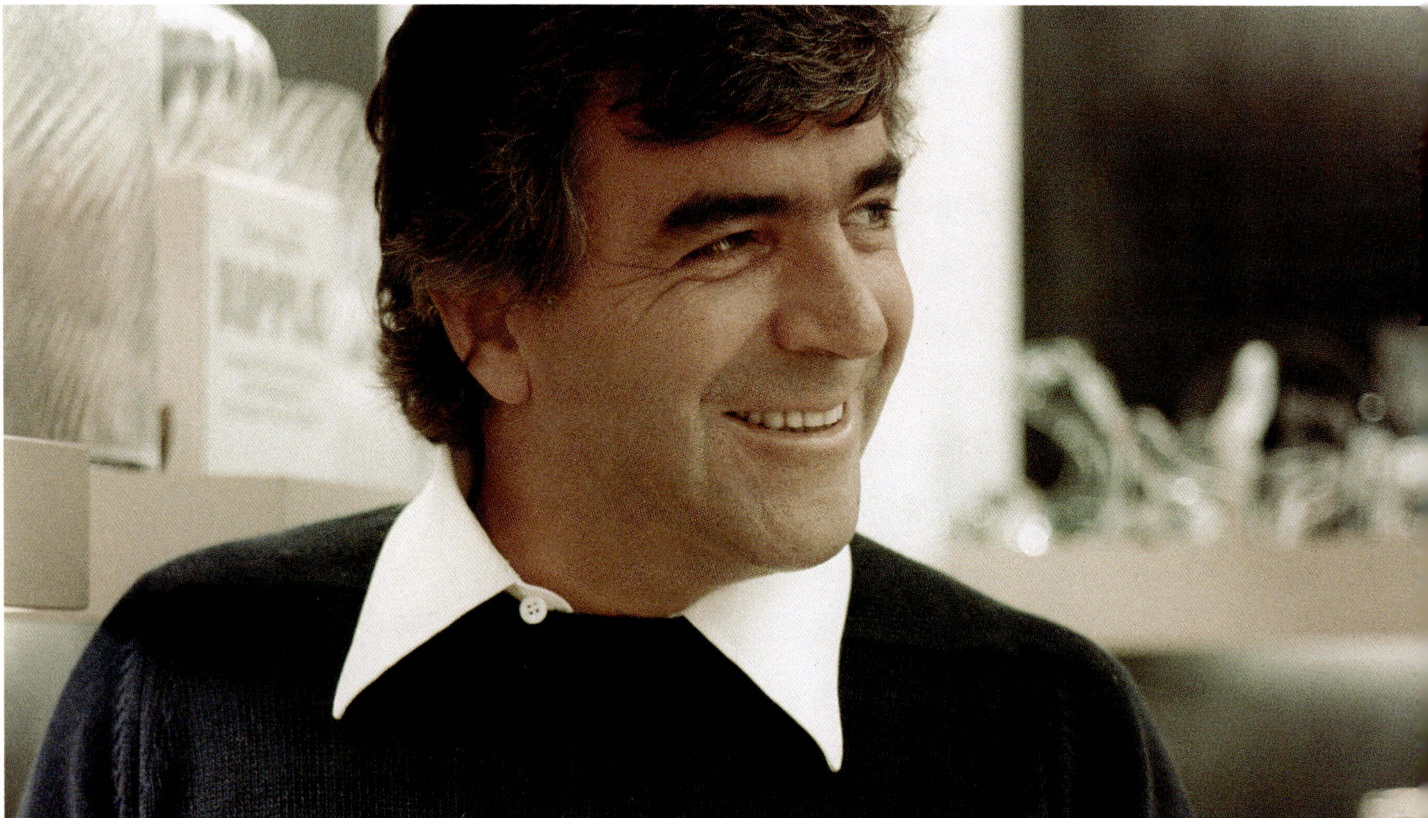

Fig. 76: Frank Thrower

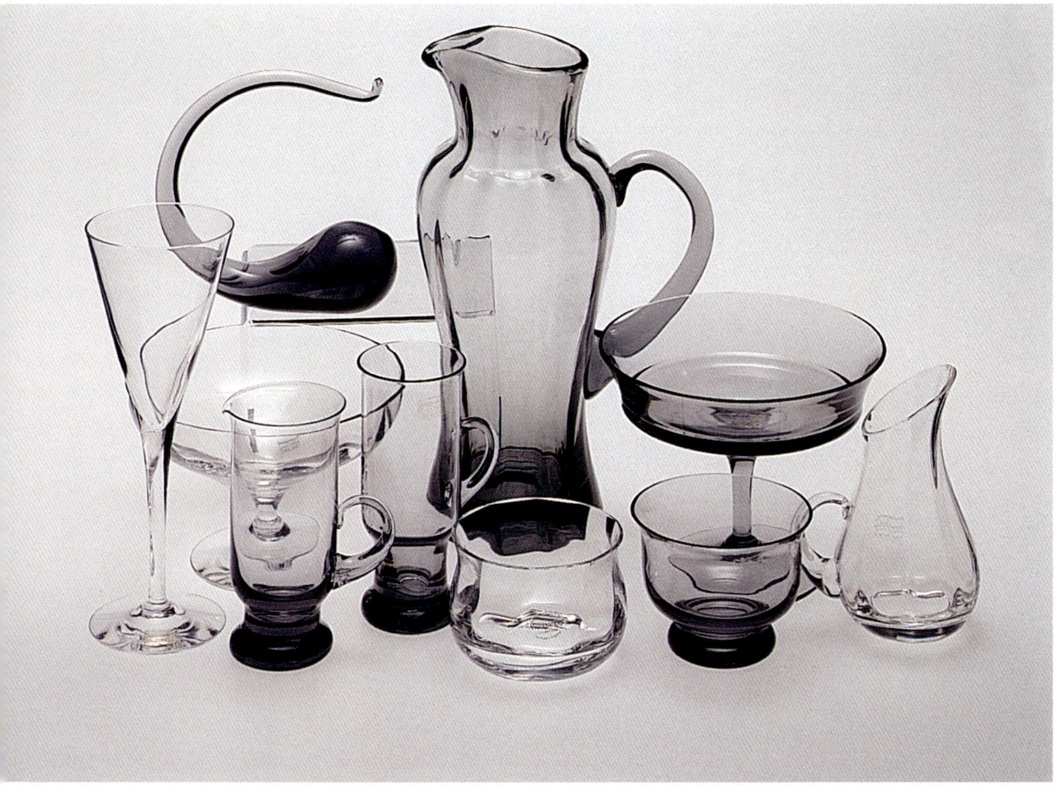

Fig. 77: Wedgwood Crystal Table and Gift Ware — Clockwise from the back: Pesce *bracelet holder (midnight),* Zelda *cocktail mixer (midnight optic),* Helene *comport (midnight),* Devon Collection *creamer (clear optic),* Genevieve *sugar basin (midnight),* Devon Collection *sugar basin (clear optic),* Seamus *Irish coffee mug (midnight),* Genevieve *creamer (midnight),* Devon Collection *comport (clear optic),* Olivia *champagne flute (clear).*

Fig. 78: Devon Collection *cut floral design lidded box, ring candy box.*

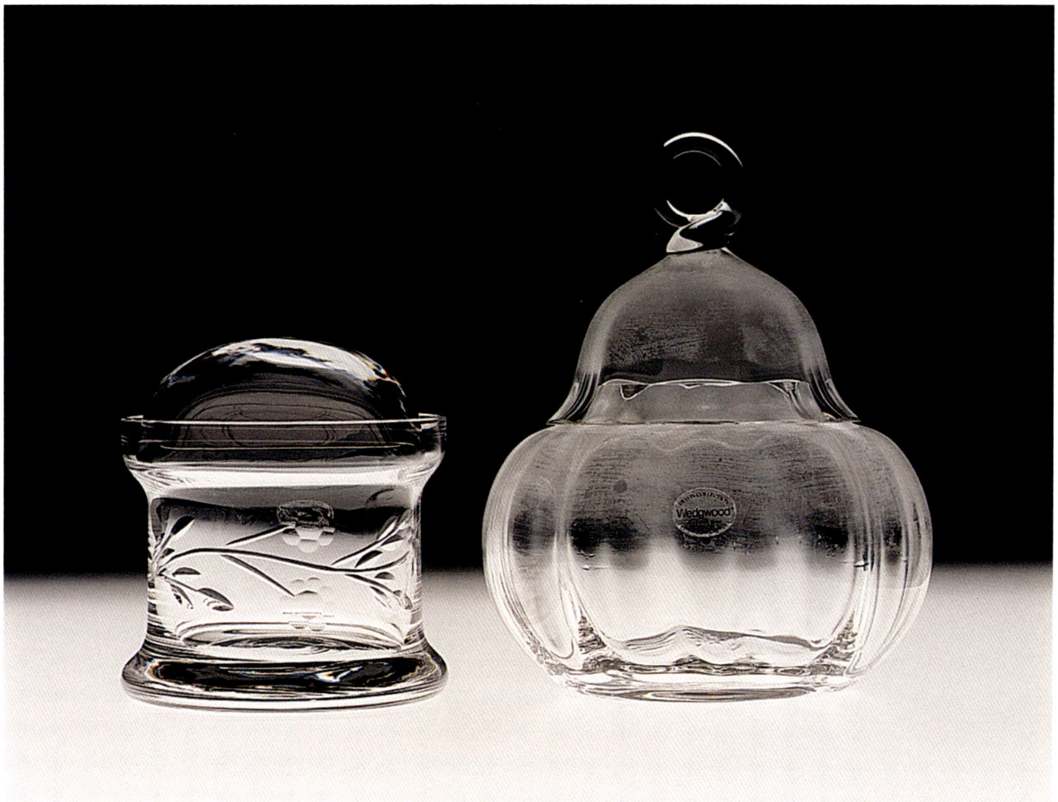

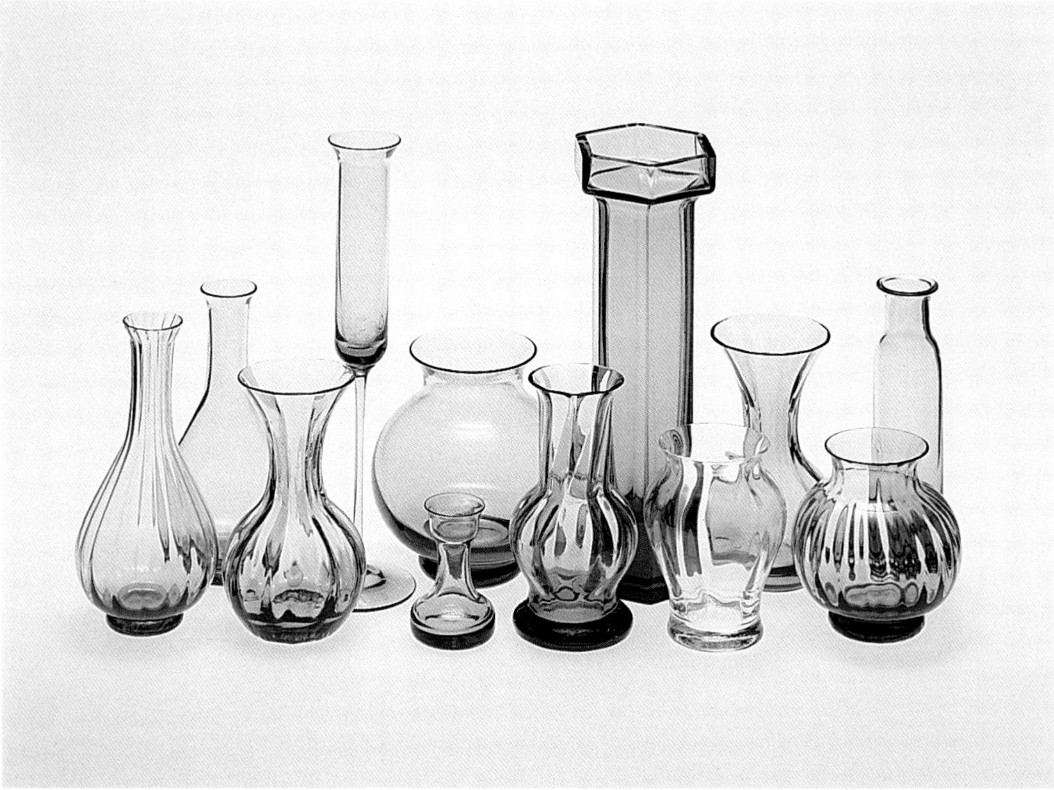

Fig. 79: Wedgwood Crystal Vases — Back row: Sarah *(midnight)*, Grace *(midnight)*, Orson *(midnight)*, Brutus *(midnight)*, Devon *floral vase (midnight optic)*, Adam *(midnight)*;
Front row: Sarah *(midnight optic)*, Devon *bouquet vase (midnight optic)*, Acorn *(midnight)*, Ming *(midnight optic)*, Adriana *(clear optic)*, Orson *(midnight optic)*.

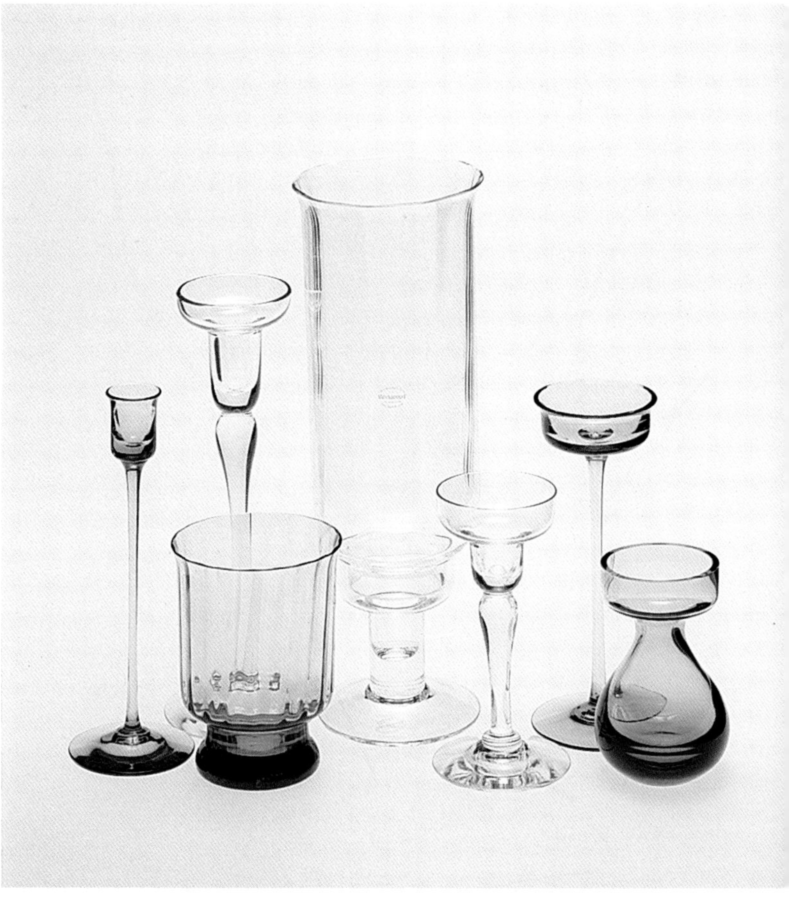

Fig. 80: Wedgwood Crystal candlesticks and candleholders — Back row: Diana *(midnight)*, Devon Collection *10 in/255mm (clear)*, Devon Collection *cylinder hurricane lamp (clear optic)*, Arthur *(midnight)*;
Front row: Celia *night light (midnight optic)*, Devon Collection *8 in/205 mm (clear)*, George *(midnight)*.

suites designed to do this was the 'Devon Collection' *(Fig. 78)*. (Though it was comprised of a range of different pieces produced primarily for the United States market, several shapes from the collection were sold in Canada and Australia). There was a fluted carafe produced in two sizes, half litre and one litre. The smaller size was available in the two colours and both forms, plain and optic, while the larger was only available in midnight optic. To match the carafe were also hurricane candlelamps in three heights in clear, clear optic and midnight optic, hurricane cylinder lamps in clear and midnight, and hurricane lamps in clear and optic midnight. The matching creamer and sugar basin, the bud vase and floral vase were in clear optic and midnight optic, while the lidded ring candy box was in clear, midnight and midnight optic. The mini candy box was only in midnight optic as was the wine cooler. Several clear vases and lidded boxes from the 'Devon Collection' were decorated with hand-cut floral and leaf patterns.

As well as the plain or optic tableware patterns, Frank Thrower extended the use of several shapes by having them produced in hand-cut crystal in the pattern, 'Justine'. It included the traditional suite of stemware—port, sherry, claret, goblet, tall champagne, and brandy balloon—accompanied by two sizes of old fashioned and two highball tumblers, two whisky glasses, a tankard and an Irish coffee mug. There were three decanters—ship's, square spirit and wine, two jugs, two bowls—for individual use and for serving salad/fruit—and a comport. Most pieces in the 'Justine' range were similar to the shapes previously produced. In stemware it was 'Philippe', with the exception of the brandy balloon which was the same shape as 'Napoleon'. The wine decanter was also in the 'Philippe' shape. There were two styles of old fashioned and highball tumblers. One was the same as 'Rufus' while the other was the same as 'Tarquin'. The shape of the tankard and the Irish coffee mug were same as that of 'Falstaff' and 'Dougall' respectively, (although in the uncut range 'Dougall' was classified as a Gaelic coffee mug). The ship's decanter was in the 'Horatio' shape and the larger jug in 'Nautilus'. The items unique to the cut crystal ranges—'Justine', also 'Sandringham' and 'Walsingham'—were a square spirit decanter, the smaller jug and three traditional pieces—whisky, old fashioned and highball tumblers.

In 1986, Wedgwood Crystal introduced two new collections of cut crystal stemware, bar ware, and giftware, 'Sandringham' and 'Walsingham'. The same types of item, but in different decorative cutting, were produced in both collections. They were stemware for port, sherry, claret, a goblet, a champagne flute, and a brandy balloon. All these were totally new shapes and were different in each suite. To accompany them on the table were a whisky glass, a highball and an old fashioned tumbler in the traditional shape complemented by the wine and square spirit decanters. As previously stated, all these pieces were the same shape as used in the 'Justine' suite. The third decanter was the same shape as uncut version, 'Horatio', an admiral's decanter. There were two sizes of jugs, the smaller being the same shape as the uncut 'Roberta' and the larger the same as 'Nautilus'.

During the 1980s, some glass blown in Yugoslavia and West Germany under contract to Wedgwood was imported as blanks to be cut in King's Lynn. Several of the patterns were 'Majesty', 'Imperial', 'Monarch', 'Sovereign', 'Tiara' and 'Dynasty'. The designs were Frank Thrower's, but foreign production enabled the items to be sold in a lower price range. One pattern, 'Royal Gold' came with the drinkware rims decorated with a quarter-inch (0.5 cm) band of gold. Collections included stemware—port, sherry, claret, champagne, and a goblet, as well as matching tumblers, decanters, and bowls. There were also vases, small dishes and small covered bowls in a range of shapes. Some crystal pieces already cut were imported. This raised the issue of how it could be labelled as there might be very little, if any, British involvement in its production.

Decorative Wares

The greatest variety in decorative wares was in vase patterns. 'Grace' was a tall drawn-stemmed vase in two sizes, while 'Adam' was a tall bud vase. Both came in midnight. For 'Orson', which was described as a Chinese vase, there were three sizes in each of midnight and midnight optic. 'Sarah' was a footed bud vase in clear optic, midnight and midnight optic. A rose bowl in midnight and midnight optic was called 'Juliet'. The midnight vase titled 'Acorn' resembled a miniature ship's decanter without its stopper. Where in tableware 'Brutus' was octagonal, as a vase shape 'Brutus' was hexagonal and came in three tall, thin vases and a short, broad vase. All shapes came in midnight. Fluted 'Ming' came in three sizes in clear optic, midnight and midnight optic *(Fig. 79)*.

Vases 'Adriana', 'Alexis' and 'Antigone' came in two sizes and both forms—clear optic and midnight optic. Flower bowls 'Claire', 'Fleur', 'Maria', and 'Tara' each came in clear optic and midnight optic.

Pattern choice also was available in candlesticks and candleholders *(Fig. 80)*. In three heights, 170mm, 200mm, and 240mm, 'Diana' was a fine drawn-stemmed candlestick, while 'Arthur' was a drawn-stemmed candleholder whose three heights were 130mm, 190mm and 265mm. Both patterns were available only in midnight. Candleholder 'George' came in two heights and two colours—clear and midnight. It could also have been used as a posy vase. Other patterns included 130mm candlestick, 'Cleo' and a 75mm high candleholder described in advertising fliers as of the 'bountiful shape of an antique rummer', 'Rory'. There was a nightlight, 'Celia', and a 365mm oil lamp, 'Lucifer'. All these patterns were in midnight. 'Caligula' and 'Stella' were both candlelamps and came in clear and midnight.

A bell designed for Christmas 1987 was not produced.

A pair of delicate items for the bedroom were a branch bracelet holder and a ring swing, 'Pesce'. Both were in available in clear and midnight. To accompany them was a choice of scent/perfume bottles in different shapes and heights, 'Danielle' 95mm, 'Sylvie' 100mm or 'Simone' 110mm in clear or midnight.

Cut crystal decorative items were also produced in 'Justine' and followed the same procedure as tableware in that design, i.e. reuse of some previous shapes. There were vases in three heights—12.75 cm, 18 cm, and 21.75 cm, a large and small footed bowl, a comport, a ring candy box, and hurricane lamp. The three vases were the same shape as 'Alexis' which had originally been in one height only, 12.75 cm. Both the footed bowls were in the 'Cybill' shape, the comport was in the 'Helene' shape, the candlelamp was the same as 'Stella', and the ring candy box was from the 'Devon Collection'.

Small bowls for individual use and a large fruit/salad serving bowl were shapes available in the three cut crystal suites. Items unique to 'Sandringham' and 'Walsingham' were the sugar basin and creamer, a small bell, a large and small rose bowl, a candlelamp, a bud vase, and a lidded candy box. The base of this last piece was similar to the uncut ring candy box from the 'Devon Collection' with the exception of the knop. In the cut crystal shapes there was no ring with which to lift the lid. The final pieces in the cut crystal suites were three different sized vases in the uncut 'Alexis' shape.

Wedgwood Crystal Limited printed a price list for 'English Hand Cut Polished Lead Crystal 1st February 1987', for both 'Sandringham' and 'Walsingham'. There was also a 'Retail Price Indicator' for the cut crystal ranges 'Torquil', 'Tarquin' and 'Justine', but the agreement between shareholders of Waterford and Wedgwood in December 1986 meant these price lists were the final ones.

13

MARKS AND LABELS

From the days of Josiah I, all items made by Wedgwood were meant to bear the company's name, and glass items were no different. Just as the Wedgwood mark varied over the years, so too, did those used on glass, but there were no special marks for different shapes. It seems also that no particular marks were used during particular years. Because of the size of or decoration on the base of some pieces, the etched mark on first quality items may be difficult to see initially, but careful examination will locate it. Probably the marks most difficult to find are those on the incised base of paperweights and drinkware or on matt finished animals or fruit. Not difficult to find, but unusually positioned, is the mark on the tail of a hippopotamus, rhinoceros or pig. Both coloured glass bells and delicate crystal bells normally had no etched mark but bore an oval or a circular foil label. An exception to this was the amethyst bell produced in 1977 for the Queen's Jubilee of accession to the throne. It was etched with the special commemorative stamp on the interior wall behind the cameo.

All marks were sand-etched. The first used and most decorative mark is the Portland vase below which is written on two lines 'Wedgwood England'. Much less decorative is the most commonly used mark. It includes the same etched words used alone. This time 'Wedgwood' is arched above, 'England' curved below, while even another uses the words 'WEDGWOOD MADE IN ENGLAND' etched in three horizontal lines. All words for all marks are etched in upper case.

The original commemorative tankard has 'RS-W' and the item number (out of five hundred) scratched, rather than engraved, into the base.

On some limited edition items, the company mark is, as usual, etched, but with it is the item number, finely wheel engraved into the base.

Special base marks are etched on Royal Commemoratives of 1977 and 1978, on the former in three horizontal lines are 'WEDGWOOD' 'MADE IN' 'ENGLAND'. Encircling them is 'QUEEN'S SILVER JUBILEE 1952—1977'. On the latter is the same company identifier, but encircling it is 'CORONATION ANNIVERSARY 1953—1978'. (Additional to the special mark, the smoky blue goblet has etched below it 'WESTMINSTER ABBEY', while on an amethyst goblet for sale in Australia is etched the special coronation base mark and below it 'AUS-

TRALIA'). All words are in capital letters *sans serif.* Not all commemorative pieces for either event bear the special mark.

Commissions for The Wedgwood Collectors' Society bore its special etched logo — the profile of Josiah Wedgwood within an oval formed by the words 'THE WEDGWOOD COLLECTORS SOCIETY' — on items only available through the Society and only available in certain countries.

On a special commission made for the Danbury Mint, the mark used on the Bird Crystals and the Stag Crystal differs from all other marks in several aspects. The usual 'WEDGWOOD' is arched above, but 'CRYSTAL' is curved below. Etched between them is the Danbury Mint logo. There is no etched 'England'.

Crystal items from Galway bore dual names — GALWAY and Wedgwood, both *sans serif.*

The final etched mark is simply 'Wedgwood' in upper and lower case. This is found only on items designed and produced during the association between Wedgwood Crystal and Dartington Glass. It appears on the base of items designed by Frank Thrower *(Fig. 76).* (Some of these items bore not only the word 'Wedgwood' but also an alphanumerical inspector's code, e.g. A/1, B/1, C/1, D/1 below the Company name). Friggers, seconds and copies of Wedgwood glass have reached the market. Friggers were never sold by the company, but seconds were available through the factory shops and through retail outlets particularly during the end of season sales. More than a decade after they were produced, seconds still packed in and probably never removed from their original boxes give clear evidence of the use of the label only.

To double up on identification of Wedgwood Glass, the etched mark was usually accompanied by a label. The type of paper, its shape and the wording written on labels for glass items is even more varied than the etched mark. There is the:

- Oblong black paper bisected by a white line. Above is written 'Wedgwood'. Below is 'England'. All writing is also white. This label came in two sizes and was one of the earliest used.
- Oblong black paper, with 'Wedgwood' written horizontally across the top. Approximately one third of the way down and below 'Wedgwood' is a horizontal line. Across the centre is 'England', and below that is 'Full lead hand-cut crystal'. This label was used on crystal produced during the early years at King's Lynn. All writing is white.
- Circular-arched paper, with the outside edge being coloured blue, while the interior is white. 'Wedgwood' is written in white around the outer edge of the arch. 'England' in blue is written horizontally across the base of the inner arch. Both words are in upper case.
- Oval gold foil bisected by a horizontal blue line with 'Wedgwood' written above and 'England' below. Both words are written horizontally and printed in blue.
- Oval gold foil, arched around the top is 'Wedgwood Glass'. Curved round the bottom is 'Made in England'. All writing is blue.
- Oval gold foil (and less frequently, silver foil), arched around the top is 'Wedgwood Glass'. Curved around the bottom is 'England. Hand Made'. All writing is blue.
- Oval gold foil, arched around the top is 'Wedgwood Crystal'. Written horizontally across the centre is 'Hand Made'. Curved around the bottom is 'England'. All writing is blue.
- Oval gold foil, arched around the top is 'Wedgwood Glass', written horizontally across the centre is 'Hand Made Crystal' and curved around the bottom 'England'. All writing is blue.
- Circular gold foil, arched around the top is 'Wedgwood'. Written in three horizontal lines across the centre is 'FULL LEAD' 'HAND CUT CRYSTAL' 'ENGLAND'. All these words

are in upper case. Curved around the bottom also is 'Wedgwood'. All writing is blue.

- Circular gold foil, arched around the top is 'Wedgwood'. Written in three horizontal lines across the centre is '30% FULL LEAD' 'HAND CUT CRYSTAL' 'ENGLAND'. All these words are in upper case. Curved around the bottom also is 'Wedgwood'. The company name, as on all other foil labels, is in upper and lower case. All writing is blue.
- Circular clear plastic round the top of the circumference is 'Wedgwood Glass', while round the base is 'England'. Written horizontally in two lines across the centre is 'Crystal' 'Hand Made'. All writing is blue.
- Circular silver foil bearing in the centre the specially designed symbol for Galway Crystal. Around the top is written 'Wedgwood Irish Crystal' and around the base 'from Galway Ireland'. The writing and symbol are blue.
- Circular plastic bearing exactly the same details as silver foil label for Galway Crystal.
- Oblong clear plastic on which 'Wedgwood®' is written horizontally on the top, 'Lead Crystal' across the centre, and 'England' on the bottom line. The writing is gold, the first two lines being in upper and lower case, while 'ENGLAND' is in upper case only. This label was used on pieces designed during the years of Wedgwood's association with Dartington. It may appear alone on an item which is not etched.
- Oblong clear plastic, similar to the previous label in every way, for the same pieces and for bells, but on which the writing is white.
- Oblong clear plastic, similar to the previous two labels in every way and which was used on crystal bells, but the writing is silver.
- Oval clear plastic which bears not only company details but also the name of the collection. Arched around the top is 'DEVON COLLECTION'. Written horizontally across the centre, 'Wedgwood ®', below which '24% Lead Crystal', is also written horizontally. Curved around the bottom is 'Handmade in England'. The printing is in gold. 'Devon Collection' is in upper case and all letters bear serifs.
- Oblong clear plastic which bears on three horizontal lines 'Wedgwood Crystal' 'Made in England for' 'the Danbury Mint'. The writing is in black in both upper and lower case. The top and middle lines are printed using a serif. The bottom line is cursive. (Used only on the commissions for the Danbury Mint, i.e. on the Bird Crystals and Stag Crystal).

Items made in Yugolsavia and West Germany also bear the etched single company name 'Wedgwood' and a clear oval label similar to that of the Devon Collection. Arched around the top is 'Full Lead Crystal'. 'Wedgwood ®' is written horizontally across the centre. Curved round the bottom is 'Yugoslavia' or 'West Germany'.

There are at least two totally different paper labels probably used in 1969. One is rectangular, predominantly black but with a narrow white border and white writing—'Wedgwood CRYSTAL'. The second is oval, black with the words written in white. Arched around the top is 'WEDGWOOD CRYSTAL LTD', horizontally across the centre is 'HANDMADE' and curved around the base is 'ENGLAND'. Items bearing these labels are clearly from Wedgwood Glass Limited, King's Lynn, yet neither the company name nor the use of 'crystal' is correct for many of the items which bear the stickers. The pieces are the same in colour and shape as items etched with one of the standard marks used. The finish is perfect but no piece bearing these types of labels seems to bear an etched base mark.

Although there is a range of style and wording among the variety of marks used on Wedgwood glass and crystal, most etched or written marks, with the exception of those listed, are *sans serif*. With the exception of the Danbury Mint commissions, there is usually no particular mark for particular items.

EPILOGUE

By the mid-1970s the King's Lynn factory was in full production due to the manufacture of commemorative items for the Queen's Jubilees. The popularity of these items stimulated interest by individuals, organisations and firms to order special designs of glassware for themselves or their clients. There was also an increase in orders for standard products which sold well in the Wedgwood Rooms. Unfortunately this did not last long enough. By the early 1980s, Wedgwood Glass was suffering from the general economic recession. According to the Sales Director, Richard Midwinter, it was given another shot in the arm through production of items for the wedding of Prince of Wales to Lady Diana Spencer in 1981. This was only a temporary relief, and the staff was frequently reduced to short-time working. Demand for Christmas items was an annual relief as staff could return to a full working week.

Though both sites were relatively small, staff relationships and quality of product at both King's Lynn and Torrington were not always the best, particularly in the mid-1980s. A report which focussed on the glasshouses indicated that problems with personnel were partly the result of transition from what could be described as a craft culture to a medium-sized organisation which could lose a sense of community spirit, intimacy and respect for the highly-skilled craftsmen. There was also concern about the volatility of the overseas market with the possibility of its collapse. Further concerns were the small size of management within an expanding factory with its greater volume of work, friction between blowers and finishers, and that skills were lost when certain personnel were promoted, for example, the glassblower who became a foreman. Insufficient training for new blowers resulted in some members of teams lacking skills necessary for basic tasks. Other problems voiced included illogical and sometimes haphazard placement of new equipment and machinery within the existing floor space, and the lack of care in the storage of moulds and batches of raw materials. These latter practices could result in damage to the moulds (or workers being unable to find them) and impurities contaminating batches. Consultation was an issue at all levels, but particularly with Frank Thrower, regarding new product development where minor design amendments could make life easier for blowers and finishers. Everyone would have liked to have a larger share of his time.

Problems related to inferior products were ultimately found to have been caused by the use of wrong quality sand. Production of bad glass could have a dual effect—loss of bonus earnings for the glass blowers and a negative impact on the Company's commercial fortune. The report stated that people who bought Wedgwood products expected quality. At the same time it was not true that purchasers of Dartington glass were happy with second best. It was more likely that they were less familiar with the latter brand.

Somewhat ironically, by March 1986 the prospect for Wedgwood Crystal seemed to be in cut crystal. The idea was to market it as handmade, hand-cut and hand-polished to establish a niche in the marketplace. Wedgwood Crystal produced blanks relatively less expensively than its competitors, but hand polishing to finish cut glass was labour intensive. Some other English glass manufacturers finished their work with acid polishing. There seemed no reason why this process would not be possible at King's Lynn.

To perform acid polishing, consideration was given to the use of the semi-automatic Saltzer system with several adaptations. This system used larger acid baths into which larger trays holding items could be immersed automatically thereby reducing manual effort. Consequently the number of items that could be polished at one time would be greatly increased.

To set up an acid polishing system, all relevant local authorities, e.g. the local Council and Water Board, needed to be consulted, but it was not proposed for the immediate future. Diamond hand-cutting and acid polishing were the cheapest means of decoration, particularly for heavily cut large items, but more research into the process and its possible application at King's Lynn were essential. Without that, thousands of pounds would be wasted. Products would be inferior, the Company's reputation severely damaged and financial losses incurred. Properly controlled, the resultant products would be quality items. Such was not to come to fruition.

Lest it be thought that problems dogged Wedgwood Glass/Crystal, there were more times of co-operation and production of quality items than the opposite. Though the problems of the 1980s are closest in time, memory and the reports of research into the status of operation, working relationships on the factory floor and between glassmakers and management for most of the eighteen years of production were amicable. As in any workplace, there is usually some friction between individuals or between groups at various times, but on the whole, many past employees of Wedgwood Glass remember more readily the co-operation, companionship and a desire to produce items that were of top quality. Evidence that this happened is obvious in the awards several of the products received during the life of the factories and the popularity many items have retained, particularly in the secondary market.

The relationship between Wedgwood and Dartington continued till February 1987, at which time Josiah Wedgwood and Sons was bought by Waterford Crystal. At that point, the partnership between Wedgwood Crystal Limited and Dartington Crystal Limited was formally dissolved, the latter continuing as a separate company with its factory in Torrington, North Devon. It maintained many of Frank Thrower's designs, and gradually expanded its range of items with the works of later designers. The products continued to be sold on the home and foreign markets.

Following the purchase, production of glass at King's Lynn factory ceased. All employees were made redundant. Some glassmakers were able to find employment in Norfolk either at Caithness Glass Limited or Langham Glass. Others had to relocate to stay in the glass industry. Four men, Otmar Schoss, Ken Tiler, Helmut Morgenfurt, and John Dowe, who remained for about six weeks after the other employees finished, were responsible for the completion of the *Bird Crystals* for the Danbury Mint. When this had been done, Jack Snell, engineering manager, cooled down the furnaces gradually and finally turned them off. The doors at Wedgwood Crystal Limited, King's Lynn, closed for the last time. Products from the warehouses and factory shop were sold, and the production of the first identifiable 'Lynn Glassware' ceased.

Though Wedgwood produced glass for fewer than twenty years, much of its production conformed to long-held company policy of quality design. Limited editions always sold out and several Wedgwood glass pieces met national design standards. Wedgwood glass was used for prizes in local and national competitions, was given as gifts to Royal persons and a Pope, and complemented many of the Company's tableware designs. In his Chairman's address as reported in the *Counterpoint* Supplement, Spring 1984, Sir Arthur Bryan reinforced the tenet—'Design has always been a fundamental part of Wedgwood business ... it has been an unswerving policy of the company ... to aim for good design, excellent design ... that has been of paramount importance in both our home and export business for well over two centuries ...The real and final test of good design is the market place.' Let the last words go to Josiah Wedgwood who wrote to his partner, Thomas Bentley, in 1769 (two hundred years before the establishment of Wedgwood Glass), 'We will fashion our products after their own hearts and captivate them with elegance and simplicity'.

BIBLIOGRAPHY

Counterpoint. Wedgwood's News for Retailers. Spring 1971; Spring 1972; Special Summer 1972; Christmas 1973; Spring 1974; Christmas 1974; Christmas 1975; Special Silver Jubilee, Autumn 1976; Spring 1977; Spring 1978; Spring 1979; Spring 1980; Spring 1981; Spring 1982; Spring 1983; Spring 1984; 1985; Spring 1986.

Elville, E. M. 'Coronation History in Glass' in *Country Life Coronation Number* London, June 6, 1953.

Mackay, James, *Glass Paperweights.* Ward Lock Limited: London, 1973.

Melhman, Felice, *The Illustrated Guide to Glass.* Peerage Books: London, 1985.

Newman, Harold, *An Illustrated Dictionary of Glass.* Thames & Hudson: London, 1977.

Richards, Paul, *King's Lynn.* Philimore & Co: Chichester, 1997.

Riley, Robin, *Wedgwood: The New Illustrated Dictionary.* Antique Collectors' Club Ltd: Suffolk, 1988.

Riley, Robin & Savage, George, *The Dictionary of Wedgwood.* Antique Collectors' Club: Suffolk, 1980.

Sandon, John, *Antique Glass.* Antique Collectors' Club: Woodbridge, Suffolk, 1999.

Schofield, Robert E., *The Lunar Society of Birmingham. A Social History of Provincial Science and Industry in Eighteen Century England.* Oxford: Clarendon Press, 1963.

Stennett-Willson, Ronald, *Modern Glass.* Studio Vista: London, 1975.

Stennett-Willson, Ronald, *The Beauty of Modern Glass.*The Studio Limited: London, 1958.

Wedgwood Review, Vol 4, No 11, June 1969; Vol 4, No 12, September 1969; Vol 5, No 1, December 1969; Vol 5, No 2, March 1970; Vol 5, No 7, June 1971; Vol 6, No 5, August 1974; Vol 6, No 6, December 1974; Vol 6, No 7, April 1975; Vol 6, No 8, August 1975; Vol 6, No 12, December 1976; Summer 1977; January 1979; August 1979; January, 1980; February, 1981; September 1981; Summer 1982; January 1987.

Who Was Who A. & C. Black (Publishers) Limited, 1996.

Newspapers

Eastern Daily Press. November 23, 1976; April (undated) 1977; October 15, 1979; April 3, 1981; April (undated) 1982; November 27, 1988.

Eastern Evening News Lynn Special. Wednesday, April 30, 1969; Friday, June 28, 1974.

Evening Sentinel. April 30, 1969.

Express & Star. April 30, 1969; July 25, 1974.

Design Magazine. January 27, 1975.

Financial Times. April 30, 1969; May 17, 1969.

Gifts. January, 1975.

Glass. December, 1974.

Investors' Guardian. May 9, 1969.

Irish Builder & Guardian. April, 1975.

Lynn News & Advertiser. May 13, 1969; June 28, 1974.

Morning Telegraph. March 1, 1975.

Sentinel. June 27, 1974; June 29, 1974; July 25, 1974; October 10, 1986; October 13, 1986; October 17, 1986.

Stone Guardian. May 2, 1969.

The Financial Post. (Toronto, Ontario) May 24, 1969.

The Lady. July 11, 1974.

The Sunday Press (Dublin). February 23, 1975.

The Times. April 30, 1969; June 27, 1974.

Western Mail. July 25, 1974.

Correspondence

Berrington, Brian, Marketing Director, to retailers, January 1977; March 1977; March 1978.

Eccles, Michael D., Managing Director, to R. A. McIntosh of McIntosh & Watts Ltd, Ottawa, Ontario, 12 February, 1973.

Lydeard, William U., Sales Director, to retailers June 1974.

Woodcock, S., Product Assistant (Danbury Mint)—no date.

Wedgwood Price Books and Price Lists

April, 1972; August, 1972.

October, 1974.

June, 1976.

January, 1978.

April, 1982.

February, 1987; Spring, 1987.

Catalogue

Wedgwood Irish Crystal from Galway, October 1977.

Friedrich & Scheibler Farbglashutte GMBH Kugler Colors®

Wedgwood c1979; 1987.

Wedgwood Home Sales Invoices
September 1972.
September 1976.
January 1977; July 1977; August 1977; November 1977.
July 1978.
February 1979.
August 1980.

Reports
Dowe, J., *Report on Visit to Dartington Glass, Torrington*, 2—5 March, 1986.
McLean, Adrian, *Skills, Change and Succession—Issues in the growth and development of English County Crystal, Part II Dartington Glass Limited*, April, 1985.

Personal Correspondence and Articles
Dancer CBE, Eric, 3 January 2000.
Dowe, John.
Lewis, P. N., *The Origins of Dartington Glass* A paper given to the Scottish Glass Society, 2 July 1994.
Stennett-Willson, Ronald.

APPENDICES

Appendix 1 — Made at King's Lynn

Code	Shape	Colour	Design
RSW1/1	Liqueur	Clear, Blue or Topaz	'Tower'
RSW1/3	Sherry	″	″
RSW1/4	Cocktail	″	″
RSW1/5	Claret	″	″
RSW1/7	Champagne	″	″
RSW1/8	Goblet	″	″
RSW1/9	Beer Goblet 11 oz/30 cl	″	″
RSW1/19	Sundae Dish	″	″
RSW1/20	Brandy 5 oz/14 cl	″	″
RSW1/23	Brandy 20 oz/57 cl	″	″
RSW2/1	Liqueur 5.5 cl	Clear	'Brancaster'
RSW2/3	Sherry 8.5 cl	″	″
RSW2/4	Port/Cocktail	″	″
RSW2/5	Claret 5 oz/14 cl	″	″
RSW2/6	Tall Hock 6 oz/14.5 cl	″	″
RSW2/7T	Champagne, Tall 5 oz/14 cl	″	″
RSW2/7B	Champagne, Bowl 20 cl	″	″
RSW2/8	Goblet 20 cl	″	″
RSW2/8L	Goblet, Large 25 cl	″	″
RSW2/10	Tumbler, 5 oz/14 cl	″	″
RSW2/11	Tumbler, 9 oz/25 cl	″	″
RSW2/12	Tumbler, 10 oz /28.5 cl	″	″
RSW2/13	Highball, 12 oz/34 cl	″	″
RSW2/14 (ST14)	Decanter	″	″
RSW2/14S (ST14S)	Ship's Decanter	″	″
	Jug, .5 Pint/28 cl	″	″
	Jug, 1 Pint/57 cl	″	″
	Jug, 2 Pint/1.2 litres	″	″
RSW2/19	Sundae	″	″
RSW2/24	Ice Pail	″	″
	Grapefruit	″	″
RSW4	Tumbler, 8oz/23 cl	Clear, Blue, or Topaz	
RSW5	Tumbler, 9 oz/25 cl	″	
RSW6/1	Liqueur	Clear, Blue, Amethyst or Topaz	'Sandringham'
RSW6/3	Sherry	″	″
RSW6/4	Port/Cocktail	″	″
RSW6/4R	Port/Cocktail, Round	″	″
RSW6/5	Claret	″	″
RSW6/5R	Claret, Round	″	″
RSW6/6	Tall Hock	″	″

RSW6/7	Champagne	"	"
RSW6/8	Goblet	"	"
RSW6/12	Highball	"	"
RSW6/19	Sundae Dish	"	"
	Fruit Bowl	"	"
RSW8/1	Candlestick	Clear, Blue, Amethyst or Topaz	
RSW8/2	Candlestick	"	"
RSW9/21 (SG9/21)	Brandy Glass 8 oz/23 cl	Clear	
RSW9/22 (SG9/22)	Brandy Glass 12 oz/34 cl	"	
RSW9/23 (SG9/23)	Brandy Glass 20 oz/57 cl	"	
RSW10	Vase with sheared top	Clear, Blue, Amethyst, Topaz, Cranberry, Orange, or White Opal	
RSW11/1 (SG11/1)	Domed Paperweight	Clear, Blue, Amethyst, Topaz, Yellow, Pink, Pale Blue, White, Opal, Green Blue Speckle, Pink Speckle Turquoise Speckle or Green Speckle	
RSW11/2	Domed Paperweight	"	
RSW11/3	Domed Paperweight	Clear	
RSW11/4	Domed Paperweight	Clear	
RSW13/1 (SG13/1)*	Candleholder (1 ring) 3.5 in/9 cm	Clear, Blue, Amethyst, Topaz or Green	'Sheringham'
RSW13/2 (SG13/2)*	Candleholder (2 ring) 4.75 in/15 cm	"	"
RSW13/3 (SG13/3)*	Candleholder (3 ring) 6 in/15.5 cm	"	"
RSW13/5*	Candleholder (5 ring)	"	"
RSW13/7*	Candleholder (7 ring)	"	"
RSW13/9*	Candleholder (9 ring)	"	"
RSW14	Cut Paperweight	Clear, Blue, Amethyst, Topaz, Yellow, Pink, Pale Blue, White Opal or Green	'Galaxy'
RSW15/1 (SG15/1)*	Candleholder 5.5 in/ 14 cm	Clear, Blue, Amethyst or Topaz	'Brancaster'
RSW15/2 (SG15/2)*	Candleholder 8 in/20.5 cm	"	"
RSW15/3 (SG15/3)*	Candleholder 11 in/28 cm	"	"
RSW16/1*	Candleholder 4.25 in/ 11 cm	Clear, Blue, Amethyst, Topaz or Green	'Cromer'
RSW16/2*	Candleholder 6 in/15.5 cm	"	"
RSW16/3*	Candleholder 8.25 in/21 cm	"	"
RSW19/1	Salad Bowl, 6 in/15.5 cm	"	

RSW19/2	Salad Bowl, 8 in/20.5 cm	″	
RSW20/1/2/3 (SG20/1)	Cylindrical Vase, 7.75 in/20 cm	Clear, Blue, Amethyst, Topaz, Cranberry, Orange or White Opal	
RSW21/1/2	Lipped Vase	″	
RSW22/1 (SG22/1)*	Candlestick, 5 in/12.75 cm	Clear, Blue, Amethyst, Topaz or Green	'Sandringham'
RSW22/2 (SG22/2)*	Candlestick, 6.5 in/17 cm	″	″
RSW22/3 (SG22/3)*	Candlestick, 7.75 in/20 cm	″	″
RSW22/4 (SG22/4)*	Candlestick, 9.5 in/24 cm	″	″
RSW25 (SG25)	Textured Tall Vase, 10 in/25.5 cm	Blue or Topaz	
RSW26	Textured Posy Vase	Clear, Blue, Amethyst or Topaz	
RSW27 (SG27)	Embossed Dish, 5 in/ 12.75 cm	Clear, Blue, Amethyst, Topaz or Green	
RSW30	Rose Vase	Clear, Blue, Amethyst or Topaz	
RSW31 (CT31)/18	Spirit Decanter	Clear	'Rushton'
RSW32 (CT32)/18	Spirit Decanter	″	'Denford'
RSW33 (CT33)/18	Spirit Decanter	″	'Ashbourne'
RSW34 (CT34)/18	Spirit Decanter	″	'Alton'
RSW35/1	Plain or Cut Dish 5 in/ 12.75 cm	Clear, Blue, Amethyst, Topaz or Cranberry	
RSW35/2	Plain or Cut Dish 7 in/ 18 cm	″	
RSW35/3	Plain or Cut Dish 9 in/ 23 cm	″	
RSW36 (ST36)	Small Sherry 6 cl	Clear	'Fenland'
	Large Sherry 8 cl	″	″
	White Wine 17 cl	″	″
	Red Wine 20 cl	″	″
	Goblet 25 cl	″	″
RSW37/1 #(CT32/CT33/CT37)/1	Liqueur	Cut Lead Crystal Clear	'Norfolk' only 'Denford' (32), 'Ashbourne'(33) 'Norfolk' (37)
RSW37/3	Sherry	″	″
RSW37/5	Claret	″	″
RSW37/6	Hock	″	″
RSW37/7T	Champagne, Tall	″	″
RSW37/7B	Champagne, Bowl	″	″

RSW37/8	Goblet	"	"
RSW37/8L	Goblet, Large	"	"
RSW37/10	Tumbler, 5 oz/14 cl	"	"
RSW37/11	Tumbler, 10 oz/28.5 cl	"	"
RSW37/13	Highball, 12 oz/34 cl	"	"
RSW37/14 (CT/14)	Wine Decanter	"	('Norfolk' only)
RSW37/14S (CT/14S)	Ship's Decanter	"	"
RSW37/18 (CT/18)	Spirit Decanter	"	"
	Grapefruit	"	"
	Jug, 1 Pint/28 cl	"	"
RSW37/24	Ice Bucket	"	"
RSW37/25	Martini Mixer	"	"
RSW38/1			
#(CT31/CT34/CT38)/1	Liqueur 5.5 cl	Cut lead crystal Clear	('Blakeney' only) 'Rushton' (31) 'Alton' (34) 'Blakeney' (38)
RSW38/3	Sherry 8.5 cl	"	"
RSW38/5	Claret 14 cl	"	"
RSW38/6	Hock 14.5 cl	"	"
RSW38/7T	Champagne, Tall 14 cl	"	"
RSW38/7B	Champagne, Bowl 20 cl	"	"
RSW38/8	Goblet 20 cl	"	"
RSW38/8L	Goblet, Large 34 cl	"	"
RSW38/10	Tumbler, 5 oz /14 cl	"	"
RSW38/11	Tumbler, 10 oz /28.5 cl	"	"
RSW38/13	Highball, 12 oz /34 cl	"	"
RSW38/14 (CT38/14)	Wine Decanter	"	('Blakeney' only)
RSW38/14S(CT38/14S)	Ship's Decanter	"	"
RSW38/18 (CT38/18)	Spirit Decanter	"	"
	Grapefruit	"	"
	Jug, 1 Pint /57 cl	"	"
RSW38/24	Ice Bucket	"	"
RSW38/25	Martini Mixer	"	"
RSW39/1 (SG39/1)	Squat Tankard 15oz/ 35 cl	Clear, Blue, Amethyst or Topaz	
RSW39/2	Tankard 20 oz/57 cl (4 in/ 10.25 cm)	"	
RSW43 (SG43)	Decanter with stopper entrapping air bubbles	Clear, Blue or Topaz	
RSW44	Footed Decanter	"	'Sandringham'
RSW46	Claret Jug	"	
RSW47/10	Tumbler, 5 oz/14 cl	Clear	

RSW47/11	Tumbler, 10 oz/28.5 cl	Clear	
RSW52	Stemmed Fruit Bowl	Clear, Blue, Amethyst or Topaz	
RSW53	Compote	″	
RSW54/3	Sherry	Clear	'Breckland'
RSW54/5	Claret	″	″
RSW54/8	Goblet	″	″
RSW54/8L	Large Goblet	″	
RSW55/1	Bowl, 5 in/12.75 cm	Clear, Blue, Amethyst or Topaz	
RSW55/2	Bowl, 7.5 in/19 cm		
RSW55/3	Bowl, 8.5 in/21.75 cm	″	
RSW57	Oil/Vinegar Bottle	Clear, Blue, Amethyst or Topaz	
RSW58 (SG58)*	Candleholder/ Posy Vase 4 in/10.25 cm	Clear, Blue, Amethyst, Topaz or Green	
RSW60 (SG60)	Whisky Decanter with Dimpled base	Clear, Blue or Topaz	
RSW70 (SG70)	Small Bird	Assorted Colours	
RSW71 (SG71)	Large Bird	″	
	Large Bird Set of 4	Assorted Speckled Colours	
RSW72 (SG72)	Penguin	Assorted Colours	
RSW73 (SG73)	Long-tailed Bird	Cream-brown Speckle	
	Long-tailed Bird Set of 4	Assorted Speckled Colours	
RSW74 (SG74)	Fish (set of four)	Assorted Specked Colours	
RSW75	Tumbler, 9 oz/25 cl	Clear, Blue or Topaz	
RSW90/2/3	Vases Clear or Tortoise-shell		
RSW102/1/2	Bowls	Clear, Blue or Topaz	
RSW103/1/2/3	Vases (three sizes)	Rose/Rose, Blue/Blue, Green/Green, Orange/ Yellow	
RSW103/4	Tall Vase	″	
RSW103/5	Globe Vase	″	
RSW103/6	Bowl	″	
RSW110	Vases - set of 4	Assorted Speckled Colours	
RSW122	Vase	Clear, Blue, Amethyst or Topaz	
RSW125/5	Claret	Clear	'Atlantic'
RSW125/10	Tumbler (Pony), 5 oz/14 cl	″	
RSW125/11	Old Fashioned (Beer)	″	″

RSW125/13	Highball	″	″
RSW125/5	Claret	Blue	'Blue Pacific'
RSW125/10	Tumbler (Pony), 5 oz/14 cl	″	″
RSW125/11	Old Fashioned (Beer)	″	″
RSW125/13	Highball	″	″
RSW125/5	Claret	Topaz	'Sterling'
RSW125/10	Tumbler (Pony), 5 oz/14cl	″	″
RSW125/11	Old Fashioned (Beer)	″	″
RSW125/13	Goblet	″	″
RSW128/13	Boxed Pair Tumblers		
RSW140 (SG140)	Owl	Assorted Colours	
RSW141	Egg	Clear or Speckled Brown	
RSW152 (SG152)*	Candleholder, 4.5 in/ 11.5 cm	Clear, Blue, Topaz or Green	
RSW156/25 (SG156)/25	Martini Mixer	Clear	
RSW157 (SG157)	Tankard, 10 oz/28.5 cl	Clear or Blue	
RSW161/14 (SG161)/14	Spirit Decanter	Clear or Green	
RSW167/5	Claret	Clear	'Stonehenge'
RSW167/8	Goblet	″	″
RSW167/19	Sundae Dish	″	″
RSW173 (SG173)*	Table Lantern, 6in/ 15.5 cm	Clear, Blue or Green	
RSW191 (SG191)*	Candleholder, 11 in/ 28 cm	Clear or Tortoise-shell	
RSW203	Cameo Goblet	Blue	
RSW206/3	Sherry	Lead Crystal	'Ely'
RSW206/5	Claret	″	
RSW206/6	Hock	″	″
RSW206/8	Goblet	″	″
RSW206/8L	Goblet, Large	″	″
RSW206/10	Tumbler, 5oz/14 cl	″	″
RSW206/11	Tumbler, 10oz/28.5 cl	″	″
RSW206/12	Tumbler, 12oz/34 cl	″	″
RSW207/3	Sherry	″	'Brandon'
RSW207/5	Claret	″	″
RSW207/6	Hock	″	″
RSW207/8	Goblet	″	″
RSW207/8L	Goblet, Large	″	″
RSW207/10	Tumbler, 5oz/14 cl	″	″
RSW207/11	Tumbler, 10oz/28.5 cl	″	″
RSW207/12	Tumbler, 12oz/34 cl	″	″
RSW217	Pendant	Crystal—Clear, Clear/ Blue, /Amethyst, /Topaz, /Green	

RSW219 (SG219)	Mushroom	Assorted Colours	
RSW225/1	Vase	Blue, Topaz or Green	
RSW225/2	Plain Dish, 10 in/25.5cm	″	
RSW225/3	Round Bowl	″	
RSW225/4	Oval Bowl	″	
RSW230 (SG230)	Apple	″	
RSW231 (SG231)	Pear	″	
RSW232 (SG232)	Duck	″	
RSW233 (SG233)	Partridge	″	
RSW234 (SG234)	Whale	″	
RSW236/1	Small Mouse	″	
RSW236/2	Large Mouse	″	
RSW237 (SG237)	Seal	″	
RSW251/1/2/3	Square Vases	Clear, Tortoise-shell, Speckled Blue or Speckled Green	
RSW252/1/2/3	Hexagonal Vases	Clear, Tortoise-shell, Speckled Blue or Speckled Green	
RSW261	Ashtray, Large or Small	Lead Crystal	'Blakeney'
RSW267 (SG267)	Polar Bear	Assorted Colours	
RSW268/3	Sherry	Lead Crystal	'Norwich'
RSW268/5	Claret	″	″
RSW268/6	Hock	″	″
RSW268/8	Goblet	″	″
RSW268/8L	Goblet, Large	″	″
RSW268/10	Tumbler, 5oz/14 cl	″	″
RSW268/11	Tumbler, 10oz/28.5 cl	″	″
RSW268/12	Tumbler, 12 oz/34 cl	″	″
RSW268/16	Spirit Decanter, Round	″	″
RSW269/3	Sherry	Lead Crystal	'Burnham'
RSW269/5	Claret	″	″
RSW269/6	Hock	″	″
RSW269/8	Goblet	″	″
RSW269/8R	Goblet, Large	″	″
RSW269/10	Tumbler, 5oz/14 cl	″	″
RSW269/11	Tumbler, 10oz/28.5 cl	″	″
RSW269/12	Tumbler, 12oz/34 cl	″	″
RSW270/3	Sherry	Lead Crystal	'Dereham'
RSW270/5	Claret	″	″
RSW270/8	Goblet	″	″
RSW270/8L	Goblet, Large	″	″
RSW270/10	Tumbler, 5 oz/14 cl	″	″

RSW270/11	Tumbler, 10 oz/28.5 cl	″	″
RSW270/12	Tumbler, 12oz/34 cl	″	″
RSW270/16	Spirit Decanter, Round	″	″
RSW280 (CG280)	Vase	Lead Crystal	
RSW281 (CG281)	Spirit Decanter, Round	″	'Matlock'
RSW282	Cake Stand	″	″
RSW290 (CG290)*	Candlestick	″	
RSW291 (CG291)*	Candlestick	″	″
RSW403 (SG403)	Hedgehog	Assorted Colours	
RSW404 (SG404)	Frog	″	
RSW405 (SG405)	Elephant—Trunk up	″	
RSW406 (SG406)	Cat	″	
RSW409 (SG409)	Elephant—Trunk Down	″	
RSW410 (SG410)	Squirrel	″	
RSW411 (SG411)	Seashell	″	
RSW412 (SG412)	Paperweight	″	'Spindrift'
RSW413	Rabbit	″	
RSW414 (SG414)	Heart Paperweight	Clear, Blue, Amethyst Topaz or Green	
RSW416 (SG416)	Otter	Assorted Colours	
RSW422	Leaping Dolphin	Lead Crystal	
RSW423 (SG423)	Spherical Paperweight	Topaz and White	'Seafern'
	Spherical Paperweight	Amethyst and White	″
	Spherical Paperweight	Blue and White	″
	Spherical Paperweight	Green and White	″
	Spherical Paperweight	Pink and White	″
	Spherical Paperweight	Turquoise and Green	″
RSW424 (SG424)	Spherical Paperweight	Blue and Lilac	'Stardance'
	Spherical Paperweight	Green and Pink	″
	Spherical Paperweight	Pink and Lilac	″
	Spherical Paperweight	Pink and Blue	″
	Spherical Paperweight	Topaz and Lilac	″
	Spherical Paperweight	Topaz and Blue	″
RSW425 (SG425)	Duckling	Assorted Colours	
RSW429 (SG429)	Fledgling	″	
RSW600 (SG600)	Tankard, 20 oz/57 cl	Clear or Blue	
RSW626	Textured Vase, 8.25 ins/ 21 cm	Clear, Blue, Topaz or Green	
RSW627	Textured Bowl	″	
RSW628/24 (SG628)/24	Ice Bucket, 4.25 in/11cm with Stainless Steel Handle	Clear	
RSW807	Lipped Vase	Blue/Green	
RSW808	Lipped Vase	″	

RSW809	Shell Vase (Cornucopia)	Assorted Speckled Colours	
CG110/11	Old Fashioned 28.5 cl	Lead Crystal	'Derwent'
CG110/18	Spirit Decanter	"	"
CG111/11	Old Fashioned 28.5 cl	Lead Crystal	'Dove'
CG111/18	Spirit Decanter	"	"
CG126	Textured Vase	"	
CG142	Marmalade Pot	"	
CG143	Honey Pot	"	
CG144	Bud Vase	"	
CG146	Posy Vase, Large	"	
CG148	Posy Vase, Small	"	
CG150	Stem Vase	"	
CG151	Bottle Vase	"	
CG251/C	Cream	Lead Crystal	
CG251/S	Sugar Bowl	"	
CG252/C	Cream	"	
CG252/S	Sugar Bowl	"	
CG281	Spirit Decanter	"	'Matlock'
CG312/B	Tea Bell	"	'Bakewell'
	Tea Bell	"	'Denford'
	Tea Bell	"	'Ashbourne'
	Tea Bell	"	'Buckingham'
	Tea Bell	"	'Windsor'
	Tea Bell	"	'Balmoral'
CG324/B	Ring Stand	"	
CG325/B	Dinner Bell	"	'Denford'
	Dinner Bell	"	'Ashbourne'
	Dinner Bell	"	'Matlock'
CG328	Beer Tankard, 1 pint/57 cl	"	
CG329	Lager Tankard, .5 Pint/ 28 cl	"	
CG337/11	Old Fashioned Tumblers (pair)	"	
CG337/22	Brandy Balloons (pair) 12oz/34 cl	"	
CG338	Rose Bowl, Large	"	
CG339	Rose Bowl, Small	"	
CG340	Bowl, Large	"	
CG341	Bowl, Small	"	
CG357	Mustard Pot	"	
CG363	Salt/Pepper Pair	"	
SG4	Tumbler 23 cl	Clear	
SG5	Tumbler 25 cl	"	

SG14	Decanter	Lead Crystal	
SG14S	Ship's Decanter	"	
SG216	Town Crier Bell	Blue, Amethyst, Topaz or Green	
SG268	Snail	Assorted Colours	
SG325	Abbey Bell	Lead Crystal	
SG412	Spherical Paperweight	Assorted Colours	'Spindrift'
SG414	Heart Paperweight	Clear, Blue, Amethyst, Topaz or Green	
SG415	Zodiac Paperweight	Clear	Twelve signs
SG417	Dolphin	Assorted colours	
SG418	Scotty Dog/Terrier	"	
SG420	Seated Dog/Puppy	"	
SG421	Panda	Dark and White	
SG422	Rabbit Medium Sized	Assorted colours	
SG427	Hare	"	
SG428	Parrot	Blue/Yellow, Blue/Pink, Blue/Green	
SG430	Spherical Paperweight	Clear encasing Pink, Blue or Yellow 'ribbons'	'Maypole'
SG431	Spherical Paperweight	Assorted Colours	'Harlequin'
SG432	Stoat	Assorted Colours	
SG434	Small Penguin	"	
SG435	Spherical Paperweight	"	'Galactic'
SG438	Robin	Red and Brown	
SG439	Pig	Assorted Colours	
SG442	Leaping Dolphin	Lead Crystal	
SG449	Teddy Bear	Assorted Colours	
SG450	Baby Elephant	Clear, Speckled Pink	
SG451	Jumbo	Speckled Pink	
SG461	Hippo	Assorted Colours	
SG462	Candlestick S/S–Floral	"	'Aztec'
SG463	Candlestick M/S	"	"
SG601/1*	Candlestick, 4 in/ 10.25 cm	Clear, Blue, Amethyst, Topaz or Green	'Helix'
SG601/2*	Candlestick, 5.5 in/ 14 cm	"	"
SG601/3*	Candlestick, 7 in/18 cm	"	"
SG602 *	Candlestick, 3.5 in/9 cm	"	'Whorl'
SG615/1	Candlestick Floral 5.5 in/ 14 cm	"	'Brancaster'
SG615/2	Candlestick Floral 8 in/ 20.5 cm	"	"

SG615/3	Candlestick Floral 11in/ 28 cm	″	″
SG622/1	Candlestick Floral 5 in/ 13 cm	″	'Sandringham'
SG622/2	Candlestick Floral 6.5 in/ 16.75 cm	″	″
SG622/3	Candlestick Floral 7.75 in/ 20 cm	″	″
SG622/4	Candlestick Floral 9.75 in/ 25 cm	″	″
SG801	Vase, 7.5 in/19 cm	″	
SG802	Vase	Speckled Blue/Green	
SG803	Vase, 6.5 in/16.75 cm	″	
SG804	Vase	″	
SG900	Elephant Ring Stand	Lead Crystal	
CJG112	Cameo Drum Paperweight 3.5 in/ 8 cm	Lead Crystal	
CJG114	Cameo Pumpkin Paperweight 3.5 in/8 cm	″	
SJ13/1	Royal Blue/White Jasper Cameo Queen Elizabeth Candlestick—1 ring	Amethyst	'Sheringham'
SJ39/2	Royal Blue/White Cameo Tankard—Queen Elizabeth/ Prince Philip	Amethyst	
SJ39/2	Etched Tankard	″	
SJ161	Silver Jubilee Royal Coat of Arms Etched Decanter	Clear	
SJ211	Silver Jubilee Etched Goblet	″	
SJ215	Silver Jubilee Royal Blue/ White Cameo Bell	Amethyst	
SJ302	Light Blue/White Cameo Goblet—Queen Elizabeth/ Prince Philip	Blue	
SJ331	Royal Blue/White Queen Elizabeth Cameo Orb Paperweight	Lead Crystal	

SJ415	Royal Blue/White Queen Elizabeth II Cameo Paperweight	″	
SJG39/1	Light Blue/White Jasper Cameo (G1000) Tankard	Blue	
	Black/White Jasper Cameo (G4000) Tankard	Topaz	
SJG191	Decanter	Clear	
SJG211	Goblet	″	
SJG215	Light Blue/White Jasper Cameo Bells	Blue with Clear Handle	
	Black/White Jasper Cameo Bell	Topaz with Clear Handle	
SJG415	Inset Paperweight	Lead Crystal	
218	Christmas Goblet	Clear	
312	Anniversary Bells	Lead Crystal	
314	Anniversary Goblets	″	
426	Anniversary Plaques	″	
600	Anniversary Tankards	″	
5001	Apple	Lead Crystal—Clear and Assorted Colours	'Lilliput'
5002	Dolphin	″	″
5003	Duck	″	″
5004	Duckling	″	″
5005	Elephant	″	″
5006	Mushroom	″	″
5007	Owl	″	″
5008	Penguin	″	″
5009	Polar Bear	″	″
5010	Shell	″	″
5011	Snail	″	″
5012	Whale	″	″
5013	Long-Tailed Bird	″	″
5014	Squirrel	″	″
5015	Frog	″	″
5016	Hippo	″	″
5017	Hedgehog	″	″
5018	Hare	″	″
5019	Norfolk Pig	″	″
5020	Pear	″	″
5021	Miniature Leaping Dolphin	″	″
5022	Teddy Bear	″	″

*candles were available in white, blue, purple, amethyst, orange, green, pink, and red to co-ordinate with and fit candlesticks and candleholders.

In the mid-1970s though the existing number for current items remained the same, the alphabetical code was changed from RSW to SG. Additional codes—CG, CJG, SJ (Silver Jubilee of Queen Elizabeth's accession—1977), SJG, and ST—were introduced from that time also.

All documentation in the early 1970s used the imperial system. As the change to the decimal system occurred during the period of production and in keeping with the convention of using dual measurements—imperial and metric—after the latter's introduction, both systems have been applied to items originally measured only in the imperial system. In the later years of the decade and into the 1980s the decimal system was in universal use. Many suites of drinkware never indicated the volume of the glasses or jugs. No attempt has been made to give the measures.

Appendix 2 — Galway Crystal Gift Items (1978)

Code	Shape	Design
B1101	Salad Bowl 9 in/23 cm	'Clifden'
B1102	Salad Bowl 8 in/20.5 cm	'Blarney'
B1103	Footed Bowl	'Avoca'
B1106	Fruit Basket	'Galway Sunset'
B1107	Fruit Basket	'Dublin'
B1108	Flower Basket s/s	'Kilcogan'
B1109	Flower Basket s/s	"
B1110	Salad Bowl 6 in/15.5 cm	'Ballymagibbon'
D1501	Georgian Bottle	
D1503	Claret Jug	'Galway Sunset'
D1505	Oblong Decanter	'Dublin'
D1507	Square Decanter	'Ronayne'
D1508	Yachtsman's Bottle	
D1511	Ship's Decanter	'Sealord'
D1512	Square Decanter	'Westport'
D1513	Square Decanter	'Ardee'
D1514	Square Decanter	'Dromoland'
D1515	Claret Jug	'Brandon'
D1516	Claret Jug	'Galway Bay'
E1609	Craftsman's Bowl	
E1612	Chalice	
J1701	Jewellery Heart	'Orla'
J1702	Jewellery Prism	'Grainne'
J1703	Jewellery Prism	'Sinead'
J1704	Jewellery Oblong Cross	'Fiona'
J1705	Jewellery Oblong Star	'Cliona'
J1707	Jewellery Harp	'Mairin'
J1709	Jewellery Pyramid	'Roisin'
J1710	Jewellery Cone	'Siobhan'
L2001	Lamp Base 14 in/35.5 cm	'Belfast'
L2002	Lamp Base 14 in/35.5 cm	'Donegal'
L2003	Lamp Base 18 in/46 cm	'Ballycastle'
L2004	Lamp Base 18 in/46 cm	'Antrim'
M1301	Honey Jar	'Blarney'
M1304	Candlestick 4 in/10.25 cm	'Tuam'
M1320	Candlestick 4 in/10.25 cm	'Connemara'
M1305	Candlestick 7 in/18 cm	'Shannon'

M1321	Candlestick 7 in/18 cm	'Blarney'
M1322	Brandy Glass	'Barna'
M1329	Liqueur 6 Pack	'Erin'
M1330	Dinner Bell	'Killary'
M1331	Dinner Bell	'Roscam'
M1332	Dinner Bell	'Shandon'
M1335	Salt	'Rosslare'
M1336	Pepper	"
M1337	Mustard	"
M1338	Covered Mustard	"
M1339	Coaster	'Leitrim'
M1340	Candy Box	'Bunratty'
M1341	Marmalade Pot	'Kells'
M1343	Sugar Bowl	'Dingle'
M1344	Cream Jug	"
M1345	Covered Sugar Bowl	'Kilronan'
M1346	Footed Cream Jug	"
M1347	Tankard	'Dunloe'
M1348	Ring Holder	'Kerry'
M1349	Ginger Jar	'Cara'
M1350	Water Jug—.5 pint/28 cl	'Blarney'
M1351	Bonbonnier	'Old Cork'
M1352	Compote 6 in/15.5 cm	'Clifden'
M1353	Compote 6 in/15.5 cm	'Donegal'
M1354	Ginger Jar	'O'Malley'
M1355	Candlestick 4 in/10.25 cm	'Navan'
M1356	Oil/Vinegar Bottle	'Ballinrobe'
M1357	Bon-bon Dish 8 in/20.5 cm	'Bantry'
M1359	Shot Glass	'Barna'
M1360	Ice Bucket	'Ballina'
M1362	Dinner Bell	'Burren'
M1364	Tea Bell	'Roscam'
M1365	Tea Bell	'Burren'
M1366	Marmalade Pot	'Clifden'
M1367	Open Salt	'Adare'
M1368	Butter Dish 4 in/10.25 cm	'Achill'
S1401	Cigarette Box/Ashtray Lid	'Ronayne'
S1416	Cigarette Urn	'Cleggan'
S1417	Ashtray 5 in/12.75 cm	'Corrib'
S1418	Ashtray 7 in/18 cm	"
S1419	Ashtray 5 in/12.75 cm	'Shannon'
S1420	Ashtray 5 in/12.75 cm	'Delga'
S1421	Ashtray 5 in/12.75 cm	'O'Connell'
S1422	Footed Cigarette Urn	'Claddagh'

S1424	Ashtray 4 in/10.25 cm	'Ballyroan'
V1201	Vase 9 in/23 cm	'Gaelic'
V1204	Vase 10 in/25.5 cm	'Tralee'
V1205	Vase 9 in/23 cm	'Wicklow'
V1207	Violet Vase 3 in/7.75 cm	'Lynch'
V1216	Bud Vase 6 in/15.5 cm	'Ardagh'
V1217	Vase 8 in/20.5 cm	'Kinrara'
V1218	Vase 11 in/28 cm	'Bantry'
V1219	Bud Vase 7 in/18 cm	'Old Cork'
V1220	Bud Vase 7 in/18 cm	'Salthill'
V1221	Violet Vase 3 in/7.75 cm	'Mallow'
V1222	Vase 9 in/23 cm	'Westport'
V1223	Vase 6 in/15.5 cm	'Sligo'
V1224	Vase 6 in/15.5 cm	'Sheelin'
V1235	Presentation Vase	'Antrim'
V1237	Vase 9 in/23 cm	'Lahinch'
V1238	Vase 9 in/23 cm	'Fermoy'
V1239	Vase 6 in/15.5 cm	'Kanturn'
V1240	Vase 9 in/23 cm	'Kilkenny'
V1241	9 in/23 cm	'Clare'
V1242	Vase 7 in/18 cm	'Mayo'
V1243	Vase 4 in/10.25 cm	'Athlone'
V1244	Vase 6 in/15.5 cm	"
V1245	Vase 8 in/20.5 cm	"
V1246	Vase 6 in/15.5 cm	'Moy'
V1247	Vase 7 in/18 cm	'Clonmel'
V1249	Violet Vase 3 in/7.75 cm	'Larne'
V1250	Vase 10 in/25.5 cm	'Furbo'

Appendix 3 — Galway Crystal (1978)

Code	Shape	Pattern
1	Decanter	'Aran', 'Ashford', 'Burren', 'Castlerosse', 'Claddagh', 'Clifden', 'Galway Oyster', 'Killarney', 'O'Brien', 'O'Donnell', 'Old Galway', 'O'Malley', 'Royal Irish'
2	Water Jug	All patterns
2A	Carafe	All patterns with the exception of 'Galway Oyster' and 'Royal Irish'
3	Saucer Champagne	All patterns
3A	Tall Champagne	All patterns with the exception of 'Burren' and O'Malley
4A	Goblet L/S	All patterns
5	Wine L/S	"
6	Sherry/Port	"
7	Tall Hock	All patterns with the exception of 'Burren' and O'Malley
8	Liqueur	All patterns
9	Wine S/S	All patterns with the exception of 'Burren' and O'Malley
11	Small Whiskey	All patterns
12	Tumbler	"
12A	Tumbler L/S	"
13	Highball	"
14	Brandy	All patterns with the exception of 'Galway Oyster' 'Royal Irish', 'Old Galway' and 'Killarney'
16	Nut Bowl	All patterns

Appendix 4 — English County Crystal

Code	Australian Code	Canadian Code	Shape	Colour	Design
FJT2/1	6435-640		Stem Bud Vase S/S 235 mm	Midnight	'Grace'
FJT2/2	6435-641		Stem Bud Vase M/S 265 mm	Midnight	″
FJT2/3			Stem Bud Vase L/S 286 mm	Midnight	″
FJT3	6435-645		Bud Vase 170 mm	Midnight	'Adam'
FJT4	6435-650		Footed Bud Vase 160 mm	Midnight	'Sarah'
FJT4/M/O			Footed Bud Vase 160 mm	Midnight Optic	″
FJT4/C/O			Footed Bud Vase 160 mm	Clear Optic	″
FJT4/C		- 221/8520	Footed Bud Vase 190 mm	Clear	″
FJT5/1	6435-660		Chinese Vase S/S 100 mm	Midnight	'Orson'
FJT5/2	6435-661		Chinese Vase M/S 125mm	Midnight	″
FJT5/3	6435-662		Chinese Vase L/S 150 mm	Midnight	″
FJT5/1/M/O			Chinese Vase S/S 100 mm	Midnight Optic	″
FJT5/2/M/O			Chinese Vase M/S 125mm	Midnight Optic	″
FJT5/3/M/O			Chinese Vase L/S 150 mm	Midnight Optic	″
FJT6/1	6435-655		Hexagonal Vase S/S 160 mm	Midnight	'Brutus'
FJT6/2	6435-656		Hexagonal Vase M/S 210 mm	Midnight	″
FJT6/3	6435-657		Hexagonal Vase L/S 255 mm	Midnight	″
FJT6/4	6435-675		Fruit Bowl 190 mm wide	Midnight	″
FJT6/5	6435-676		Serving Bowl 150 mm wide	Midnight	″
FJT6/6	6435-677		Cocktail Dish 105 mm wide	Midnight (pair)	″
FJT6/7	6435-691		Ice Bucket 135 mm	Midnight	″
FJT6/8	6435-690		Vase 110 mm	Midnight	″
FJT7/1*	6435-620		Candleholder S/S 110 mm	Midnight (White)	'George'
FJT7/1/C*			Candleholder S/S 110 mm	Clear (White)	″
FJT7/3*	6435-621		Candleholder L/S 140 mm	Midnight (Red)	″
FJT7/3/C*			Candleholder L/S 140 mm	Clear (Red)	″
FJT7/CDL/W			Candle for 'Arthur/George'	White	
FJT7/CDL/R			Candle for 'Arthur/George'	Red	
FJT8	6435-665		Rose Bowl 120 mm	Midnight	'Juliet'
FJT8/M/O			Rose Bowl 120 mm	Midnight	″
FJT9	6435-625		Nightlight 125 mm	Midnight	'Celia'
FJT9/M/O			Nightlight 125 mm	Midnight Optic	″
FJT9/NL			Nightlight for 'Celia'	White	
FJT12	6435-630		Candlelamp 175 mm	Midnight	'Rory'
FJT12/M/O			Candlelamp 175mm	Midnight Optic	″
FJT13/M			Admiral's Decanter 1.1 litres	Midnight	'Horatio'
FJT13/C	6424-600		Admiral's Decanter 1.1 litres	Clear	″
FJT13/JUS			Admiral's Decanter 1.1 litres	Cut Crystal	'Justine'
FJT13/SAN			Admiral's Decanter 1.1 litres	Cut Crystal	'Sandringham'
FJT13/WAL			Admiral's Decanter 1.1 litres	Cut Crystal	'Walsingham'

FJT14/M		Decanter 70 cl	Midnight	'Gaston'
FJT14/M/O		Decanter 70 cl	Midnight Optic	″
FJT14/C	6424-601	Decanter 70 cl	Clear	″
FJT14/C/O		Decanter 70 cl	Clear Optic	″
FJT15/M		Decanter 75 cl	Midnight	'Marcel'
FJT15/M/O		Decanter 75 cl	Midnight Optic	″
FJT15/C	6424-602	Decanter 75 cl	Clear	″
FJT15/C/O		Decanter 75 cl	Clear Optic	″
FJT16/M		Water Jug 85 cl	Midnight	'Alexander'
FJT16/M/O		Water Jug 85 cl	Midnight Optic	″
FJT16/C	6424-610	Water Jug 85 cl	Clear	″
FJT16/C/O		Water Jug 85 cl	Clear Optic	″
FJT20/M	6425-415	Irish Coffee 17.5 cl	Midnight (pair)	'Seamus'
FJT20/M/O		Irish Coffee 17.5 cl	Midnight Optic	″
FJT21	6435-635	Sugar & Cream	Midnight	'Genevieve'
FJT22/1/M		Sherry 13 cl	Midnight (pair)	'Philippe'
FJT22/2/M		Claret 28 cl	Midnight (pair)	″
FJT22/3/M		Champagne 21 cl	Midnight (pair)	″
FJT22/4/M		Goblet 40 cl	Midnight (pair)	″
FJT22/5/M		Port 10 cl	Midnight (pair)	″
FJT22/6/M		Decanter 1 l	Midnight	″
FJT22/7/M	6425-420	Claret/Tasting Glass 28 cl	Midnight (pair)	″
FJT22/1/C	6424-480	Sherry 13 cl	Clear (pair)	″
FJT22/2/C	6424-481	Claret 28 cl	Clear (pair)	″
FJT22/3/C	6424-482	Champagne 21 cl	Clear (pair)	″
FJT22/4/C	6424-483	Goblet 40 cl	Clear (pair)	″
FJT22/5/C	6424-484	Port 10 cl	Clear (pair)	″
FJT22/6/C	6424-488	Port/ Sherry Decanter 1 litre	Clear	″
FJT22/7/C		Claret/Tasting Glass 28 cl	Clear	″
FJT22/1/JUS		Sherry 13 cl	Cut Crystal	'Justine'
FJT22/2/JUS		Claret 28 cl	Cut Crystal	″
FJT22/3/JUS		Champagne 21 cl	Cut Crystal	″
FJT22/4/JUS		Goblet 40 cl	Cut Crystal	″
FJT22/5/JUS		Port 10 cl	Cut Crystal	″
FJT22/6/JUS		Wine Decanter 1 litre	Cut Crystal	″
FJT23/1/C		Sherry 8 cl	Clear (pair)	'Rebecca'
FJT23/2/C		Claret 18 cl	Clear (pair)	″
FJT23/3/C		Champagne 14 cl	Clear (pair)	″
FJT23/4/C		Goblet 30 cl	Clear (pair)	″
FJT23/1/M		Sherry 8 cl	Midnight (pair)	″
FJT23/2/M		Claret 18 cl	Midnight (pair)	″
FJT23/3/M		Champagne 14 cl	Midnight (pair)	″
FJT23/4/M		Goblet 30 cl	Midnight (pair)	″

FJT24/1/M		Sherry 8 cl	Midnight (pair)	'Olivia'
FJT24/2/M		Claret 19 cl	Midnight (pair)	"
FJT24/3/M		Champagne 16 cl	Midnight (pair)	"
FJT24/4/M		Goblet 26 cl	Midnight (pair)	"
FJT24/1/C	6424-440	Sherry 8 cl	Clear (pair)	"
FJT24/2/C	6424-441	Claret 19 cl	Clear (pair)	"
FJT24/3/C	6424-443	Champagne 16 cl	Clear (pair)	"
FJT24/4/C	6424-442	Goblet 26 cl	Clear (pair)	"
FJT25/1		Hand-cut O-F Tumbler 22 cl	Clear	'Torquil'
FJT25/2		Hand-cut Double O-F Tumbler 34 cl	Clear	"
FJT25/3		Hand-cut Highball 25 cl	Clear	"
FJT25/4		Hand-cut Decanter 85 cl	Clear	"
FJT26/1/M	6425-470	Sherry 8 cl	Midnight (pair)	'Theo'
FJT26/2/M	6425-471	Claret 22.5 cl	Midnight (pair)	"
FJT26/3/M	6425-473	Champagne 19 cl	Midnight (pair)	"
FJT26/4/M	6425-472	Goblet 34 cl	Midnight (pair)	"
FJT26/1/C	6424-470	Sherry 8 cl	Clear (pair)	"
FJT26/2/C	6424-471	Claret 22.5 cl	Clear (pair)	"
FJT26/3/C	6424-473	Champagne 19 cl	Clear (pair)	"
FJT26/4/C	6424-472	Goblet 34 cl	Clear (pair)	"
FJT27/1/M	6425-450	Sherry 7.5 cl	Midnight (pair)	'Portia'
FJT27/2/M	6425-451	Claret 25 cl	Midnight (pair)	"
FJT27/3/M	6425-453	Champagne 12.5 cl	Midnight (pair)	"
FJT27/4/M	6425-452	Goblet 34 cl	Midnight (pair)	"
FJT27/1/C	6424-450	Sherry 7.5 cl	Clear (pair)	"
FJT27/2/C	6424-451	Claret 25 cl	Clear (pair)	"
FJT27/3/C	6424-453	Champagne 12.5 cl	Clear (pair)	"
FJT27/4/C	6424-452	Goblet 34 cl	Clear (pair)	"
FJT30/1	6425-460	O F Tumbler 24 cl	Midnight (pair)	'Rufus'
FJT30/2		Highball 30 cl	Midnight (pair)	"
FJT30/3	6424-460	O F Tumbler 24 cl	Clear (pair)	"
FJT30/4		Highball 30 cl	Clear (pair)	"
FJT30/5		Hand-cut O-F Tumbler 24 cl	Clear	'Tarquin'
FJT30/6		Hand-cut Highball 30 cl	Clear	"
FJT30/7		Hand-cut Decanter 85 cl	Clear	"
FJT30/3/JUS		O F Tumbler 24 cl	Cut Crystal	'Justine'
FJT30/4/JUS		Highball 30 cl	Cut Crystal	"
FJT30/9/JUS		Whisky	Cut Crystal	"
FJT31/M	6435-670	Bracelet Branch 150 mm	Midnight	'Pesce'
FJT31/C		Bracelet Branch 150 mm	Clear	"
FJT32/M	6435-671	Ring Swing 85 mm	Midnight	"
FJT32/C		Ring Swing 85 mm	Clear	"
FJT33/87		Christmas Bell	Cut Crystal	

FJT40	6435-664	Vase 70 mm	Midnight	'Acorn'
FJT41/M	6425-416	Gaelic Coffee 17.5 cl	Midnight (pair)	'Dougall'
FJT41/C		Gaelic Coffee 17.5 cl	Clear (pair)	"
FJT41/JUS		Irish Coffee 17.5 cl	Cut Crystal	'Justine'
FJT42/M		Brandy Balloon 30 cl	Midnight (pair)	'Napoleon'
FJT42/M/O		Brandy Balloon 30 cl	Midnight Optic (pair)	"
FJT42/C		Brandy Balloon 30 cl	Clear (pair)	"
FJT42/C/O		Brandy Balloon 30 cl	Clear Optic (pair)	"
FJT42/JUS		Brandy Balloon 30 cl	Cut Crystal (pair)	'Justine'
FJT43/1/M		Vase S/S 110 mm	Midnight	'Ming'
FJT43/1/M/O	6436-640	Vase S/S 110 mm	Midnight Optic	"
FJT43/1/C/O		Vase S/S 110 mm	Clear Optic	"
FJT43/2/M		Vase M/S 140 mm	Midnight	"
FJT43/2/M/O	6436-641	Vase M/S 140 mm	Midnight Optic	"
FJT43/2/C/O		Vase M/S 140 mm	Clear Optic	"
FJT43/3/M		Vase L/S 180 mm	Midnight	"
FJT43/3/M/O		Vase L/S180 mm	Midnight Optic	"
FJT43/3/C/O		Vase L/S 180 mm	Clear	"
FJT44/M		Ale Tankard 70 cl	Midnight	'Falstaff'
FJT44/C		Ale Tankard 70 cl	Clear	"
FJT44/JUS		Ale Tankard 70 cl	Cut Crystal	'Justine'
FJT45/M	6425-605	Carafe Half Litre	Midnight	'Devon'
FJT45/M/O	6426-605	Carafe Half Litre	Midnight Optic	"
	6426-606	Carafe 1 Litre	Midnight Optic	"
FJT45/C	6424-605	Carafe Half Litre	Clear	"
FJT45/C/O		Carafe Half Litre	Clear Optic	"
FJT46/M	6435-632	Avocado Dish 45 mm	Midnight	'Desmond'
FJT46/C		Avocado Dish 45 mm	Clear	"
FJT49	6435-692	Ice Bucket 130 mm	Midnight	'Eugene'
FJT51/M	6435-626	Oil Lamp 365 mm	Midnight	'Lucifer'
FJT62/M	6435-627	Candlestick 135 mm	Midnight	'Cleo'
FJT62/C		Candlestick 135 mm	Clear	"
FJT62/CDL		Candle for 'Cleo'	White	
FJT63/1/C/O		Sherry	Clear Optic (pair)	'Nicole'
FJT63/2/C/O		Claret	Clear Optic (pair)	"
FJT63/3/C/O		Champagne	Clear Optic (pair)	"
FJT63/4/C/O		Goblet	Clear Optic (pair)	"
FJT65/1/M/O		Vase S/S 105 mm	Midnight Optic	'Alexis'
FJT65/1/C/O		Vase S/S 105 mm	Clear Optic	"
FJT65/2/M/O		Vase M/S 130 mm	Midnight Optic	"
FJT65/2/C/O		Vase M/S 130 mm	Clear Optic	"
FJT65/2/JUS		Vase S/S 135 mm	Cut Crystal	'Justine'
FJT65/3/JUS		Vase M/S 165 mm	Cut Crystal	"

FJT65/4/JUS	Vase L/S 215 mm	Cut Crystal	"
FJT65/2/SAN	Vase S/S 135 mm	Cut Crystal	'Sandringham'
FJT65/3/SAN	Vase M/S 165 mm	Cut Crystal	"
FJT65/4/SAN	Vase L/S 215 mm	Cut Crystal	"
FJT65/2/WAL	Vase S/S 135 mm	Cut Crystal	'Walsingham'
FJT65/3/WAL	Vase M/S 165 mm	Cut Crystal	"
FJT65/4/WAL	Vase L/S 215 mm	Cut Crystal	"
FJT66/1/M/O	Vase S/S 100 mm	Midnight Optic	'Adriana'
FJT66/1/C/O	Vase S/S 100 mm	Clear Optic	"
FJT66/2/M/O	Vase M/S 125 mm	Midnight Optic	"
FJT66/2/C/O	Vase M/S 125 mm	Clear Optic	"
FJT67/1/M/O	Vase S/S 100 mm	Midnight Optic	'Antigone'
FJT67/1/C/O	Vase S/S 100 mm	Clear Optic	"
FJT67/2/M/O	Vase M/S 125 mm	Midnight Optic	"
FJT67/2/C/O	Vase M/S 125 mm	Clear Optic	"
FJT68/M	Candlelamp 215 mm	Midnight	'Stella'
FJT68/C	Candlelamp 215 mm	Clear	"
FJT68/JUS	Candlelamp 215 mm	Cut Crystal	'Justine'
FJT68/CDL	Candle for 'Stella'/'Justine'	White	
FJT69/M	Scent Bottle 95 mm	Midnight	'Danielle'
FJT69/C	Scent Bottle 95 mm	Clear	"
FJT70/M	Scent Bottle 100 mm	Midnight	'Simone'
FJT70/C	Scent Bottle 100 mm	Clear	"
FJT71/M	Scent Bottle 110 mm	Midnight	'Sylvie'
FJT71/C	Scent Bottle 110 mm	Clear	"
FJT73/M	Salt & Pepper 110 mm	Midnight	'Tessa'
FJT73/C	Salt & Pepper 110 mm	Clear	"
FJT75/1/JUS	Rose Bowl S/S 80 mm	Cut Crystal	'Justine'
FJT75/2/JUS	Rose Bowl M/S 115 mm	Cut Crystal	"
FJT76/JUS	Jug .725 litre	Cut Crystal	'Justine'
FJT77/1/JUS	Whisky Tumbler 15 cl	Cut Crystal	"
FJT77/2/JUS	O F Tumbler 25 cl	Cut Crystal	"
FJT77/3/JUS	Highball 29 cl	Cut Crystal	"
FJT77/1/SAN	Whisky Tumbler 15 cl	Cut Crystal	'Sandringham'
FJT77/2/SAN	O F Tumbler 25 cl	Cut Crystal	"
FJT77/3/SAN	Highball 29 cl	Cut Crystal	"
FJT77/1/WAL	Whisky Tumbler 15 cl	Cut Crystal	'Walsingham'
FJT77/2/WAL	O F Tumbler 25 cl	Cut Crystal	"
FJT77/3/WAL	Highball 29 cl	Cut Crystal	"
FJT78/JUS	Square Spirit Decanter 85 cl	Cut Crystal	'Justine'
FJT78/SAN	Square Spirit Decanter 85 cl	Cut Crystal	'Sandringham'
FJT78/WAL	Square Spirit Decanter 85 cl	Cut Crystal	'Walsingham'
FJT81/JUS	Large Bowl 235 mm dia	Cut Crystal	'Justine'
FJT81/SAN	Large Bowl 235 mm dia	Cut Crystal	'Sandringham'

FJT81/WAL		Large Bowl 235 mm dia	Cut Crystal	'Walsingham'
FJT82/JUS		Small Bowl 105 mm dia	Cut Crystal	'Justine'
FJT82/SAN		Small Bowl 105 mm dia	Cut Crystal	'Sandringham'
FJT82/WAL		Small Bowl 105 mm dia	Cut Crystal	'Walsingham'
FJT84/1/M/O		Flower Bowl 125 mm dia	Midnight Optic	'Claire'
FJT84/1/C/O		Flower Bowl 125 mm dia	Clear Optic	"
FJT85/1/M/O		Flower Bowl 125 mm dia	Midnight Optic	'Maria'
FJT85/1/C/O		Flower Bowl 125 mm dia	Clear Optic	"
FJT86/1/M/O		Flower Bowl 125 mm dia	Midnight Optic	'Tara'
FJT86/1/C/O		Flower Bowl 125 mm dia	Clear Optic	"
FJT87/1/M/O		Flower Bowl 125 mm dia	Midnight Optic	'Fleur'
FJT87/1/C/O		Flower Bowl 125 mm dia	Clear Optic	"
FJT88/1		Footed Bowl—Small 145 mm	Clear	'Cybill'
FJT88/2		Footed Bowl—Large 200 mm	Clear	"
FJT88/1/JUS		Footed Bowl—Small 145 mm	Cut Crystal	'Justine'
FJT88/2/JUS		Footed Bowl—Large 200 mm	Cut Crystal	"
FJT89/C		Beer Tankard 65 cl	Clear	'Brendan'
FJT90/C		Small Jug 32.5 cl	Clear	'Clifford'
FJT91/C		Small Jug 37.5 cl	Clear	'Roberta'
FJT91/SAN		Small Jug 37.5 cl	Cut Crystal	'Sandringham'
FJT91/WAL		Small Jug 37.5 cl	Cut Crystal	'Walsingham'
FJT92/1C		Jam/Honey Pot S/S 95mm	Clear	'Georgia'
FJT92/2C		Jam/Honey Pot L/S 105 mm	Clear	"
FJT93/C		Cheese Bell 200 mm	Clear	'Louise'
FJT94/SAN		Small Bell	Cut Crystal	'Sandringham'
FJT94/WAL		Small Bell	Cut Crystal	'Walsingham'
AWH50/1/M	6435-680	Salad/Fruit Serving Dishes 145 mm dia	Midnight (pair)	'Wave'
AWH50/2/M	6435-681	Salad/Fruit Bowl 210 mm dia	Midnight	"
AWH50/3/M	6435-682	Shallow Salad/ Fruit Bowl 245 mm dia	Midnight	"
AWH50/4/M	6435-683	Large Salad/Fruit Bowl 270 mm dia	Midnight	"
AWH50/5/M		Butter Platter 190 mm dia	Midnight	"
AWH50/6/M		Cheese Platter 255 mm dia	Midnight	"
AWH50/7/M		Small Plate 190 mm dia	Midnight	"
AWH50/8/M		Large Plate 255 mm dia	Midnight	"
AWH50/1/C		Salad/Fruit Serving Dishes 145 mm dia	Clear (pair)	"
AWH50/2/C		Salad/Fruit Bowl 210 dia	Clear	"
AWH50/3/C		Shallow/Salad Fruit Bowl 245 mm dia	Clear	"
AWH50/4/C		Large Salad/Fruit Bowl 270 mm dia	Clear	"

AWH50/5/C			Butter Platter 190 mm dia	Clear	"
AWH50/6/C			Cheese Platter 255 mm dia	Clear	"
AWH50/7/C			Small Plate 190 mm dia	Clear	"
AWH50/8/C			Large Plate 255 mm dia	Clear	"
W22/CDL/W*			Candle for 'Diana'	White	
W22/CDL/R*			Candle for 'Diana'	Red	
W29/1/MW*	6435-600		Candlestick 130 mm	Midnight (White)	'Arthur'
W29/1/MR*			Candlestick 130 mm	Midnight (Red)	"
W29/2/MW*	6435-601		Candlestick 190 mm	Midnight (White)	"
W29/2/MR*			Candlestick 190 mm	Midnight (Red)	"
W29/3/MW*	6435-602		Candlestick 265 mm	Midnight (White)	"
W29/3/MR*			Candlestick 265 mm	Midnight (Red)	"
W29/1/CW*			Candlestick 130 mm	Clear (White)	"
W29/1/CR*			Candlestick 130 mm	Clear (Red)	"
W29/2/CW*			Candlestick 190 mm	Clear (White)	"
W29/2/CR*			Candlestick 190 mm	Clear (Red)	"
W29/3/CW*			Candlestick 265 mm	Clear (White)	"
W29/3/CR*			Candlestick 265 mm	Clear (Red)	"
W30/2/MW*	6435-610		Candlestick 130 mm	Midnight (White)	'Diana'
W30/2/MR*			Candlestick 130 mm	Midnight (Red)	"
W30/3/MW*	6435-611		Candlestick 200 mm	Midnight (White)	"
W30/3/MR*			Candlestick 200 mm	Midnight (Red)	"
W30/4/MW*	6435-612		Candlestick 240 mm	Midnight (White)	"
W30/4/MR*			Candlestick 240 mm	Midnight (Red)	"
W30/2/CW*			Candlestick 130 mm	Clear (White)	"
W30/2/CR*			Candlestick 130 mm	Clear (Red)	"
W30/3/CW*			Candlestick 200 mm	Clear (White)	"
W30/3/CR*			Candlestick 200 mm	Clear (Red)	"
W30/4/CW*			Candlestick 240 mm	Clear (White)	"
W30/4/CR*			Candlestick 240 mm	Clear (Red)	"
WUS100/1/M/O	6436-600	-200/8510	Hurricane Candlelamp S/S 225 mm	Midnight Optic	'Devon'
WUS100/2/M/O	6436-601	-201/8510	Hurricane Candlelamp M/S 285 mm	Midnight Optic	"
WUS100/3/M/O	6436-602	-202/8510	Hurricane Candlelamp L/S 365 mm	Midnight Optic	"
		-203/8510	Hurricane Cylinder Lamp 190 mm	Midnight Optic	"
		-203/8520	Hurricane Cylinder Lamp 190 mm	Clear	"
WUS100/1/C		-200/8520	Hurricane Candlelamp S/S 225 mm	Clear	"
WUS100/2/C		-201/8520	Hurricane Candlelamp M/S 285 mm	Clear	"

WUS100/3/C		-202/8520	Hurricane Candlelamp L/S 365 mm	Clear	″
WUS100/1/C/O			Hurricane Candlelamp S/S 225 mm	Clear Optic	″
WUS100/2/C/O			Hurricane Candlelamp M/S 285 mm	Clear Optic	″
WUS100/3/C/O			Hurricane Candlelamp L/S 365 mm	Clear Optic	″
		-219/8520	Hurricane Lamp 210 mm	Clear	″
		-219/8510	Hurricane Lamp 210 mm	Midnight Optic	″
WUS103/M			Carafe 1 Litre	Midnight	″
WUS103/M/O			Carafe 1 Litre	Midnight Optic	″
WUS103/C			Carafe 1 Litre	Clear	″
WUS103/C/O			Carafe 1 Litre	Clear Optic	″
		-205/8510	Carafe 1.2 litres	Midnight Optic	″
		-205/8520	Carafe 1.2 litres	Clear	″
WUS104/M/O		-204/8510	Sugar & Cream	Midnight Optic	″
WUS104/C/O		-204/8520	Sugar & Cream	Clear Optic	″
WUS106/S/M/O	6436-645		Bud Vase 145 mm	Midnight Optic	″
WUS106/S/C		-208/8520	Bud Vase 145 mm	Clear	″
WUS106/L/M/O	6436-646		Floral Vase 220 mm	Midnight Optic	″
WUS106/S/C/O			Bud Vase 220 mm	Clear Optic	″
WUS106/L/C/O		-200/8520	Floral Vase 220 mm	Clear Optic	″
		-211/8510	Posy Vase 165 mm	Midnight Optic	″
		-211/8520	Posy Vase 165 mm	Clear	″
		-212/8510	Bouquet Vase 190 mm	Midnight Optic	″
		-212/8520	Bouquet Vase 190 mm	Clear	″
WUS111/SAN			Candy Box	Cut Crystal	'Sandringham'
WUS111/WAL			Candy Box	Cut Crystal	'Walsingham'
WUS120/M			Ring Candy Box 165 mm	Midnight	'Devon'
WUS120/M/O	6436-620	-218/8510	Ring Candy Box 165 mm	Midnight Optic	″
WUS120/C		-218/8520	Ring Candy Box 165 mm	Clear	″
WUS120/JUS			Ring Candy Box 170 mm	Cut Crystal	'Justine'
		-213/8520	Candlestick 150 mm	Midnight	'Devon'
		-214/8520	Candlestick 205 mm	Midnight	″
		-215/8520	Candlestick 255 mm	Midnight	″
		-206/8510	Salad Bowl 235 mm	Midnight Optic	″
		-210/8510	Rose Bowl 145 mm	Midnight Optic	″
		-216/8520	Jam Pot & Spoon 115 mm	Clear	″
		-217/8510	Mini Candy Box 115 mm	Midnight Optic	″
		-220/8510	Wine Cooler 210 mm	Midnight Optic	″
WUS121/1/M	6435-686		Individual Fruit/Salad Bowl 135 mm dia	Midnight	'Marcus'

WUS121/1/C		Individual Fruit/Salad Bowl 135 mm dia	Clear	"
WUS121/2/M	6435-685	Large Fruit/Salad Bowl 230 mm dia	Midnight	"
WUS121/2/C		Large Fruit/Salad Bowl 230 mm dia	Clear	"
WUS122/M	6435-689	Pudding/Sweets Dishes 132 mm dia	Midnight (pair)	'Charlotte'
WUS122/C		Pudding/Sweets Dishes 132 mm dia	Clear (pair)	"
WUS123/M	6435-615	Tall Comport 155 mm	Midnight	'Helene'
WUS123/C		Tall Comport 155 mm	Clear	"
WUS123/JUS		Tall Comport 155 mm	Cut Crystal	'Justine'
WUS123/M	6435-616	Comport 205 mm dia	Midnight	'Harry'
WUS123/C		Comport 205 mm dia	Clear	"
WUS125/M	6435-628	Candleholder 78 mm	Midnight	'Caligula'
WUS125/C		Candleholder 78 mm	Clear	"
WUS125/CDL		Candle for Caligula	White	
WUS126/C	6424-612	Jug/Pitcher 1.2 Litres	Clear	'Nautilus'
WUS126/C/O		Jug/Pitcher 1.2 Litres	Clear	"
WUS126/JUS		Jug/Pitcher 1.2 Litres	Cut Crystal	'Justine'
WUS126/SAN		Jug/Pitcher 1.2 Litres	Cut Crystal	'Sandringham'
WUS126/WAL		Jug/Pitcher 1.2 Litres	Cut Crystal	'Walsingham'
WUS127/M/O		Cocktail Mixer & Stirrer 1.1 Litres	Midnight Optic	'Zelda'
WUS127/C/O		Cocktail Mixer & Stirrer 1.1 Litres	Clear Optic	"
	6427-615	Cocktail Mixer & Stirrer 1.1 Litres	Clear	"
WW500/1/SAN		Sherry 13 cl	Cut Crystal	'Sandringham'
WW500/2/SAN		Claret 28 cl	Cut Crystal	"
WW500/3/SAN		Champagne Flute 21 cl	Cut Crystal	"
WW500/4/SAN		Goblet	Cut Crystal	"
WW500/5/SAN		Port 10 cl	Cut Crystal	"
WW500/6/SAN		Wine Decanter	Cut Crystal	"
WW500/8/SAN		Brandy 30 cl	Cut Crystal	"
WW501/SAN		Bud Vase	Cut Crystal	"
WW601/WAL		Bud Vase	Cut Crystal	'Walsingham'
WW502/2/SAN		Candlelamp	Cut Crystal	'Sandringham'
WW602/2/WAL		Candlelamp	Cut Crystal	'Walsingham'
WW503/SAN		Sugar & Creamer	Cut Crystal	'Sandringham'
WW603/WAL		Sugar & Creamer	Cut Crystal	'Walsingham'
WW504/1/SAN		Rose Bowl S/S	Cut Crystal	'Sandringham'
WW504/2/SAN		Rose Bowl L/S	Cut Crystal	"

WW604/1/WAL	Rose Bowl S/S	Cut Crystal	'Walsingham'
WW604/2/WAL	Rose Bowl L/S	Cut Crystal	"
WW600/1/WAL	Sherry 13 cl	Cut Crystal	"
WW600/2/WAL	Claret 28 cl	Cut Crystal	"
WW600/3/WAL	Champagne Flute 21 cl	Cut Crystal	"
WW600/4/WAL	Goblet	Cut Crystal	"
WW600/5/WAL	Port 10 cl	Cut Crystal	"
WW600/6/WAL	Wine Decanter	Cut Crystal	"
WW600/8/WAL	Brandy 30 cl	Cut Crystal	"

* Refers to the colour of the candles that were available as part of the candlestick and candle-holder sets, not the glass which was midnight, midnight optic, clear or clear optic.

In the above listing, some numerals are missing. All designs were assigned a code, but not all designs went into production.

Items coded WUS were intended mainly for sale in the United States although many were also sold using a different code through retail outlets in Australia and Canada as is clear from extant pattern books and retail posters.

Codes for cut crystal JUS, SAN, and WAL were for 'Justine', 'Sandringham', and 'Walsingham' respectively.

In Australia the four defining codes were 6424, 6425, 6426, 6427, 6435 and 6436.

6424—Clear;

6425—Midnight items which were sold in pairs (with the exception of one half-litre carafe);

6426—Midnight Optic used only for two carafes, a half-litre and one litre;

6427—only for the 'Zelda' two-piece Cocktail Mixer and Stirrer;

6435—Midnight single items with the exception of cocktail, salad, and pudding dishes which were sold as matching pairs with the larger serving dishes;

6436—Midnight Optic.

Clear Optic does not appear in catalogues for items sold in Australia.

In Canada, 8510 indicated an item was Midnight Optic, while 8521 was for Clear, in the 'Devon Collection'.

Unfold to view Appendix 5

Appendix 6 — Lilliputs

Lilliputs	Code	Clear	Sapphire	Topaz	Lilac	Speckled Turquoise	Speckled Pink
Apple	L5001	+		+	+		+
Dolphin	L5002	+	+	+	+	+	
Duck	L5003	+		+			+
Duckling	L5004	+			+		+
Elephant	L5005	+	+	+	+		
Mushroom	L5006	+					
Owl	L5007	+	+	+			
Penguin	L5008	+					
Polar Bear	L5009	+	+				
Shell	L5010	+					
Snail	L5011	+		+			
Whale	L5012	+			+	+	
Bird	L5013	+	+	+	+		
Squirrel	L5014	+		+			
Frog	L5015	+			+	+	
Hippo	L5016	+		+			
Hedgehog	L5017	+		+			
Hare	L5018	+	+	+			
Pig	L5019	+		+	+		
Pear	L5020	+		+	+	+	+
Teddy Bear	L5021	+		+			
Long-Tailed Bird	L5022	+	+				+

INDEX

Appendix 5

Figurines	Code	Clear	Sapphire	Topaz	Lilac	Speckled Green	Speckled Pink	Speckled Turquoise	Cream Brown	Speckled Brown	Grey	Red Brown	Dark White	Blue Yellow	Blue Pink	Blue Green	White	W Br
Apple #	RSW230/SG230	+	+		+	+	+	+		+	+						+	
Baby Elephant	SG450	+					+											
Bird	RSW70/SG70	+	+	+	+	+	+	+										
Bird L/S	RSW71/SG71		+	+			+	+	+			+						
Cat	SG440		+	+	+		+		+	+			+					
Cornucopia	RSW809								+				+					
Dog (Seated)	SG420			+			+	+		+								
Dolphin	SG417	+	+	+	+	+	+	+										
Dome Paperweight	RSW11/SG11	+	+	+	+	+	+	+									+	
Duck	RSW232/SG232	+	+	+	+	+	+	+		+								
Duckling	SG426		+	+	+		+	+		+								
Egg	RSW141									+								
Elephant Ring Stand	RSW900																	
Elephant -Trunk Down	RSW409/SG409		+	+	+	+	+	+			+						+	
Elephant-Trunk Up	RSW405/SG405		+	+	+	+	+	+			+						+	
Fish	RSW74/SG74		+	+			+	+	+	+								
Fledgling	SG429	+	+	+	+	+	+	+				+						
Frog	SG404	+	+	+		+	+	+		+								
Hare	SG427		+	+	+		+	+		+								
Hedgehog	SG403								+									
Hippo	SG461		+	+							+							
Jumbo	SG451						+											
Large Rabbit	SG413			+			+	+									+	
Leaping Dolphin	SG442																	
Long-Tailed Bird	RSW73		+						+									
Mouse	RSW236	+									+						+	
Mushroom	RSW219/SG219	+	+	+			+	+	+	+							+	
Otter	SG416		+	+							+		+					
Owl	RSW140/SG140		+	+	+		+		+	+	+							
Panda	SG421												+					
Parrot	SG428													+	+	+		
Partridge	RSW233/SG233	+								+								
Pear#	RSW231/SG231	+			+	+	+	+		+	+							
Penguin	SG434		+	+	+	+				+			+					
Penguin	RSW72		+	+									+					
Pig	SG439	+	+	+	+													
Polar Bear	RSW267/SG267	+	+	+	+												+	
Rabbit	SG422		+	+	+		+	+		+							+	
Rhino#		+		+							+							
Robin	SG438											+						
Scotty Dog/Terrier	SG418		+	+			+	+		+								
Seal	RSW237/SG237	+	+	+	+	+		+			+							
Seashell	SG411		+						+									
Snail #	RSW268/SG268	+	+	+		+	+	+		+								
Squirrel	SG410	+	+	+	+						+							
Stoat	SG432			+		+	+			+								
Teddy Bear	SG449	+		+	+													
Whale	RSW234/SG234	+	+	+	+		+	+										

Elephant ring stand & leaping dolphin were produced in crystal only
Also with frosted surface

—Animals

hite own	White Pink	White Turquoise	Speckled Topaz	Green	White Cream	Speckled Grey	Speckled White	Yellow	Blue Dark	Yellow Brown	Speckled Amethyst	Powder Blue	Powder Green	Powder Pink	Midnight
				+			+								
				+											
								+	+			+	+	+	
			+												
	+														
				+				+				+	+	+	
+	+								+						
							+								
+	+														
+	+								+						
			+		+	+				+					+
				+											
				+											
				+											
															+
							+								
										+					
+	+	+													
															+